Well, Here We Are!

Well, Here We Are!

◆

The Hansons and the Becks

J. Robert Beck

iUniverse, Inc.
New York Lincoln Shanghai

Well, Here We Are!
The Hansons and the Becks

iUniverse books may be ordered through booksellers or by contacting:

iUniverse
2021 Pine Lake Road, Suite 100
Lincoln, NE 68512
www.iuniverse.com
1-800-Authors (1-800-288-4677)

ISBN-13: 978-0-595-35772-7 (pbk)
ISBN-13: 978-0-595-80245-6 (ebk)
ISBN-10: 0-595-35772-5 (pbk)
ISBN-10: 0-595-80245-1 (ebk)

Printed in the United States of America

Contents

FOREWORD. vii

CHAPTER 1   MY GREAT-GRANDPARENTS AND BEFORE. 1

CHAPTER 2   MY GRANDPARENTS 15

CHAPTER 3   SIBLINGS OF MY GRANDPARENTS. 29

CHAPTER 4   MY FATHER: JOHN LENNART ANDERSON BECK 38

CHAPTER 5   MY MOTHER: MABEL LEILA HANSON BECK 45

CHAPTER 6   MY FATHER'S SIBLINGS—My Aunts and Uncles 52

CHAPTER 7   MY MOTHER'S SIBLINGS—My Aunts and Uncles 63

CHAPTER 8   MY HANSON COUSINS 72

CHAPTER 9   MY BECK COUSINS 77

CHAPTER 10   MOUNTAIN IRON, MINNESOTA My Home Town as I Saw It 91

CHAPTER 11   GROWING UP IN MOUNTAIN IRON 106

CHAPTER 12   COLLEGE AND THE NAVY 115

CHAPTER 13   MY CAREER AT KODAK. 122

CHAPTER 14   INTO EACH REIGN SOME LIFE MUST FALL 129

CHAPTER 15   RETIREMENT 138

CHAPTER 16   OBSERVATIONS 143

AFTERWORD 149

APPENDIX A   NOTES AND ST. URHO 151

APPENDIX B   THE MEMOIRS OF ALEXANDER KETO 161

APPENDIX C   THE WORLD WAR JOURNAL OF J. LENNART BECK 191

APPENDIX D   DESCENDANTS 223

APPENDIX E   FAMILY TREES 229

FOREWORD

This is written for my children and their children and any Becks, Hansons or others who may find it interesting or useful.

Whoever happens to read this must remember that this is written from the point of view of one person. I saw what I saw and think what I think about our ancestors and relatives based on my own observation or what I was told or overheard. These observations were from limited samples and my own bias, which I have made little attempt to filter out. Much of it is necessarily hearsay which carries the double risk of inaccuracies in the memories and bias of the tellers as well as in the memory of the hearer.

In spite of these limitations, I think this is a sufficiently accurate account to provide a good chance for you to know something about your roots. I hope it is important for you to be linked to the past through someone who knew the people in our past. I hope I have been able to make them more than just names.

You can be proud of our ancestors. They were almost without exception good, honorable, honest, and proud people. They were not without some human failings, but not really serious ones. Their genes have given us a good chance for better than average intelligence and longer than average lives.

I hope I have succeeded in portraying these lives accurately, fairly and honestly. I hope perhaps even more that you will find this inspiring as well as entertaining.

J. Robert Beck
January 2005

1

MY GREAT-GRANDPARENTS
AND BEFORE

Before Great-Grandparents

I am indebted to Virginia Bygden Fox and June Pelo, relatives on the Bygden side of my family, for some information about the ancestors of that branch of the family. That was the Swedish branch, all of whom, it seems, lived in Finland, at least after about 1700. Virginia Bygden Fox was my father's first cousin, the daughter of Charles Bygden, my grandmother Hulda Bygden Beck's brother.

Virginia was about three years older than I, and died in 2001. June Pelo's great-grandmother and one of my great-great-grandfathers in the Bygden line were sister and brother; she says that makes us fifth cousins, and I will accept that.

Virginia and June were avid genealogists and have provided me with some interesting stories about our ancestors as well as a genealogy tracing at least a few lines back to about 1460 (some 19 generations).

Lars Andersson Friis was my great-grandfather six times over. He was born on April 2, 1696 in Ingermanland, Sweden. He came from a military background with his father, Anders Frijs, an ensign with Wrangel's Regiment and his mother the daughter of an armor keeper. Lars became a soldier and endured a life of hardship during the Stora Ofreden (Great Strife), the Northern wars of 1700-1721.

Lars was a volunteer with Wästerbotten's Regiment in Sweden, advanced to grenadier staff sergeant 1st class and was sent to Finland by the military as a spy. This was a dangerous assignment. The Czar was mad at the Swedes for prolonging the war and was in the process of ruining the east coast of Sweden, burning villages, murdering citizens, and taking captives. Lars survived, however, and married Malin Olofsdotter of Grisbacka, Sweden. They settled in Palo, Karleby,

Finland, and took one of the many deserted homes in Karleby left from the war. Lars and Malin had 10 children before she died at age 33 in 1738. He remarried that same year to Maria Jacobsdotter Jurvelius.

Maria's grandfather, Michael Balt, is believed to have come from France, and was a famous wood carver in Finland.

Lars remained a farmer in his post-military life and fathered another eleven children with Maria. Thirteen of his 21 children were still living when he died of gallstones or kidney stones at age 73. It's no wonder that many members of the Swedish Finn Historical Society are descendant of the children from both of Lars Friis' marriages. (Quote from Hans Ettlingar, *Lars Frijs I Karleby.*) His widow gave the church a donation for ringing the bell and the bier clothing. His last resting place was not under the church floor nor even in the churchyard. Toward the close of the 1700s prominent people were still buried under the church floor, but spaces were limited. So poor Lars was buried in the usual way in a temporary grave. The practice was to leave the body in its grave for about three years and then to exhume the body, empty the coffin by shoveling the contents into a bone basket where anything other than bones that remained were air and sun dried. The bones then sank down through the bottom of the bone basket into a walled cellar in the ground.

Typical of the message on a bone basket:
You wretched child of a human,
Who the world's path shall wander
Consider yourself mortal, and see
Now how it is for others,
Your haughtiness and what
Your world built in the name of bliss.
Here is found a poor farmer
Who would like to rest with those
Of higher station.
These plentiful bones
All have here a haven.

He left, besides thirteen children, a silver bowl and a mug, Russian rubles and Swedish Karoliners, a schnapps boiler, 4 pewter bowls, 6 flat pewter plates, 1 pewter beer pot and many iron hooks. There was fishing gear and a sea boat with sail, 2 net boats, 1 skiff and a fish house. Also left were a Bible and two psalm books. There were 3 horses, 17 cattle and 17 sheep. His leather saddle is now in the Museum of History in Vasa and his silver spurs are in the Österbotten Historical Museum in Vasa. There was a little furniture, clothing and linens.

His widow died 14 years later at age 76.

A 5th cousin 3 times removed (is that still a relative?) was Johan Ludvig Runeberg. He was born in Jakobstad on February 5, 1804. He became Finland's national poet and is regarded in both Finland and Sweden as Finland's greatest poet. He wrote an epic poem called Tales of Ensign Stol (Steel) in Swedish, telling stories about persons and events in the War of 1808-09, where Finns and Swedes fought side by side against the Russians. The first part began with the song Vart Land (Our Country) which expressed a deep love of the homeland in all its varied natural aspects and under all social conditions. Sung to a melody by Pacius, it soon became and is still the National Anthem of Finland.

He had a Ph.D. and taught Latin and Greek literature at Borga College, which probably was necessary for poets who wanted to eat. He liked to eat well enough to have a favorite cake. It's still traditional in Finland that everyone eats a Runeberg Cake on Johan's birthday, February 5th.

A 7th cousin is Tapio Wirkkala, the glass designer. His work can be seen on the net: http://www.memorieoffinland.com.

A 6th cousin, Fritz Jakobsson, is a well-known artist who was commissioned recently to paint a portrait of Pope John Paul and was present at its unveiling in the Vatican in 1998. Some Catholics wondered why a Lutheran artist was selected to paint a portrait of the Pope. Fritz was also selected to paint a portrait of Queen Silvia of Sweden.

Considering that our ancestors and living relatives number in the thousands, it is not surprising that a couple of them have been considered notable. I wonder what our genealogists could have dug up if they were looking for the notorious instead of the notable.

The first ancestor to use the name Bygden was my great-great-great grandfather Pehr Bygden. He was born in Sweden in 1777 and married Maglena Olofsdotter Öberg. He worked for the glassworks in Strömbäck, Sweden, first as a skipper of a boat, then as an overseer, then as a glassblower in Piteå. He returned to Strömbäck and worked there as a glassblower until he was 70 years old. After that he continued to work in the glassworks until he died in a cholera epidemic in 1853. His wife Maglena died in 1857 and was described in the parish records as poor.

My great-great grandparents included Pehr's son Johan Bygden. He was educated in high school and college and went to work as a journalist and a printer. Doctors advised him to leave the printing business because he had weak eyesight and might become blind if he stayed. Then, he said, I chose something that was worse. He became a glassblower like his father had been and worked first in the Raume [sic] factory in Finland and later in the Yttersfors (Sweden) Glass Factory. He did lose his job when the factory closed in 1878, and was described in parish notes as poor and blind and when he died in 1894 was labeled a pauper. His wife Anna Kristina, who had borne them seven children, had died in 1887 with the parish noting that she was deaf. Johan's promising early education did not save them from sad and difficult endings.

Lovisa Lexabak Eriksson
Mother of Maria Eriksson Bygden
Grandmother of Hulda Bygden Beck
My Great-great grandmother

Lovisa and Johann Eriksson, the grandparents of my grandmother Hulda Bygden Beck.

All I know about the Eriksson family is that they had nine children, five of whom lived long enough to be married. They married off one child, my great-grand-mother Maria in Finland so they could afford to emigrate to Michigan without her, but apparently she and many other members of this family were either born or reunited in Michigan. It is my impression from Virginia Bygden Fox that even though most of the Eriksson descendants and the Bygden branch lived in Michigan they had relatively little contact with each other and were not interested in their family ties. Uncle Charles Beck and Aunt Lillian Beck Fuller sought out more of the family members of these branches and made more contacts from their homes in Minnesota than those who lived near each other in Michigan were interested in pursuing. Virginia Fox said that that was the Swedish way of doing things, but the Becks were half Swedish and half Finnish and I can't believe that they got their curiosity from either. Uncle Charlie and Aunt Tommy were just born nosy and sociable.

Johann Petter and Maria Eriksson Bygden—Parents of My Grandmother Hulda Bygden Beck.

I met my great-grandparents Johann Petter and Maria Bygden who lived in East Tawas, Michigan. I really never got to know them, but I did see them once or twice. All of my other great-grandparents were dead when I was born.

Maria Emelia Eriksson was born on December 31, 1861 to John Eriksson and Lovisa Lexabak Eriksson in the Raumo district of Himango, near Karleby, Finland. When she was 16 years old in 1878 her parents arranged her marriage with Johann Petter Bygden, one of the seven children of Johan and Anna Kristina Bygden. The Erikssons did this so they could emigrate to the United States and leave Maria because they could not afford to take her. It has been reported in family legend that she never forgave her parents for either her marriage or her abandonment.

This must be somewhat of an exaggeration, since Maria and Johann joined Maria's parents in East Tawas, Michigan, after they left Finland in the mid-1880s. Her great-granddaughter, Virginia Bygden Fox, sent the photograph of an elderly Lovisa Lexabak Eriksson to me. Virginia said that one of her uncles found his grandmother Lovisa frozen to death in their back yard in Michigan on Christmas Eve, 1904. Apparently she had been trying to visit the Bygden farm and never quite made it. The Eriksson farm was near the Bygden farm on Timmerick Road in Wilbur Township, Michigan, and she had apparently walked from her farm to her daughter's.

Even though Johann and Maria were born and married in Finland, both the Erikssons and the Bygdens were Swedish. Johann Bygden, born in 1850, was 11 years older than his bride. He had been a sailor in his earlier years, but had settled down in Karleby as a glass blower at the time of his marriage. His grandfather Pehr and his father Johan had also worked as sailors and glassblowers.

Their first child, Hulda Marie, was born in Finland (then part of Russia) on August 28, 1879, and became my grandmother. There is some vagueness in the records, but it is believed that the Bygdens emigrated to the United States in 1887 after the Raumo Glasbruk went bankrupt. Three of their children were born and died in Finland, and Hulda was the only one who lived to emigrate. Seven more children were born in Michigan.

Johann and Maria Bygden lived in East Tawas, Michigan. Johann died in 1937 and Maria in 1947 at ages 87 and 86, respectively. I vaguely remember their visiting my grandmother in Mountain Iron, Minnesota, in 1935 or 1936. I remember visiting and staying at my great grandmother's house in East Tawas in 1938 after Johann had died. The house in East Tawas was fairly large and old and near the center of that small town, but in 1938 still had an outdoor privy as its only toilet and a pump in the kitchen sink as its source of water.

The Bygden Family, June 1908, East Tawas, Michigan
Back Row: Charles, Hulda, Emil
Front Row: Joel, Johann Petter, Hilma, Maria, Emma

Hulda was my grandmother, the mother of John Lennart Beck
Johann Petter (1850–1936) and Maria (1860–1947)
were my great-grandparents
At the time this picture was taken, Hulda had a son (my father) who was 14
years old, only two years younger than Hulda's brother Charles and older
than Joel, Hilma and Emma, his uncle and aunts.

My Aunt Lillian described her grandfather Johann Petter Bygden as an alcoholic; his granddaughter Virginia Bygden Fox described him as the town drunk. There were hints that the marriage between Johann and Maria was less than idyllic even though it produced 11 children and lasted 60 years, ended only by Johann's death. Johann was apparently educated and worked as a bookkeeper for the lumber company keeping track of their shipping into East Tawas on Lake Huron. His drinking, however, made him unreliable as either a father or a provider, so the burden of raising a family fell on Maria.

One of the family stories told by Maria about her husband Johann was that he took a horse and wagon filled with produce from their farm to town to sell. He sold the produce and spent the money on booze; then he sold the wagon and drank all that money; then he sold the horse and ended up penniless in the drunk tank where Maria had to go to get him out.

Johann became quite blind in his later years. This was blamed on his career as a glassblower, but that career was brief, only between his being a sailor and his emigration to Michigan where he was a bookkeeper. When his eyesight failed and the lumber mills moved west he became a farmer. His father Johan had died blind after a long career as a glassblower, but he apparently had had eye problems before he became a glassblower. Johann Bygden's granddaughter, Virginia Bygden Fox, rarely saw her grandfather, but had heard of his telling that he had sailed the seven seas, had studied for the Lutheran ministry, and that he read the Bible daily.

Virginia Fox got better acquainted with her grandmother after her grandfather had died. "I remember her as a very energetic and cheerful tiny little lady with a wonderful sense of humor and a great story-teller," she wrote. "Maria was a healer. She cured [a neighbor's child] of weeping eczema…Maria put a pot on the wood stove with water from three different wells in it, she added coins of different metals, a lead weight and she spit in it. Then she put in a straight pin; if it stood upright, the solution was ready. She bathed [the girl] with it and before she got home she had begun to clear up. [As part of the process] Maria had to dump this concoction at the end of a dead end street where three streets intersected to form a T.

"Maria had no trouble with the English language, she spoke it quite colorfully. Someone asked her what a friend had died of. She said, 'He had a kangaroo in his foot.' This translates to gangrene.

"This wonderful little lady worked very hard. She had a large loom upstairs where she wove rag rugs. The man next door saw her frequently run around the outside of the house as fast as she could. Finally, he could stand it no longer and asked her why she was doing this. She said, 'Why, it's the warp,' meaning this was how she measured the cord for the loom. He said, 'Why do you run?' She said, 'Why not?'

"She had the majority of the responsibility for the children and a frequently errant husband. She instilled them with good Christian values and an honest work ethic. She was a fine woman."

The Ketos—The Parents of My Father's Father.

While Aunt Lillian Beck Fuller in a hand-written family genealogy-history showed their names as Andrew and Wilhelmina Korpi, in other places she uses

Keto as their last name. A memoir written (in Finnish) by John Beck's younger brother, Alexander Keto, gives his parents' names as Antti and Wilhelmiina Keto, which I think is most likely correct. (See Appendix B). In that book he writes that his father Antti Keto bought a house in Oulu, Finland, named Korpi. I expect that is where Lillian got the name she occasionally ascribed to her grandparents. Alexander retained the name Keto throughout his life. John and another brother, Oscar, adopted the name Beck some time after they moved to the United States. Her death certificate indicates that my great-grandmother was using the name Wilhelmiina Keto when she died, and that certificate was signed by her son, my grandfather, John Beck.

I now believe this about the Finnish great-grandparents on my father's father's side: Their names were Antti Keto and his wife, Wilhelmiina. They were both born in 1849. Wilhelmiina's parents were Jaako and Anna Katharine Antilla who lived in Kortesjarvi, Finland. Of the seven children of Antti and Wilhelmiina Keto born in Inankyla, Finland, the third was my grandfather John (Johan) born on May 16, 1873.

Jaako Antilla was very poor and sent his daughter to live near Kauhavalle with an uncle, Elias Kleimola, who was better able to support her. She met and married Antti Keto after she had left her uncle's house to work as a housemaid near Lake Evijarvi.

Antti Keto worked as a fisherman and sometimes carpenter, but was very poor in Russian Finland. His children, including my grandfather, had to go to work as children to help support the large family. Having heard about getting rich in America, Antti left his family and went to work in a sawmill in East Tawas, Michigan, for a few years and returned home rich enough to make a down payment on a house (the one named Korpi) in Oulu, Finland.

He decided that he should return to Michigan and accumulate enough money so that he could return to Finland and pay off the mortgage. On that second trip he brought my grandfather John to East Tawas with him. Money accumulated too slowly, and the house in Oulu was lost to foreclosure. Antti changed his plans to return and instead sent money to bring his wife and youngest daughter Emelia to the U. S., leaving Alexander, Oscar and Nikolai in Finland. Alex and Oscar later arrived in Michigan on their own; Nikolai never left Finland.

Antti died in Michigan on December 18, 1901 (age 52). Alexander joined his mother and his sister Emelia in Michigan about a year later and the three of them soon moved to Minnesota to live near an older sister, also named Wilhelmina but known as Minnie.

They were later joined in Mountain Iron, Minnesota, by my grandfather John Beck and his family. My great-grandmother Wilhelmiina, because she had tuberculosis, was not housed with my grandparents and their many children but was provided with a separate one-room abode in their back yard. My father Lennart and his brother Leo, the two oldest grandchildren, took turns as her companions and caretakers in this isolated bedroom until she died in 1907 at the age of 58. Surprisingly, neither Lennart nor Leo contracted tuberculosis. This assignment may have been what made my father fluent in the Finnish language. John's youngest sister, Emelia, who was only two years older than her nephew Lennart, lived with the John Beck family and fit in as a sibling rather than an aunt.

Alex Keto, in his memoir, *Shoemaker's Apprentice,* gives a different view of this arrangement, saying that he built the one-room house for his mother and his sister, and he takes sole credit for caring for them, not even mentioning his brother John Beck and his family. It is true that Alex Keto and his mother and sister lived in Mountain Iron for a couple of years before the John Beck family arrived.

Johannes and Ragnild Odegaard (Johnson)
Parents of Bertha Johnson Hanson

Johannes Johanneson Odegaard and his wife, Ragnild, were both born in Norway in 1830. Their first child was born in Norway, but the other five were born in Wisconsin. The family name was changed to Johnson when they entered the United States.

Johannes (by then he was plain John Johnson from Wisconsin) was drafted and served in the Union Army in the Civil War, but only from Oct. 19, 1864 to June 2, 1865. He was with the regiment that took part in the siege of Atlanta and the March to the Sea. Ragnild was so lonesome during his absence that she took up smoking and until her death nearly sixty years later she was still smoking a pipe using a very cheap and vile tobacco. My father told me he won my mother's grandmother's heart by giving her a tin of Prince Albert tobacco, a big improvement over her usual Peerless. Ragnild (sometimes known as Rachel) was the only grandparent my mother and her sister Ethel knew. Ethel said that she was unable to communicate with her grandmother because Ragnild never learned English even though she had lived in the United States for at least 60 years.

I picture Johannes and Ragnild as a rustic pair—smart, but naïve—whose goal in life was to raise fruit, vegetables, meat, and children on their Wisconsin farm. They did that successfully. And they must have been very good people and parents, because the four of their children I knew were the most lovable, warm and wonderful people I have ever known. I cannot picture Johannes being comfortable in Sherman's army marching—and pillaging, and worse—through Georgia.

The farm continued in the family through at least two more generations.

The Kjustads—Parents of My Mother's Father.

Marta Arnson (Hanson) and Christian Hansen Kjustad
Parents of Bernt (Bans) Hanson
My great-grandparents

On my mother's father's side were Christian Hansen Kjustad and his wife Marta Arnson (aka Arnsdotter), both born in 1832 in or near Fetsund, Norway. They had three children: Bernt, my grandfather (known later as Bans or Ben); Charles; and a daughter Dikka. Even though he was reported to be well off and successful in Norway, Christian was an adventurer unable to resist the lure of the New World, so he and his family emigrated to the United States. He may have been disillusioned, since he never became more than a millwright in a sawmill in Eau Claire, Wisconsin. The family name was changed to Hanson when they entered the United States.

Kristian (Norwegian spelling) had a grandfather named Kristoffer Arnesen N Kjustad. I believe that it was common to use the name of the farm as part of one's name, hence the Kjustad. Kristian's father, the son of Kristoffer was named Hans Kristoffersen. Kristian, the son of Hans, was named Kristian Hansen, and that is how my grandfather and his children got to be Hansons. (For some reason the spelling was changed from-sen to-son.) If they had followed the old Norwegian practice, my grandfather would be named Christianson, and his children might have been Berntson or Bansson or Benson.

Kristian (Christian) was one of eight children. Two were named Kristian, but the first one was born and died in 1826 so the name was recycled when my great-grandfather was born in 1832. A daughter died in infancy in 1827. A third son was named Arne and he managed to live for five years, dying in 1834. So the second Kristian was the first to survive to maturity, and the only one of the eight children to live a full life and produce heirs. A second Arne and a daughter Anne Marie were both born in 1834; this Arne lived for two years and Anne Marie lived long enough to marry but died childless in 1857 at age 23. There is no report that Arne and Anne were twins. Peder was born and died in 1837. Bernt was born in 1840 and died in 1848. So only one of the eight children of Hans and Anne Dortea lived to extend the lineage.

Martha Arnson, Christian Hanson's wife, lived on a neighboring farm before they were married. They had been born the same year, so we can assume they were childhood playmates or schoolmates if those things existed in Norwegian farm country in the early 19th century.

Christian and Martha lived comfortably in Eau Claire, however, in a nice home. They had a stable and kept horses, which took them about town and to church. According to their grandson, my Uncle Harry Hanson, the horses were beautiful with polished harnesses and were used to draw an immaculate carriage. (Remember that Harry's memoirs were written almost a hundred years later and may have been somewhat embellished by those who reported it to him.)

I cannot picture my grandfather Bans in this environment. He was an adventurous iconoclast whom I will describe more fully later. Fancy horses and churches and pretense of any kind were far from his lifestyle. Perhaps the only trait he shared with his father was his desire for adventure.

His brother Charles, too, had a problem with his family. Charles fell in love with Frances, a Roman Catholic. Charles was supposedly a dedicated Lutheran like his parents, but he converted to the Catholic faith for Frances. Uncle Harry writes: Because of his devotion to his fiancée, he sought and was received into membership of Frances' church. This change on Uncle's [Charles Hanson's] part would have been almost intolerable to the centuries-old religious background of Lutheran fellowship on the part of my grandparents. Therefore, they were never told about it, and the wedding of Uncle Charles to Aunt Frances (at least as far as we knew) was delayed until after his parents' deaths.

This was a different era that we may find hard to comprehend. To me, the differences between the Roman Catholic faith and the Lutheran faith appear quite insignificant, and even their rituals are similar. It is also difficult to see how the fear of risking parents' disapproval could outweigh the chance to pursue living a perfectly reasonable and happy life. And I wonder how many centuries or even generations back the Lutheran tradition in the family went. Christianity came rather late to the far northern reaches of Europe, and it probably wasn't too many generations before when our ancestors were worshiping trees and fire. I do know that Bans, my grandfather, did not seriously subscribe to either the Lutheran or other Christian religious traditions, but he didn't worship trees or fires either.

2

MY GRANDPARENTS

I got to know my grandparents well, because both pairs lived in my hometown of Mountain Iron, Minnesota, where I lived until I was 19 years old. I am now grateful for that opportunity which seemed normal at the time, but which I now realize is fairly rare. It was also generally accepted that all members of both sides of my family who happened to be there were included in all major events such as holidays.

John Anderson Beck, My Father's Father.

This grandfather was known in Mountain Iron during my life as John Beck. He had been born in Finland to parents named Keto. The Ketos had difficulty supporting their children in Russian-dominated Finland and the children had to go to work as soon as they were able. My grandfather most likely had a childhood of hard labor and a marginal diet, which could possibly account for his small stature—about 5 ft. 2in. and never more than 100 pounds.

His father brought him to the United States when he was about 17 years old. Since his father was Antti (Andrew) Keto, John's American name became Anderson (son of Andrew). He married Hulda Bygden and their first child, my father, was born in 1894 and registered as John Lennart Anderson in East Tawas, Michigan. By the time their second child, (Emil Lionel, always known as Leo) was born two years later in Oscoda, Michigan, they had changed the family name to Beck. The reason for the change was not documented, but it was probably because there were too many John Andersons where they were living.

The name Beck is not Finnish. Grandpa John Beck spoke English with such an accent that I had trouble understanding him. I assumed he selected Beck as a name because it was easy to spell. Some members of the family say it came from a Finnish name Raambekka (Rombeck) which was a farm in Finland where Grandpa spent his childhood working. Some say that Beck was selected because my grandparents went into the hotel business and needed a sign painted. Since the sign painter charged by the letter, they selected a short name. In any case, Keto became Anderson became Beck, which caused my father some problems in later years when he had to produce proof of his birth and to convince the world that John Lennart Anderson was really John Lennart Beck. No one has ever attempted to explain why the family did not use the name Keto as John's younger brother Alex and sister Emelia did.

While John appeared to be relatively uneducated and illiterate in English, my Uncle Roland, his youngest son, said his father had a good education as a child in Finland, even in those days a highly literate country. He learned to read and write English, too, and read faithfully the Duluth *Herald* along with the Finnish daily *Paivalehti,* and the Finnish weekly *Minnesota Uutiset.* If Alex Keto's *Shoemaker's Apprentice* is accurate, however, it is unlikely that any of the Keto children ever saw the inside of a school and must have been mostly self-educated.

To me, John Beck was the least of my grandparents, not only in stature, but in every way. His thick Finnish accent made it difficult for me to understand him. He was either shy or diffident, because he tended not to acknowledge me when we met on the streets of our very small village. I found this baffling when I was 9 or 10, and it certainly did not endear him to me. He and his wife Hulda raised seven children of the ten born to them (three died in infancy), and lived in a reasonably nice house, so he must have been a good provider, although during the years I knew him he never had anything but a menial job. I suspect that John and Hulda survived with great sacrifice and never had much money. I do remember that during the depression of the 1930s Grandma would make doughnuts and Grandpa would peddle them door-to-door around our village for pennies apiece, and that may have been their main source of income during some years.

Uncle Roland said that his father's first jobs in Michigan and Minnesota were with the Weyerhaeuser lumber company, and that he moved from East Tawas to Oscoda in Michigan to Cloquet, Minnesota, following the movement of the clear cutting of the northern forests. The beginning of iron mining on the Mesabi Range made him decide to abandon lumbering for mining, although he did not spend much time working in the mines. Finns were not welcome as employees by the mining companies after many of them joined a radical labor union. Like many other Finns, John Beck was politically conservative, certainly anti-socialist, but just because he was a Finn he was judged by the mines to be an unemployable radical.

John Beck's efforts at running his own businesses were unsuccessful. His most notable talent was in landscape gardening. He spent many years planting and maintaining the school grounds and village parks in Mountain Iron as an employee of either the village or the school district and did a good job.

Grandpa Beck did not have expensive vices. I never saw him drink alcohol, but he chewed snuff. My cousin, Bruce Fuller, who lived with him until he died when Bruce was about eight years old, says that Grandpa Beck did not avoid alcohol. He would take Bruce with him on walks to a local saloon where he would drink a bit and buy candy for Bruce. I am sure he kept this a secret from his wife who was vigorously opposed to alcohol. He smoked a pipe on very special occasions. He liked to play games like cribbage and checkers and I think he would cheat to win if he could. When I was about 12 years old I was shocked to observe him cheating my 5-year-old brother at checkers. I expected grandparents to cheat to help their grandchildren win, not the other way around.

He was elected to the office of Mountain Iron Village Assessor for one term, which seems like a somewhat noteworthy accomplishment. He was also an avid radio fan and I remember his having the biggest and best radio I had ever seen.

Grandpa John Beck was never close to me, and as far as I could tell not to any of his grandchildren and perhaps not to his children. This is understandable not only because being distant is considered typically Finnish, but because he had probably not had a normal family upbringing in the Russian serfdom economy of his childhood Finland. I have no memory of how close his children felt toward him, although he was seldom mentioned as a major factor in their lives.

He died of heart disease in 1940 at the age of 66.

Hulda Bygden Beck and John (Keto/Anderson) Beck
My grandparents, parents of John Lennart Beck
At their wedding in 1893 Hulda was 14, John was 20

John, Leo, Lennart, and Hulda Beck
about 1898

◆   ◆   ◆

Hulda Bygden Beck, My Father's Mother.

Fortunately for their children and probably for us, their grandchildren, Hulda was as much a giant in all respects as John was a midget. She was somewhat bigger than he was physically, so none of their children were as small as John, but more important was that she was brilliant, had very high ethical and moral standards, and was able to provide the leadership and guidance her children needed for their successful lives.

Hulda was born in Finland of Swedish parents (Johann Petter Bygden and Maria Eriksson Bygden) and came to the United States with them when she was about eight years old. She married John (Keto) Anderson, a recent immigrant, when she was 14 and had her first child, my father, before she was 16. In time she bore ten children, seven of whom survived infancy and lived longer lives than either of their parents.

It does not sound auspicious to be married at 14 and have 10 children. But Hulda spoke English flawlessly with no accent and as far as I could tell was equally fluent in Swedish and Finnish. It is probably a family fable that she read every book in the Mountain Iron library, but it is true that she read a lot. This did not keep her from keeping her house clean, from weaving rugs, from keeping her children fed and clothed, nor from stretching the few pennies of family income incredibly far.

Uncle Roland reports that she translated stories and articles from magazines such as the *Saturday Evening Post, Colliers* and *Ladies Home Journal* into Finnish for the *Paivalehti* publishers, but this career was soon thwarted by copyright law problems.

She insisted (over her husband's objections, I have been told) that all of her children not only finish high school but also go to college. Not all of them finished college, but all of them were intelligent and appeared well educated.

I do not remember Grandma Beck as a warm person, or even as much of a grandmother to me, especially compared to my Grandma Hanson. Perhaps by the Swedish standards of her forbears she would have been judged very warm, indeed. My limited contact with her is not surprising when you consider that when I was born she was only 45 years old and still had four school-age sons at home, the youngest only 11. By the time the last of her sons had left, her daughter (my Aunt Lillian) had ditched her husband and moved into her parents' home with two infants. So Grandma, while Lillian worked, took care of two more children and did so until she died of a stroke when those children were only 13 and 11. She never had much time to be a grandmother to any of the rest of us.

What I do remember about Grandmother Beck is that in the limited time she had available to notice me, she showed a sincere interest and pride in my intellectual and academic accomplishments, and not only encouraged me but reinforced my parents' message that higher education was the only way to go. I also suspect that she didn't even notice that I was on the high school football team; she may not even have been aware that there was such a thing, although she lived less than a block from the field and at least five of her sons had also played on that field in their high school days.

She died suddenly of a stroke a couple of weeks after she had attended my graduation from junior college in June 1943, at age 63.

The Extended Family of John and Hulda Beck
about 1906
From left to right: Leo, John, Lennart, Lillian, Wilhelmiina
(John's mother), Hulda
and Emelia (John's youngest sister)

Aunt Lillian's Account of the Becks' Early Life in Mountain Iron

I believe it was in 1908[1] that we moved to Mountain Iron from Cloquet, Minnesota, where I had been born. Our first home in Mountain Iron was a tarpaper house in the part of town called Costin (after a John Costin who originally owned the land). In Costin there were several saloons, a jail, and two bordellos. I remember seeing the fancy dressed ladies with large plumed hats ride by in fancy carriages into town. Dad worked in the mine and when he was on the night shift Mother would push the old Singer Sewing Machine in front of the kitchen door (our only outdoor entrance) and we always had a shotgun loaded hanging out of reach of us kids.

---

1.   It was 1906 or 1907

Mother and Dad belonged to the Finnish Temperance Society and Dad 'The Modern Woodmen' and Mother 'The Royal Neighbors.' The latter two had a funeral insurance plan of sorts.

After a year our dad gained employment in the local grocery store which also had clothing and a post office. Dad's job was to go from house to house taking orders for groceries from the housewives. There were no telephones in those days. Dad had no formal education in the U. S., having emigrated from Finland when he was 16 years old and immediately had to work. At eighteen he met and married Mother. Mother had gone to school through the sixth grade and was employed as a dressmaker in a shop in Michigan. Father would bring the order book home and Mother would transcribe them from Dad's Finglish. An example: 1 pauna putter would be 1# butter, etc. It's a miracle that the housewives received the proper items. Then after the groceries were packed my dad delivered them and sometime we got to ride with him (on a horse-drawn wagon). We especially liked it when he had to go to the lumber camps and were privileged to ride along, because we would be fed pie and huge cookies.

One cold night in January the young people organized a sleighride party. My dad drove the horses and my two older brothers and aunt were to go along. The party would ride four miles to Virginia, a nearby town. During the night our house caught fire. Mother, I, and two younger brothers were home. Father came home to a pile of ashes. We had been taken in by neighbors. Everything was gone! We even had a piano. My mother was determined that one of us should learn to play the piano and no matter what kind of a house we had it must have a piano. I know as soon as the insurance paid for the fire damage the first piece of furniture was a piano, and I, being the only girl, had to take lessons.

The Christmas before the fire I remember our usual trek to the Finnish Temperance Hall for the festivities. All Temperance Finns gathered there bringing presents and children. There would be a large Christmas tree lit with candles. The Hall was over a hardware store and had only one exit. I think the good Lord really watched over us—there was never a fire. Men would stand by the tree watching the candles with buckets of water.

In our town there was a Temperance Society and a Socialist Society. Each had its own hall and they were next to each other with only an alley between. The Temperance people were straitlaced and temperate; the Socialists imbibed and by and large were agnostic.

The Temperance Hall was the center for social activities. The men, both single and married, met weekly to exercise, hoping some day to achieve the muscle and build of Karhun Saari, the famous Finnish athlete. The young girls would meet to make paper flowers for the socials held on Sunday night after the *'Ohjel-mas'*. The young men also had an extemporaneous speaking society, so on Sunday evening for part of the entertainment two or three would get up and expound on topics. We kids never listened, so I couldn't tell you what they were saying. Then maybe Mrs. K. would have a piece, or *'runo'*. I can see her walking sprightly to the stage followed by 'Arne' and her dog and always there would be a gap in the back of her white blouse which didn't meet. Then there would maybe be a piano duet or solo by Mr. Kukola's piano students. After the program the paper flowers were auctioned off and the men bid and could take their best girl to coffee and biscuit or cake.

After coffee was served they would have what we called *'runki tansi'* folk dancing to the accompaniment of folk singing. Then the young fellows took their best girls home, and met again midweek for more flower making and exercising.

Mr. Kukola, a Finnish piano teacher recently from Finland, came to Mountain Iron by street car from Virginia once a week to give piano lessons at 50 cents per hour. He traveled from house to house. He couldn't speak a word of English so all we learned was notes and tempo. He about wore a spot in our living room carpet by beating time with his foot—*'yksi, kaksi, kolme...'* He was a very stern, strict teacher and many a tap I'd receive on my fingers if I struck the wrong note. It was interesting to note that nearly every Finnish home had a piano, organ, or some musical instrument. A few had *kanteles*.[2]

Bans (Ben) Hanson, My Mother's Father

When I knew him he was rather stout, about 5'8 or 5'9 with short gray hair and a yellowish mustache that resembled a short scrub brush. He walked very straight and tall and liked to help his walking with a very unusual cane made from diamond willow. He usually wore a dark suit with a vest and a necktie and kept the summer heat or the winter cold of Minnesota from his head with a gray fedora. He looked proud and to some people, forbidding. He was my Grandpa Hanson, and he was my best friend until he died when I was sixteen.

I liked to spend time with him because he loved to talk about anything and everything and I liked to listen. Although he had had very little formal education, he read newspapers thoroughly and seemed to remember and assimilate everything he read. We were both fortunate that his mind remained sharp as long as he lived. While he formed opinions and took sides on issues, I don't remember his

---

2.   A *kantele* is a Finnish plucked stringed instrument held on the player's lap.

ever being heatedly partisan nor unable to concede that opinions different from his could have merit.

Bans was born in Norway on March 20, 1859, and was brought to the United States by his family when he was eight years old. I believe his given name was Bernt but he used only Bans or Ben in this country. He learned to speak English well and with no trace of a Norwegian accent. What little accent he had was a slight Irish brogue; apparently he had learned his first English in an Irish neighborhood in New York City.

His family settled in Eau Claire, Wisconsin, and while they have been reported to have had high class pretensions it must not have included education, since Bans left school to go to work in a sawmill when he was about 14. He left there to become a photographer's helper in the very early days of photography. He met his bride-to-be when she dropped in from the farm to have her picture taken and he couldn't resist this wholesome, pleasant, plump young woman whose ancestry was also Norwegian.

Shortly after they were married they moved to Duluth, probably because the bustling port seemed much more exciting to Grandpa than staid Eau Claire. Grandma went along as the dutiful, uncomplaining proper Norwegian wife.

Grandpa found work in a haberdashery in Duluth, and in a short time discovered that Duluth could be as dull as Eau Claire. He was ready for new adventure when news came that the Merritt brothers had discovered iron and possibly gold about sixty or seventy miles north. Bans got a job on the survey crew laying out the route of the railroad to bring the ore to the port in Duluth. It took about two years to finish the railroad to Mountain Iron, and Grandma and the kids took one of the first trains and went to live there in the log cabin that Grandpa had built for them.

Grandma did sometimes complain about that move, I think. The log cabin in the woods with bears for neighbors was not always as comfortable as she would have liked, and having brought three children and fairly soon having four more, the place got pretty crowded. By about 1910, Grandpa (helped, I assume, by his older sons) built Grandma a big house with high ceilings on a big lot with hardly a tree in sight.

Grandpa Hanson learned quickly and had good mechanical aptitude, so he must have been a valuable employee in the mines. He never did rise very far above the lowest paying levels, however, and his mining days ended when he fell down a mineshaft and injured his back. When I first became aware of him he was a policeman for the Village of Mountain Iron. He later (by now in his seventies) had a one-day-a-week job as janitor in the Presbyterian Church. This was a Saturday job, so I could go with him to help, since it was difficult for him. It never occurred to me to expect to be paid for this because he needed all of what little money was paid for this small job.

What I did get out of this was the basis for a religious philosophy. Even though I attended that church every Sunday, too, I was more impressed by the Saturdays I spent there with Grandpa. Being in church probably inspired him to discuss religious philosophy with me. Although he felt reasonably sure there was a higher power of some kind that had put all of these wonderful things together, he was very skeptical of man's attempts to explain and define them. He did not hold either the rituals of the various religions nor the men who made their living administering them in very high regard. He felt that when he had any business with The Maker as he called Him, he would much rather take it up directly than through any intermediaries.

I doubt that there were any others, at least in the family, with whom he discussed his beliefs. In those days a public declaration would have been considered grossly heathen both in the family and in the town.

The special bond between us grew and strengthened as the years went on. When he was about 80 and I was 15 we occasionally discussed his impending death. He made me feel even happier for him when it occurred than sad for myself at having lost my best friend.

I faced the world with Grandpa's words always in my memory: "You can be whatever you want to be. Don't be afraid of anything. Don't depend on God, man or luck. Just believe in yourself. Beware of believing in things you can't see or prove."

He didn't teach me mathematics or chemistry or physics, but no one else made more important contributions to my happy and successful life.

He died about a week after his 82nd birthday in March 1941, from complications related to heart problems he had lived with for several years.

Bans and Bertha Hanson, 1886
My grandparents
Parents of Mabel Hanson Beck

Bertha Johnson Hanson, My Mother's Mother

Bertha Johnson was born on October 6, 1861 in Elk Creek, Wisconsin. Her father served in the Civil War but he didn't leave for military service until 1864.

Bertha married Bans Hanson on December 31, 1884, in Eau Claire, Wisconsin. They had eight children, five of whom were living in 1924 when I was born. The other three had died at ages about 20 years, 11 years, and one month, respectively.

Grandma loved life, loved people, loved to cook, and loved to ride in automobiles (or airplanes, trains, or anything else that moved.) She was totally unselfish and was incapable of seeing bad in anyone. She is nearly impossible to describe with accuracy. If someone she knew were identified to her as a burglar, prostitute, murderer, or more mildly sinful, she would merely respond with her most violent expletive, Uff Da! which meant either that nothing bad had happened or that she had just administered an oath of total forgiveness. Her door was never locked. I think it is true that she never met a person she didn't like—and this was not because she was sheltered from the many rough characters on the early iron range frontier whom most of us would consider either bad or unlikable or even dangerous.

Grandma smothered me with love. Because I was her first grandchild and for a few years the only one, and for even more years the only one who lived in the same town, I had no competition. I was perfect in her eyes and she would not allow my parents to punish me for anything. I was also there to be cooked for, and every day she dreamed up new goodies to fatten me up, which she did with unfortunately great success. She read to me until I could do so for myself; we played card and board games; I brought friends to her house to sleep over or to pick pin cherries or peas in her garden—her amazing world was open to anything and everything, no holds barred. It is difficult for me to believe that there has been another person in the world like my Grandma Hanson, and I have observed her influence on her five children. I think and hope that even a bit of it has rubbed off on me and my children.

I am happy to report that her smothering love of me didn't become more one-sided. I could have been so badly spoiled that our relationship would have been all take and no give on my part, and Grandma would never have complained if she had even noticed. My parents probably either by word or by example fortunately kept me on the right track and because I knew that Grandma would do anything she could for me, I was willing to do anything I could for her and for Grandpa. I hauled coal, oil, groceries, shoveled snow and did whatever Grandma and Grandpa needed. Helping them was part of my daily routine when I was in high school and junior college. Our idyllic relationship lasted after Grandpa's death until she died in 1950 at the age of 89, although I couldn't do the daily chores after I left town in 1943 and my 12-year-old brother had to take over.

This was not a physical relationship. Hugging and kissing were not part of their Scandinavian tradition. We knew and understood the bond and felt it, but it did not include much touching. In many cultures physical contact is part of bonding, and I think this is good. But I can't believe that any amount of bodily contact could have made the bonds I had with both Grandpa and Grandma Hanson any stronger than I remember them.

*Bans Hanson and Bertha Johnson Hanson
in 1936 at their 50th wedding anniversary*

3

SIBLINGS OF MY GRANDPARENTS

✦

(My Great Aunts and Great Uncles)

Siblings of John Anderson Beck

Grandpa John Beck had six siblings. Three I never knew: Nicholas (Matti) Keto who lived and died in Finland; Mary, who lived in Michigan, with her first husband Matt Mattson and their four children and her second husband Henry Anderson and their three children; and Emelia, who was born in 1893 and died in childbirth in 1920 after coming to Mountain Iron from Finland in 1902 and marrying August Takala a year or two before her death. (August Takala and his children by a subsequent wife were living in Mountain Iron during the years I lived there. Their children were friends and schoolmates of mine and of my brother, although we did not know then that their father had first been married to our father's aunt.)

A brother Oscar Beck lived in upper Michigan (Calumet, I think) and was married to Fanny. They had eight children, all of whose names began with E. I was not aware of his existence until he showed up at Grandpa Beck's funeral in 1940. I learned much later that Oscar had come to America in the early 1900s leaving a wife and child in Finland. His brothers John Beck and Alex Keto didn't know about this, but they did know about his American wife, Fanny, who had just been delivered of child number three when Wife One and child from Finland arrived in Mountain Iron looking for Oscar. She found only Alex and John, who, when they recovered from the shock, paid her $100 to disappear. Changing his name from Keto to Beck probably also threw Wife One off the track. Oscar also had a third wife after Fanny's death many years later.

A fifth sibling was a sister Wilhelmina (Minnie) who married Matt Rautiola and had 11 children. They lived in northern Minnesota—in Mountain Iron until I was about six years old and then on a farm a few miles north. I don't remember Minnie and Matt who rarely came in from the farm, but I did know some of their children. Their youngest, Walter, actually attended kindergarten in Mountain Iron with me, but I never saw him after that. I played in the town band with their older son Hunley for several years. A son Elmer graduated from Mountain Iron High School in 1935. During or just after his service in World War II he died of cancer. One of the Rautiola daughters, Alma, late in life and widowed, married my mother's widowed brother Ben Hanson. Alma had graduated from Mountain Iron High School in 1931 after her parents had moved out of Mountain Iron. She told me she lived with my grandparents while she was going to school and worked for my father in his post office/store, but Uncle Roland who was living in that house at that time did not remember that they were housing Alma. Considering how small the house was I am baffled at this memory lapse by one or both.

The other sibling I knew was another brother of my grandfather, Alexander Keto, who was apparently the only one in the United States who kept the family name. Alex and his wife Hulda lived next door to Grandpa John Beck and his wife, also named Hulda. Alex was about ten years younger than John. The overlapping generations put me in kindergarten with not only Walter Rautiola but also Minerva Keto, both cousins of my father (my first cousins once removed). I do not remember being aware then that we were related. I saw my great-uncle Alex often as I was growing up and I don't believe that he ever spoke a single word to me. He appeared not to know that I existed.

Neither the Ketos nor the Rautiolas were ever included in our family social gatherings. I guess these were Hanson events expanded to include the Becks, and there wouldn't have been room for either of these other large families. For whatever reason, we had little contact with the Finnish branch of my family. I don't remember ever being in their homes. My closest contact was much later with my father's cousin Minerva Keto who was my age and whom I discovered in the 1950s living in Palo Alto, California, when we lived in Los Altos. At that time she was married to Joe Smith, and we exchanged very pleasant visits a few times until we moved back to Rochester, New York, and they were divorced and left Palo Alto.

My other significant contact was in the 1990s with cousin Alma Rautiola in Alamo, Texas, who had become my aunt by marrying my mother's brother, Uncle Ben Hanson.

I think the Beck and Keto and Rautiola first cousins were fairly friendly in their generation, especially the Becks and Ketos who were next-door neighbors and near the same ages. Brothers Alex and John seemed to be friends, although their wives did not seem to have much in common. The Ketos remained Finnish Lutherans for their entire lives, which meant being confirmed in a Finnish-speaking church, and the Becks had left for the English-speaking Presbyterian church. The younger Beck children spoke little or no Finnish while all of the Ketos were bilingual. The Becks were firmly intent on becoming Americans and minimizing their Finnish/Swedish culture. The Ketos appeared to be equally intent on retaining their Finnish culture and remaining close to the Finnish community. When Alex Keto wrote his memoirs in 1953 it was published in Finnish. (See Appendix II for an English translation, which I think, is a great contribution to our knowledge of their life in Russian Finland in the late 19th century.)

Hulda Keto died in 1944, one year after Hulda Beck. Alex moved to Seattle and married a widow, Hilma Koski, in 1948. He died in Seattle in 1955.

Siblings of Hulda Bygden Beck.

This branch of the family was nearly unknown to me. Other than my grandmother I only remember meeting Emil in 1938 on his farm in Michigan, and Emma both on that trip and later at Leland Beck's first wedding in Dearborn, Michigan, in 1949. My limited impressions were entirely favorable.

It appears that this branch of the family did not travel out of Michigan very much so they didn't get to Minnesota; and we only traveled to Michigan once, in 1938. It is also true that five of the 11 siblings of my grandmother had died before I was born and one other died before our 1938 trip to Michigan.

When their mother, Maria, died in 1947 only four of her eleven children were still alive. Five died before the age of five years and a sixth died at age 35. (Four of the children died of diphtheria, three in the same year.) Even her daughter, Hulda, my grandmother, died four years before her mother. It is not surprising that I remember my great-grandmother only as a person who did not smile easily, if at all. (A much different impression than the one in Chapter I quoted from her granddaughter Virginia Bygden Fox.)

Virginia Fox was the daughter of my Grandmother Hulda Bygden's brother Charles. I did not know that she existed until I was past my 74th birthday. She had become interested in genealogy and was tracing the family of her aunt, my grandmother Hulda Bygden Beck. She supplied me with names and dates of earlier generations in exchange for information about the Becks.

She told another story of one of Maria and Johann Bygden's sons, her Uncle Joel. I have previously noted the stories of Johann Petter Bygden's love of alcohol. Apparently his son Joel was similarly inclined. Joel married a French woman who wore her hair and dressed in a way that disguised her femininity. (This was probably in the 1920s when fashionable women were called flappers and had short hair and wore mannish clothes; but East Tawas, Michigan, did not look kindly on fashionable women.) One of their sons complained to his mother that his friends taunted him by saying that when he was walking down the street with one of his parents they couldn't tell whether it was his mother or his father. His mother said, "Tell them if it staggers it's your father."

Siblings of Bans Hanson

These are relatives I did not know and who did not leave survivors, so Grandpa Hanson is the only one of this family I can describe. He had one brother, Charles (mentioned previously) and one sister, Dikka. They lived their lives in Eau Claire, Wisconsin, and if there was anything other than a dull, comfortable, middle class existence I heard nothing about it. Charles did have the aforementioned misfortune of falling in love with a Roman Catholic, so his life's challenge apparently was to keep his parents from finding this out.

Siblings of Bertha Johnson Hanson

The Jolly Johnsons: Johnny, Anna, Otto, and Bertha

This picture is of the four Johnson siblings I knew well. Bertha was my Grandmother Hanson, Anna (Olson) was her older sister, and Otto and Johnny were their two kid brothers, Johnny being the youngest.

This is the branch of my family that really kept in close touch with each other and the only part of that generation that I really got to know. Knowing them was for me a great and probably significant experience in shaping my life.

There were six children in the Odegaard (Johnson) family. The oldest, John, was born in Norway. Anna was born in Wisconsin in 1856, the year the family arrived from Norway. The other four, also born in Wisconsin, were Bergit (Bertha, my grandmother), Oline (Lena), Ole (Otto) and Johannes (Johnny—to distinguish him from his oldest brother John).

I did not know John or Oline who had probably died before I was old enough to remember them. I remember the others very well.

Aunt Annie was five years older than Grandma Hanson and was widowed before I was born. Her married name was Olson and she had at least four grown children whom we saw occasionally. Aunt Annie was quite deaf. She came to Mountain Iron from her home in Minneapolis to visit Bertha once a year and the sisters greatly enjoyed being together.

Aunt Annie was warm and friendly and laughed a lot. Her hearing aid was a speaking tube, and she enjoyed having me talk into it. She was an amateur fortuneteller and always carried her worn deck of cards. It was a family tradition when Aunt Annie arrived to have her tell your fortune and maybe some of the members believed a little, especially when she saw money in your future. It was hard for me to see how this was compatible with their Christian beliefs; and Grandpa Hanson never allowed his fortune to be told, being as skeptical of fortune telling as he was of Christianity. It was mainly a game which allowed Aunt Annie, who missed most of the conversations because of her deafness, to participate in family activities.

Annie would accept a beer on the rare occasions one was offered her, and would drink it enthusiastically, always remarking, "This is good for my stomach." Grandma did not normally take medicine, but Aunt Annie arrived with a large stock of non-prescription drugs. Every night when Aunt Annie was there, the two of them would tie their hair up in bits of cloth rags—the curlers of their day—put on their nightgowns, and sit at the kitchen table to share Annie's assortment of pills and tonics. Aunt Annie would again announce with smug satisfaction: "This is good for my stomach."

It must have been, because she lived in relatively good health other than for poor hearing and eyesight until she was about 93 years old.

Uncle Otto (Ole) Johnson was younger than Grandma. Even though he always seemed ancient to me, Grandma referred to him as the kid along with his younger brother Johnny. Otto was the only member of his family and perhaps of that generation in any of the branches of my family to have a somewhat professional skill. He was a registered pharmacist, and that, besides having no children, made him comfortably well off. This did not in any other way set him apart from the others in the family.

Uncle Otto and his wife, Aunt Ethel, lived in Parkville, Minnesota, a very small bedroom community about 2 miles from Mountain Iron. Years after I left home it was annexed by the City of Mountain Iron. It had always been part of the Mountain Iron school district. Otto worked in Virginia, which was about two miles in the opposite direction and was big enough to have a drug store or two that employed pharmacists.

Otto and Ethel were childless, probably not by choice, so they took a great interest in Bertha's children, and then later in me, the first of Bertha's grandchildren. They were always extremely good to me and I was always welcome at their house. I felt as much at home there as in my own or Grandma Hanson's house, and they were always included in the Beck-Hanson holiday gatherings. Aunt

Ethel usually tried to book one of them at her house even though it meant that 15 to 20 people without cars had to travel instead of the two of them who did have a car.

In the early years of my life it was not too inconvenient to visit the Johnsons in Parkville because an interurban streetcar, which traversed the Mesabi Range, went past our house and past their house. I vaguely remember members of our Mountain Iron families laden with cooked food and Christmas gifts boarding the streetcar in front of our house for the trip to Parkville. When the streetcar was replaced by a Greyhound bus this became much less convenient. It helped greatly when my father got a car.

The most wonderful thing about Uncle Otto and Aunt Ethel was that they had a car—the first one in our family in northern Minnesota. And it was not just a car. Most of the few people who had cars in the mid-1920s had flivvers—Model T Fords—or older touring cars with soft tops and ising glass windows. Otto had an Oldsmobile! The one I remember was very high, had large real glass windows that looked like picture windows, upholstered seats, window shades with velvet fringes, and very fancy interior lights. The top was solid and the back seat seemed to me to be a luxurious living room. It seated eight passengers, three in the front seat, three in the back, and two on jump seats that folded down from the backs of the front seat. This was probably a 1924 or 1925 model.

Quite often on Sundays, Otto and Ethel would pick up Grandma Hanson, my mother and me, and maybe Grandpa or my father and take us for a ride. Ethel did not drive, but she was very nervous when Otto drove, so she did a lot of back seat driving. It was not long before they decided to help my Uncle Ben, my mother's brother who was about 19 or 20 at the time, earn some college money by being their chauffeur. After that our rides were more frequent, longer, and more pleasant. Even after Ben left the local junior college for Ohio State another junior college student named Bill Anderson succeeded him.

They got a second Oldsmobile to replace the first. It was probably a 1928 model, not as luxurious as the first, but it probably ran better. Even though this was not as formidable a vehicle to drive, I don't think Otto ever got to be comfortable behind the wheel (at least when Aunt Ethel was in the car) and after my father got a car in 1931 the Oldsmobile didn't get a lot more use except when Otto and Ethel came to Mountain Iron to visit.

Otto's hobby was his house and yard. He built a very unusual house on his large lot (possibly two acres), and landscaped it with circular walks and a pond, a summer house, and eventually a swimming pool of sorts. He loved to do sculpture with concrete and I especially remember a couple of lions he had by his lily pond. Some years later he attempted a large sculpture of an Indian maiden, which I considered less than fine art even though he seemed quite proud of it. His procedure was to form his intended shape with steel mesh and then plaster wet cement on the form, shaping his sculpture into its ultimate form while the cement was still wet. The house and yard were placed on the National Register of Historic Places, including whatever sculpture has survived, so I was shocked on my visit in 1996 to discover that the house is no longer there, having been replaced by a large log structure.

Uncle Otto could also play the fiddle and the Jew's harp. He seemed very talented to me, but at that age I was probably no better a music critic than I was an art critic.

Aunt Ethel was the dominant force in their marriage. She was a woman of strong opinions and since Otto was quiet and not inclined to rock the boat he did whatever she planned. I suspect that he did what he wanted to do most of the time, but luckily it was the same as what she thought she wanted. One of her big things was Temperance and the WCTU (Women's Christian Temperance Union.) She was firmly opposed to alcohol and was such a strong personality that no one dared bring out booze when she was around. This meant that my father and Uncle Hap (who were not really serious drinkers) felt challenged to arrange to drink secretly at our holiday gatherings. Luckily most holidays were in the cold Minnesota winters and the cars needed to be started up frequently to keep them from freezing. The car-starting trips provided sufficient opportunity for surreptitious imbibing.

Both Aunt Ethel and Uncle Otto treated me as a highly favored grandson, even though I was only a grandnephew. I don't remember hearing a cross word or even a hint of criticism from them. When Otto had some health problems and could no longer keep up his large property, they sold it and moved to Hastings, Minnesota, fairly near St. Paul. Since they had no other reason for moving there, I assumed it was so they would be within visiting distance when I attended the University of Minnesota. And I did happily visit them in Hastings as often as I could.

Sometime during World War II after I had been graduated from the University and left for other Navy service, they moved to Wisconsin. Otto's health was failing and they headed for the old family homestead near Elk Mound where Otto's youngest brother Johnny, a bachelor, lived with a couple of bachelor nephews—Olive's sons Orville and Clarence Hedmark. They were probably happy to put up with Otto and Ethel in exchange for Ethel's cooking and housekeeping. But Otto had a paralyzing stroke and when I stopped to see them on my way home from my Navy service in 1946, Otto was unable to speak or get out of bed and he died soon after.

Ethel then moved to a rooming house in Eau Claire, and later to a retirement home. We stopped to see her on our move back to California in 1967 and she died less than a year later. I was glad that she did get to see all of my children. She must have been close to 90 when she died, although it was a family joke that she would never reveal her age.

The last and youngest member of the Johnson family was Johnny. He must have wondered why he was given the same name as his oldest brother John, but I suppose good Norwegians were not much given to idle speculation. Acceptance was part of the direct route to heaven.

Johnny inherited the family farmstead in Elk Creek, Wisconsin, and none of his siblings ever begrudged him a square inch of it. He never married and he was joined by two bachelor nephews, Orville and Clarence Hedmark. The three of them squeezed a livelihood from the land for as long as they lived in the house that was built by my great-grandfather before the Civil War.

Uncle Johnny was a typical bachelor great-uncle. He came to visit us three or four times in my lifetime and I always thought he was wonderful. He laughed a lot, played the fiddle when he was coaxed to do so, and (I found out in later years) went out nights to tour the local saloons. He rounded out the wonderful family of Grandma, Aunt Annie, and Uncle Otto—all warm, happy, friendly, optimistic, and loving in spite of the tragedies they had endured in their lives. I was only vaguely aware at the time that these were the people who were teaching me that no matter how bad or how difficult life is, it is a wonderful gift, which has been given us to be enjoyed under all circumstances.

4

MY FATHER: JOHN LENNART ANDERSON BECK

When my father was born in 1894 in Tawas City, Michigan, his father was using the name John Anderson, and my father was given his name, John, plus Lennart, plus of course, the family name Anderson.

This was changed to Beck sometime within the next two years, for reasons that were never fully explained, after the family moved to Oscoda, Michigan. For whatever reason, the change was a good one considering the oversupply of Andersons. The change gave my father some problems in later years, but he survived those and here we are in the second generation of this proud family name, which as I explained in earlier chapters should have been Keto.

Lennart, as my father was most commonly known throughout his life, moved with his parents from East Tawas, Michigan, to Oscoda, Michigan, then to Cloquet, Minnesota, and then to Mountain Iron, Minnesota, between the time he was born and the time he was about fourteen years old. They settled in Mountain Iron for the rest of their lives. Not only did his parents stay in Mountain Iron until they died, so did Lennart. While my mother, who was born and died there, warned me it would be a fate worse than death for me to do the same, my father Lennart refused to consider living elsewhere.

My mother was discussing my fate, not hers, when she said Mountain Iron was no place to plan to live in, since by that time she was resigned to her fate. But I couldn't help but think that she had wished at least a little that her husband, Lennart, hadn't been so set on living only there. Her own parents also lived in Mountain Iron until they died, so since Mother was the only one of the five children in her family who stayed there, I think for that reason she would also have been reluctant to consider moving away. But her advice to me was right on.

Lennart had gone to Mountain Iron High School and graduated in its first class along with his wife-to-be, then Mabel Hanson. She was younger than he.

He had waited two years until the school was built and opened; she had been just the right age and didn't have to wait to enter the new high school. After he had returned from World War I military service and she had returned from teaching school in Montana they were married in 1922.

Lennart's younger brother Leo, the same age as Mabel Hanson, was also a member of that same high school class. The two brothers went to Macalester College together for nearly two years and then left together to enlist in the Navy in 1917 when the United States entered the war. Lennart kept a journal of his wartime experiences, which I am including as Appendix III.

Instead of returning to college they returned to Mountain Iron after the war. Before either Lennart or his brother Leo were married, the two brothers started a business in Mountain Iron selling candy, ice cream, tobacco, magazines, non-prescription drugs and other non-essentials. In a town of less than 1,500 mostly poor immigrants this didn't produce much income. Somehow Dad managed to get appointed postmaster, and the added income kept the business afloat. Leo eventually decided it was too little income for the two of them, both by then married, so he and his wife left town and my father was stuck with the marginal business.

Dad enjoyed being his own boss, being an important personage (the postmaster) in his small town, and having endless political discussions with the men who dropped into his store. I remember that during those years he always had a callus on one elbow from leaning on the counters while he talked. Mother disliked the long hours he worked and the low income it generated, but she complained very little.

Besides the long hours at the store/post office, Dad was often away playing baseball in the summertime. He had been a baseball star in college, had played some while he was in the Navy during the war, and had been offered at least a tryout with the Crookston, Minnesota, professional team in the Class D Northern League. His mother talked him out of attempting to become a professional baseball player and he never pursued that offer. But Mountain Iron, like most of the towns on the Mesabi Range, had a baseball team. There was at least an informal league with a season schedule of home and away games, usually one evening a week and on Sunday afternoons. Evening practice and the evening games were possible without floodlights because northern Minnesota has very long summer days.

It seemed to me that Dad enjoyed playing baseball more than anything else, and he stayed on the team and played well until he was at least 45 years old. Between his store and his baseball we didn't see him at home much in the summertime, although he took me to some of his games when he thought I was old enough.

The postmastership in the fourth class post offices, even though it required a civil service examination, was a political appointment. Lennart was an outspoken and loyal Republican, so when Franklin Roosevelt and the Democrats defeated Hoover in 1932 his job was doomed. He managed to hang on until 1935, but finally was replaced by someone more acceptable to the Democrats.

His successor was the son of a U. S. Treasury agent who had been the chief enforcer of the Eighteenth Amendment in northern Minnesota. The Eighteenth Amendment made the production, sale, and consumption of alcoholic beverages illegal in the United States and was in force from about 1918 until about 1934. Not surprisingly, this law was much broken and is credited with making millionaires out of gangsters all over the country. Treasury Agents hired and assigned to enforce the law had no difficulty keeping busy.

Matt Viitala, the Treasury Agent who lived in Mountain Iron, had managed to become the richest man in town. He was never openly accused of having taken bribes, but it was hard to accept that he had been able to get that rich on only his salary from a government job.

His son, Rudy, was about 25 years old then, and had not been able to launch a career during the depression, so with Matt's help he got the appointment as postmaster. This was fortunate for my father, because Matt was willing to buy the candy and tobacco business to go along with the postmastership, and was able to pay cash for it. I remember Dad showing me the handful (I can't remember whether it was 12, or 13, or 15) of $100 bills he had been paid, a sight neither of us had ever seen. It seemed like a fortune, and, indeed, we lived quite well on it for the next year, during which Dad found very little work, as I remember.

1936 was a rather bad year for the national economy since the depression was continuing and it was a peak year for a drought that drastically hurt Midwestern farmers. But even with little other income such as Mother's substitute teaching, we took a trip to the state of Washington, had a new car—a 1934 Chevrolet to replace the 1929—and I got a new bicycle with balloon tires to replace the overweight monstrosity with clincher tires I had bought from Bill Voss for $1.50 a couple of years before. It is amazing what that $1200 or $1300 did in 1936.

By the end of that year, though, Lennart needed a steady income. He decided to run in the fall election for the job of village clerk, which paid $150 a month, or $1800 a year. The term was for two years. He won the election quite handily and had two years in a job that he not only liked, but one that fit his talents. My mother liked it, too, because it did not demand a great deal of time beyond a normal eight-hour working day. Those were probably the happiest years of their lives during the time I lived at home.

Unfortunately, Dad lost the next election. It was only by about two or four votes, but he was out of work again. He managed to get a job in the Wacootah Mine, which was not only dirty and physical but also seasonal. If Mother didn't get some work as a substitute teacher, things got pretty tight when bills came due during the winter months. Nevertheless they squeaked by and we ate every day—well, in fact—and as the war approached the mines worked longer hours and longer seasons.

I was not ever a drain on their finances. From the time I was in the fifth or sixth grade I played in the village band, which paid enough to keep me in spending money and even paid for many of my very modest clothes purchases. When I got out of high school I got a part-time job for twenty-five cents an hour in a local gas station which let me accumulate $75 which more than covered my first year college expenses including lunches, which as I remember cost me four cents a day.

After Pearl Harbor there were no further problems with money. In 1942, after my freshman year in junior college, I got a summer clerical job with the Great Northern Railway Company paying $5.05 a day for six days a week. Dad worked summers in the mine and winters on the Duluth, Missabe, and Iron Range Railroad as a track laborer.[1] His hourly railroad pay was less than mine and the hours were long. He was now almost fifty years old and working at hard labor for 12 or 14 hours a day in subfreezing, often subzero, weather. He kept us awake nights with his coughing. The cold weather, his years of cigarette smoking, and his age, to say nothing of the hard work he was doing, showed. But he felt that God and Uncle Sam were telling him that it was his duty to do this to help win the war, so he never complained.

I think it was before the war was over that he managed to get a job at the Oliver Iron Mining Company, a branch of U. S. Steel, in their warehouse. This was less physical, made at least some use of his intelligence and his mathematical aptitude, and kept him employed until he reached retirement age. He had a few years with an income above the poverty level. Unfortunately Mother had died

---

1.   Like many Indian words, Mesabi had more than one spelling. The railroad chose Missabe, and a township used Mesaba. Mesabi was the most commonly used and was used to name the sixty-mile by one-mile vein of rich iron ore and the string of mining towns known as the Mesabi Iron Range. The name came from a legendary Chief Mesabi.

before that income did her much good, and also unfortunately it came too late in life to provide him with more than a meager retirement income.

I doubt that it would be possible for anyone to live up to the Biblical Ten Commandments better than Dad did. He was totally honest and trustworthy; he never touched anything that didn't belong to him. I am sure he was a completely faithful husband. He was generous and charitable even though he had little to be charitable with. He had a civic pride, felt an obligation to be a good citizen and was always ready to volunteer for community activities. His goal in life was to be able to live with himself and he set the standards very high and lived up to those standards.

He was also intelligent. I was impressed when I transcribed his World War I journal to note that it had been written in ink, and yet I found no errors in spelling or grammar and few if any strikeovers. He read almost only works of the more serious writers—I remember Victor Hugo, for example—and he read a chapter of the Bible in several languages daily, just for fun.

With all these wonderful talents, I am disappointed that he wasn't able to make better use of them to achieve an easier and more productive life for him and for Mother. He never admitted even to himself that his life was less than satisfactory.

Why? What made him live the life he did?

In his wartime journal he wrote that because he was the oldest he felt an obligation to return home to help his father support his large family.

He also was extremely cautious and seemed to have a need to avoid the risks of change. When he decided to vote for Warren Harding and the Republicans in 1920, he made a commitment to vote the straight Republican ticket for the rest of his life, and he did. When he joined the Presbyterian Church, he never questioned that decision again. When he bought a house in 1926 he vowed never to move again, and he did not. By the time he was 30 or 35 years old he had made all of his decisions for life and from then on refused to reconsider any of them.

One of the doctrines of the Presbyterian Church he accepted was predestination. I am not sure the church hadn't modified this since the days of John Calvin, but Dad felt that he had no control over his life since it had been preordained. I always felt this was a hedge against failure. He felt it was an explanation for his having to do mindless, painful physical labor for long hours and little pay even though the God he believed in had given him the intellectual tools to perform at a far higher level.

You would think that someone who believed in the archaic notion of predestination would have been a fundamentalist Christian. Dad was not a fundamentalist, at least in the years he shared some of his beliefs with me. He did not think, at least in the 1930's, that it was necessary to believe literally in the virgin birth, the resurrection, the creation, Noah, Jonah and the whale, and many other Biblical myths to be a Christian. In those years he attended regional or state meetings of Presbyterians to defend liberal preachers who expressed doubts about Christianity requiring literal beliefs in Bible stories.

I believe that his professed belief in predestination was an excuse for lack of courage or confidence. I also have to believe that his insistence on staying in Mountain Iron in case his father's family needed him was his back-up excuse.

I admire my father for his good qualities. I was less than thrilled when, after he had helped finance his brothers through college, and it was time for me to go he said, in effect: You must go to college but I can't help you. The truth was that he knew I was capable of doing it on my own. He was right, of course, that even at age 16 I didn't need his help, but I still felt a bit betrayed having to set out for college with nothing to fall back on. I should have been flattered, I suppose.

His high ethics and morality notwithstanding, Dad was a bigot. As postmaster and village clerk he helped the immigrant Slavs and Italians and he played base-ball with their sons, but he would never have forgiven someone in our family who had married an Italian or a Slav or any other Catholic. Negroes and Jews he con-sidered even more inferior and one of his favorite sayings was that Mountain Iron had never had any serious problems because they didn't have any niggers or Jews living there. Mountain Iron, of course, had the same problems as any town of its size and none of them were caused by the Ben Solosky or the Cy Ettinger families who were Jewish and who had lived there during some of my childhood years.

I could never understand the source of his bigotry or why he believed so strongly that northern Europeans were better than southern, and Protestants bet-ter than Catholics or Jews. It is less difficult to understand his negative feelings toward non-whites, since that was pretty much the prevailing wisdom of the day and people living in northern Minnesota almost never saw anyone other than an occasional American Indian whose skin was not white. That meant there was no chance to test that prevailing wisdom with first hand experience.

How did this man stack up as a father? I think he seemed a little afraid of the responsibility and unsure of his role, but our relationship during my childhood was acceptable. He certainly set a good example of strong moral principles. He did not resort to physical punishment; in fact, I don't remember his punishing me in any way.

One of his strange quirks that I found confusing was his belief that pride was a sin and humility a virtue. I was a good student in school and got mostly A's.

Since everybody in Mountain Iron knew everything about everybody, it was not uncommon for people to comment on how smart I was when they saw my father and me together. He felt that this called for a counter remark, a put-down of some kind to reveal that I had counterbalancing weaknesses. These public revelations of my private frailties, especially unavoidable physical flaws, were not good for my self-confidence, and seemed inconsistent with his expecting me to be an A student and then apparently denying its importance.

I figured out later that he was really very proud of me, at least as a student, and was happy that the world knew it. It was just that he felt guilty to feel proud. It was probably related to the attitude that kept him accepting menial jobs instead of striving for better ones. He felt he should stick to the class into which he had been born and sometimes warned me and my brother to do likewise and not to strive to become too high and mighty in our working careers.

Dad was a very moderate drinker and alcohol was not one of his vices. He also never was fat. Tobacco, however, shortened his life. He smoked heavily from the time he was 23 or 24 years old until he died at age 75. He usually accompanied his cigarettes with coffee.

My father was easy to live with. I felt that he may have given me more from his negatives than from his positives: living in poverty made me determined not to do likewise; fumbling through life without a hint of goals for a career inspired me to do otherwise. But he also showed me that being honest, ethical, charitable and trustworthy were more important for personal satisfaction in life than being wealthy. His creed seemed to be "Always remember that you will have to live with yourself for the rest of your life, and behave accordingly."

Dad was unusual for his time in one respect. He was not a male chauvinist. He did not divide the work of the world into women's and men's, and was always willing to do any of the jobs around the house that Mother did. I think, in fact, he would have been happy to have been a househusband if Mother had been the wage earner.

John Lennart Beck in many ways approached perfection, and in many other ways he fell woefully short. He was human. Even though some of his weaknesses were disappointing to me, I have to admit that on the whole if all of humankind shared his good qualities and maybe even endured his bad ones, the world would probably get along very well, indeed.

5

MY MOTHER: MABEL LEILA HANSON BECK

John Lennart and Mabel Hanson Beck
My Parents
Lake Superior, 1949

Mabel was rather shy and quiet She tended to stay in the background. She did not become the president of the American Legion Auxiliary or the Presbyterian Ladies Aid or the P. T. A., or whatever else she belonged to. She was a hard worker and exercised leadership in small groups in her own quiet way.

This diffidence was not from lack of intelligence. She had been the valedictorian of the Mountain Iron High School class of 1915, the first graduating class from that school. Her husband, Lennart, was the salutatorian (second-highest academic rank) of the same class, but she did not ever use this academic triumph to his disadvantage.

That was probably her most typical characteristic. She was so acutely sensitive to the feelings of others that she was always careful to avoid making anyone feel at a disadvantage.

She was an elementary school teacher by profession, and perhaps the first grade was her favorite. I can picture her as being nearly ideal for the job. I see her taking 20 to 25 six-year-olds from all levels of ability and background and immaturity and molding them into readers and counters and eager seekers of knowledge.

I am sure she never ridiculed or browbeat the slower ones. I am sure she never held up the brighter kids as models. She was the kind of person who recognized everyone for what he or she had been given, and treated the kids with love and tenderness as individuals who were each doing the best they could. She had the patience to bring out the best in each of them and was not dismayed that they were not all geniuses.

This empathy carried over into all other parts of her life. It included the way she brought us up. I don't remember ever being angry with her. I don't consider that she ever criticized—only corrected. When, for example, she corrected my grammar or pronunciation—as she often did, until I got it right—it was always done quietly and politely. She never made me feel guilty or inferior about any of my mistakes (in anything, not just in language) no matter how serious or stupid they may have been. Her approach made me want to be perfect in her eyes, which would not have been the case if she had been either verbally or physically harsh.

She also tolerated my being myself even if that did not necessarily conform to what "they" did. It was not important to her when I played childish games or played with toys that others might have thought I was too big or too old for. She didn't discourage me from keeping scrapbooks or baseball statistics or writing nonsense on the typewriter. She never even hinted that she thought it was important to be like everybody else, or even like somebody else, or that to be different was bad. She obviously felt that I had the same right to be an individual at whatever age I was, as had her first graders—and, I suppose, as she herself had. Her message, though I don't remember her ever saying it, was clear: The important thing in life is not to conform to what we think are the standards of others, but is to know for ourselves what is right and to live up to our own high standards.

This was all done very subtly. In fact, I never had thought much about this until now, as I am remembering my mother 50 years after her death. It is probably not too much of a simplification to describe her as being guided principally by the Golden Rule. Because she herself was very sensitive, she applied the Golden Rule with that sensitivity. This meant that she believed that the others we were to do unto included more than just whites of northern European ancestry; it included *everybody*. This broad interpretation was not widely shared by her friends and relatives in her generation. Her first and last teaching jobs were on Indian reservations, which may have helped her see non-whites as human beings a couple of generations before it became a little more widely accepted.

I do not know how she happened to marry my father. They had, of course, been classmates in high school, but were apparently at that time no more than somewhat casual friends. My father's journal during his World War I military service mentioned several girl friends, but Mabel only casually. She had completed her course at Duluth Normal School (which later became Duluth State Teachers College, and still later the University of Minnesota at Duluth) and was teaching in Montana when he returned to Mountain Iron.

Somehow during that time they remembered each other and decided that marriage would be the right thing, so they married in 1922. I was born in 1924 and my brother Gerry in 1930. Mother died in 1952, so she and Lennart had thirty years together. During the Great Depression and World War II there were difficult years, but I think that on the whole theirs was a happy marriage that survived even difficult years surprisingly well.

Married women were not allowed to teach in those days, at least in northern Minnesota, so Mother was able to pursue her profession only occasionally as a substitute teacher. She always continued to teach Sunday school so she retained some contact with five to seven year olds, her favorite people.

My parents and I moved into the only house they ever owned in 1926 and that was where she died 26 years later. It was a very small house very poorly designed. It had no basement and was not insulated, which made it extremely uncomfortable in the cold Minnesota winters and even in the somewhat hot Minnesota summers. It had only one electrical outlet that had to be used for lamps, refrigerator, radio, iron, vacuum cleaner, toaster, and whatever else needed to be plugged in. That wasn't so bad in 1926 when the refrigerator was a non-electric icebox and they had no radio, but as the age of electricity progressed the house felt something like a giant spider web with many wires coming out of this one outlet. It was not possible to provide the one outlet with enough receptacles to keep everything plugged in all of the time and if it had been possible it would have overloaded the circuit. This meant we were constantly plugging and unplugging things.

The refrigerator had to be unplugged when the washing machine was running, for example. If you forgot to plug the refrigerator back in, the milk would turn sour or other bad things would happen.

This was only a minor inconvenience. It was more inconvenient that the house never had any kitchen counters or cabinets, so the only surface Mother had to work on was a much too low kitchen table. Even the sink had no counters beside it.

There was no space for a washing machine in the house, so it was kept outside on a back porch and had to be hauled in along with a rack and some laundry tubs for rinsing, which were stored in a detached garage. The washing machine was not automatic, but it was electric and even had an electric rather than a hand-operated wringer. The machine and the rinse tubs had to be filled by hand, and emptied by hand. Then the clothes had to be hung on a line outside, often in below-freezing weather; there were even times when the snow was so deep it was necessary to shovel paths under the lines to keep the clothes from lying on the snow.

It was a good thing Mother didn't have a job outside of home, because her work at home required a great deal of time and strength and Mother was not very big nor very strong. There were no such things as dishwashers, garbage disposals, automatic washers and dryers, permanent press fabrics, and many other labor savers we now take for granted. There were many things that could have been done to have made her life easier even in those days, but there never seemed to be money available for them, and she never complained about it.

My father helped around the house when he had time, especially with the heavier chores. I was pressed into service, too, as soon as I was big enough, doing most everything except ironing clothes.

The house was heated by a coal and wood stove located in the living room on an inside wall. The coal was kept in an outside shed at the back of the lot. One of my jobs was to mush through the snow and cold with a coalscuttle so we could keep the fire going. During some winters we couldn't afford coal so we burned free wood that we had gathered in the Minnesota forests.

After I became an avid reader and patron of the local library, I remember noting that Mother read very little, even of the newspaper. This seemed strange since she was an educated, intelligent person. It was several years later that I discovered it was because she badly needed glasses and was never willing to spend the money to get them, deciding that there were more important uses for the limited money that was available. (She did finally get glasses, about the time I finished high school.)

Mother did not, as I remember, attend competitions that I was in such as football games and speech contests. I think she must have been afraid either to see me lose or to get hurt. I think she did attend plays and at least some band concerts that I was in where there was no competition.

Perhaps she avoided public events because she was shy, or maybe just because she was busy or tired. She did not like to go to the grocery store, so I did most of the grocery shopping from the time I was 10 or 12. I didn't have to deal with money because the grocer kept a tab, which my father paid once a month. Grocery shopping was much different in those days. Mother gave me a list of the items she wanted to have. I walked to the store and read the list to a clerk who, sometimes needing a ladder to reach them, gathered the items from the shelves and put them in a bag for me to carry home along with an itemized, hand-written bill which my mother checked carefully. If there were any errors she could correct them by telephone. If she remembered something that she had forgotten while I was en route she would call the store and have it added to the list I was carrying. There weren't many choices of brands and the clerks knew which ones to select for us.

Dad tried to teach Mother to drive a car, but she never got the hang of it and gave up after she ran into a pole. Dad was not a very good driver nor teacher, and it took a fair amount of coordination to drive a 1929 Chevrolet which of course did not have automatic transmission or power steering. Apparently neither of them had the courage or the patience nor felt a strong need for Mother to learn to drive.

Mother became a cigarette smoker after we got a car. Dad was a heavy smoker and couldn't drive very far without a cigarette. He also needed both hands to drive, so Mother decided that in the interest of safety she had better light them for him. In time she grew to like smoking. She didn't smoke a lot, and I don't think it contributed to her early death. As I remember she never felt right about smoking and did so only in private, hoping that no one outside the immediate family would ever know.

She almost never drank alcohol. Maybe a little gin in lemonade on a hot summer day, or a Tom and Jerry at Christmas. She didn't even drink milk, which she apparently disliked because of some bad childhood experience. The coffee pot was always on and I suppose she consumed that, although Dad was the chief consumer of coffee.

Mother's real joy in life was simple and inexpensive: nature and the outdoors. She was awed by the dramatic seasonal changes in Minnesota. She always seemed surprised when spring emerged from the frigid winter, and was thrilled to find a blossoming trailing arbutus among patches of snow. She always brought home pussy willows to decorate the house as a symbol that spring was really there.

Her favorite sport was picking wild berries and she would happily spend the summer in the hot sun among the flies and mosquitoes picking first strawberries, then blueberries, then raspberries as they came sequentially into season. She had expert, flying fingers and could fill cans and buckets faster than anyone else. I hated the heat and the insects and those tiny wild berries; it seemed to take me forever to fill even a small cup.

When you had berries you had to do something with them. That was the wonderful part. The berry pies that Mother and Grandma made were, of course, delicious. And we had berries on cereal, and berries with sugar and cream (not milk!). After we had eaten all the fresh berries we could, and she had given away as much as possible, Mother canned or made jam and jelly of the rest. We ate some of these between the berry seasons, but sometimes the new crops were so good that the supply in storage was forgotten. I think I remember that when my father died in 1969 we found jars of canned blueberries still left from the early 1930's.

We spent a couple of weeks at a lake every summer, which was another highlight of Mother's life, especially if it coincided with the berry season. It is surprising that she never learned to swim. She went into the lake and splashed around, but never attempted to learn how to swim.

Mother also enjoyed the Minnesota fall with its colorful leaves and goldenrod and Indian paintbrush. She and Dad would drive all over the county every nice day on fall weekends or holidays. He would take a gun and look for ruffed grouse if it were hunting season, and she would enjoy the scenery.

This acute awareness of the beauties of nature probably indicates the latent artist in Mother. She had done some passably good drawing and painting in her youth but never pursued this. She was also a good pianist, but let her skills diminish at least partly because she couldn't see without the glasses she refused to admit she needed. Unfortunately she never had the time or the energy or the money for the lessons or the materials or the piano tuning that would have greatly enriched her life. She also enjoyed traveling but they could afford only a very little.

Because she was generally optimistic, I think she looked forward to an enriched life in her later years when either Dad or Gerry or I would become wealthy enough to make it possible to travel more. She never said this to me, I just felt it. Unfortunately this never happened—she died much too young. The only thing I was able to do was to take her, along with Gerry and Dad, on a trip to South Dakota's badlands and Mount Rushmore in the summer of 1949.

Mother had colon cancer and by the time she had it diagnosed and operated on it had spread to her liver and she died in April, 1952, at age 55 after three or four months of suffering. I was only 27 years old, and Gerry was only 21. She had lived a good life, but it was hard and limited. The next 20 years could have been the best.

6

MY FATHER'S SIBLINGS
—My Aunts and Uncles

Next oldest to my father was Leo, born two years later in 1896. Leo and Lennart were close friends throughout their lives. Lennart waited two years for the Mountain Iron high school to be built, so he and Leo were classmates in the first graduating class of that school. They entered Macalester College in St. Paul together, and when the U. S. entered World War I in 1917 they left college near the end of their second year and enlisted in the Navy immediately and together. The Navy did not keep them together, but after the war they went into business together in Mountain Iron.

Leo married a schoolteacher in Mountain Iron, Josephine Whitcomb, who was a bit older than he, and when they wisely decided that one small business in Mountain Iron could not support two families Leo and Jo moved to Dearborn, Michigan and Leo got a job with the United States Gypsum Company. He worked there until he retired. But Leo's heart was always in Mountain Iron and while he was still working he bought a vacation cabin on nearby Lake Leander which they visited every summer. When he retired they sold their home in Dearborn and came back to live in Mountain Iron until he died in 1970. He and his brother Lennart had almost daily contact in their retirement years.

Uncle Leo was a likable person, easygoing and tolerant of the shortcomings of others. Like his siblings he was blessed with above average intelligence and he was especially good at mathematics. He had not finished college, so I think his jobs were mostly in some less technical sales field. But he did well enough to enjoy at least a middle class life and survived the depression without ever being laid off as far as I knew. He was always looking for an easy buck and it was my impression that he did a fair amount of gambling on stocks, horses, and even ideas—good or bad—that didn't ever make him rich. But if he did gamble badly his losses were not serious enough to make him poor.

His wife, Josephine, was generally regarded as the family bitch. Her snide remarks were widely quoted at family gatherings. I remember one that was typical: He (referring to either me or one of my bachelor uncles) had better leave home or he'll end up marrying some trash from the Iron Range like the rest of the Becks. (You can imagine that this did not exactly endear her to my mother, nor to my aunts Jean, Esther, and Ellen, all of whom were raised on the Range and married Becks, and all of whom were intelligent, educated, and refined women who could not possibly have qualified as trash in any social circles.) Every contact with Aunt Jo produced enough of these vitriolic remarks to keep her extremely unpopular until the next time she appeared and renewed her reputation for spewing venom.

Leo always avoided getting involved in these gaffes, and he never showed any signs of being annoyed at or by Josephine. After he retired to Mountain Iron, however, he seemed to spend a lot more time on the streets or visiting his brother Lennart than he spent around home with Jo. Their marriage survived until Leo's death in 1970. Josephine died a few years later. They had one son, Leland Whitcomb Beck, who was born in 1926.

The only female offspring of John and Hulda to survive infancy was Lillian Augusta Wilhelmina Beck, born in 1902. She became known as Tommy because with six brothers she was always one of the boys and considered a tomboy. She became a nurse and married a doctor, Leland Stanford Fuller. They had two children, Faith and Bruce, born in 1930 and 1932, respectively.

Lillian sent her husband packing shortly after Bruce was born and Dr. Fuller returned to his boyhood home near Chicago. Lillian stayed in Mountain Iron with her parents and worked as a nurse to support her children and her parents while her mother helped raise the kids. As far as I know there was never a divorce, and neither of them remarried.

The story I heard from my mother was that Lillian had discovered that Leland Fuller had contracted syphilis in France during World War I. The implication was that he was developing paresis, but there is no evidence that this ever came to pass. It seemed as if Lillian was unable to tolerate his premarital infidelity, or perhaps she feared that syphilis was either incurable or could recur.

From my seven-or eight-year-old point of view, Leland Fuller was the most unpleasant person I had ever known. I barely remember now exactly why I disliked him so much, but I remember him seeming rude, arrogant, impatient, and unkind—not at all like my many other uncles. I heard much later that when a couple of Tommy's cousins came to visit she had to apologize to them for not offering coffee because Lee did not like for her to have visitors. (Not offering coffee to a guest in Minnesota was a most unpardonable sin.) He could tell if she had because he apparently kept track of the coffee supply. He is also reported to have counted things like potatoes to make sure she didn't use any more than she should.

It was probably during Lee and Tommy's brief residence in Mountain Iron that a cousin found a note from Tommy telling her that she had gone to the pit to commit suicide. The pit was an abandoned iron mine that had filled with water and was used as a rather dangerous swimming hole by some of the braver townspeople. This cousin and another rushed to the pit and found Tommy sitting on the bank in tears. They assumed that her problem was her husband, but Tommy was not willing to discuss it then or later. At least she did not go through with her planned suicide.

But this makes me suspicious that she had realized that this man was an unfit husband and father and she got rid of him as soon as she found an excuse.

We have to wonder how she made such a mistake as to marry so incompatibly. She had been very friendly with a man in town named Emil Mattila. He was intelligent but not highly educated and with his two brothers Eino and Heino operated the Red and White grocery store in town. The other brothers were heavy drinkers, but during all the years I knew him, Emil was a non-drinker. Emil apparently waited and did not marry until after Tommy had married Lee Fuller.

I have heard that it was Tommy's mother, my Grandma Beck, who encouraged her to marry a doctor to provide a secure financial future. Bad judgment was not characteristic of Grandma Beck, but perhaps even she made one mistake in her life.

After she freed herself of humorless Lee Fuller, Aunt Tommy became the comic relief character of the Beck family. Actually there was a lot of humor in the family in spite of their Finnish-Swedish background of unsmiling severity. Tommy became the town wit and was a regular actress in community theater, vaudeville, and other stage productions. As a comedienne she was a town and a family institution. Even well into her eighties she performed a funny hat act with her own piano accompaniment.

She was also the village Florence Nightingale. There was often no doctor available, or equally often a less than well-qualified doctor. People believed as much or more in Tommy as in the alternatives, so she became the local medical authority. Whatever she did was appreciated and I am sure she did as well as most of the doctors who were there only because they weren't skilled enough to succeed in bigger, more affluent communities. Tommy was the first person elected into the

Mountain Iron Hall of Fame, which showed that she was widely appreciated. (I believe the second person chosen was a bartender, but perhaps that doesn't represent as great a contrast as it first appeared.)

I enjoyed having her as an aunt. I liked her sense of humor and her theatrical performances and admired her medical reputation. I also enjoyed having her play the piano to accompany my playing the baritone horn. She was outspoken, brash, and totally lovable. She was apparently also not much of a parent, but at least while her mother lived that seemed not to be a serious problem.

The next younger member of the Beck family was Clarence Royal, best known as Phoxey. Poor Clarence was bowlegged from having had rickets, nearsighted, sickly, and the ugly duckling of the Beck family. Probably because of that he was the protected darling of his mother, which made him slightly resented by his siblings. He wore glasses early in life when this was unusual, and he had very blond hair. There was a comic strip called Foxy Grandpa in those days with an elderly character who wore glasses and had white hair, so when blond Clarence showed up in school with glasses he was immediately dubbed Foxy Grandpa. The dauntless Clarence never missed an opportunity to capitalize on a situation, so he eventually glorified the spelling to Phoxey and used that nickname for his entire life.

This was typical of Uncle Phoxey. He always was able to make the lemons that life handed him into lemonade or more often into Tom Collins's. We—his nephews and nieces—always loved Uncle Phoxey. He didn't marry until I was eighteen, so he was the bachelor uncle who gave instructions about how to smoke cigars and drink whiskey without getting sick. Even though I avoided both booze and tobacco until I was at least 20 or 21 years old, I was always impressed with his worldly knowledge and used his advice in later years.

Phoxey had in the 1920s attended Virginia Junior College and Ohio State University, but apparently left Ohio State without getting a degree. Both he and my uncle Ben Hanson, high school and junior college classmates, entered Ohio State University to study chemistry. Ben graduated and had a successful career in the paint industry in Dayton, Ohio. Phoxey apparently majored in phun.

Phoxey's philosophy was to avoid work and never do anything he could get someone else to do. I suppose this was something he perfected as a sickly child and capitalized on even after he had become a healthy adult. After he left Ohio State he found a woman named Bonny and it appeared that she was his main source of support during the early years of the depression. I remember getting Christmas gifts during my childhood from Phoxey and Bonny and I assumed that if she weren't already my aunt she would soon be. They never married, however, and no one ever discussed the reason for this in my presence.

His younger brother, Charles, kept a diary during the year 1930. One entry was: Phoxey helped me wash his car today.

Phoxey eventually returned to Mountain Iron to live. He managed to survive and usually avoid work by living with his parents and his sister.

Phoxey married very well when he was past his mid-thirties. His wife was a schoolteacher, Ellen Linval, nearly his age. (Phoxey was in the Mountain Iron High School class of 1923 and Ellen in 1924.) The wedding took place in 1942 and did not keep him out of World War II. He became a Seabee in the Navy and left Ellen pregnant with a daughter, Mary Ellen, who became a strikingly beautiful blonde. Shortly after the war they had a second daughter, Joyce.

After World War II he ventured into education and in 1947 was hired as principal and 5th and 6th grade teacher at an Indian Reservation in Nett Lake, Minnesota. His wife Ellen taught 3rd and 4th grades there also. When the teacher who taught the first and second grades became terminally ill, they recruited my mother to teach there for a year or two. During that time with the school being manned by one Mr. Beck and two Mrs. Becks, the Indians probably assumed they were observing bigamy in action.

Phoxey used this as a stepping stone and with a bit more education he and Ellen became, respectively, the principal and a teacher at a school in Duluth.

While they were in Duluth Phoxey got involved in an extramarital affair. Those of us who saw Phoxey as old, fat and bowlegged had a great deal of trouble visualizing this. Nevertheless it was never denied and apparently cost him more than he was making because he found it necessary to borrow money from the school's kids' lunch and milk fund to support his philandering. In due time he was arrested and fired for not repaying this money. All of the members of the family were solicited to clear the family name by contributing to a fund to reimburse what he had stolen. Much as I liked Uncle Phoxey, my reaction was that if he had stolen money and should go to jail that was what he deserved. His brothers, especially Uncle Charlie, were more distressed at the idea of having a jailbird brother than at his guilt, so they bailed him out and he was saved from incarceration.

Phoxey was considered his mother's favorite son—as is probably typical of those considered black sheep—as well as a favorite uncle. He was the sinner we accepted and perhaps envied a little. Even though I will not defend his ethics, morals, or work habits, I always found him likable and enjoyed his company.

The next member of the family was Laurence. He looked like his father, was skinny, and was not inclined to be intellectual. He left college early to marry

Esther Carlson, a high school sweetheart and classmate, when they were both very young.

Laurence and Esther lived next door to us when I was about seven or eight years old, and I became great friends with them, especially Laurence. I went over there almost every night to play card games. We remained good friends as long as he lived. Their first child died shortly after it was born. They moved from Mountain Iron to Inkster, Michigan, where they had two healthy children, Beverly and Gary. A later fourth child was stillborn.

In Michigan, Laurence first worked in a Ford factory and then left to become a mail carrier, the career that he pursued until he retired. They lived in Dearborn, Michigan, but moved to Grand Rapids, Minnesota to retire. Like his brother Leo, he felt that Minnesota was the only suitable place to live.

Laurence was drafted into the Navy in World War II even though he had two young children. His assignments in the Navy were mostly in postal service, but that doesn't mean it wasn't hazardous. Much of his duty was on ships in the Atlantic, and he went ashore on Omaha Beach a few days after D-Day to set up a post office there. He returned home unscathed, fortunately.

Some of the family considered Laurence an alcoholic, although I cannot verify this from personal observation. Esther was a compulsive neatoholic and she and Laurence spent so much time painting, wallpapering, and scrubbing that he must have had little time left for drinking. Laurence also spent a fair amount of time cooking and cleaning while Esther either went to school or worked. It was never clear to me what the goals of their lives were, but I think that it may be somewhat defined by the statement they made to one of his brothers during a visit: We have been here for two days, so we have to go home and wash our walls.

Laurence was always pleasant, tactful and friendly. I liked Esther, too, but she did have problems with her sisters-in-law over her compulsion with neatness. (She must have been an especially difficult mother-in-law.) Even though all of the relatives were above-average neat in their habits, she at some time let it be known that she thought house guests should bring their own sheets and towels. This seemed unreasonable to the rest of us until I learned in 1999 that this is customary in Sweden even now, so she was probably only echoing the practices of her Swedish family.

Laurence slipped on the ice, punctured his lungs with a broken rib and died of pneumonia or related complications when he was 80. Some members of the family think he might have lived longer if he hadn't felt compelled to leave his hospital bed far too early to go home and help Esther clean the house. Esther died a few years later.

Uncle Charlie was a medical doctor. Between lack of funds because of the depression and some academic difficulties it took him longer than normal to get his M. D. degree. Almost before he had time to start practice he was in the Army and serving in the South Pacific in World War II where he was decorated for bravery and lauded for his medical skill under fire.

Charlie completed his undergraduate work at Virginia Junior College and Macalester College, and medical school at the University of Minnesota. He kept a diary for the year 1930 when he was a freshman and sophomore at Virginia J.C., and it appeared that he majored in girls and good times, although he was also a serious student and was on the debating team. Charlie practiced general medicine and developed a reputation as a good doctor first in Harvey, North Dakota, and later in North St. Paul, Minnesota.

He married a quiet, attractive, submissive, intelligent, refined, non-assertive biology teacher at Macalester College, Gertrude Waite, the daughter of a Presbyterian minister. Charlie lived in a world of black and white in which right was right and wrong was wrong and there was no gray area. Conservative Presbyterianism was the only right way. He was outspokenly blunt and had opinions on most everything.

He believed absolutely in the superiority of white males whose ancestors had lived in northern Europe, and in his mind it was axiomatic that Italians, Jews, Slavs, Blacks, women, Asians, Indians, etc., etc., etc., were inferior. He also seemed to be convinced that Democrats, homosexuals, Catholics, and divorcees were unredeemable sinners. Uncle Charlie had the world all figured out and I suspect that as the leading elder in some Presbyterian church in North St. Paul he saw to it that any preacher they hired did not contradict his righteous beliefs.

Even though we were poles apart in our beliefs and philosophies, Uncle Charlie and I were always good friends. He was only 14 when I was born and he considered me more an equal than a nephew. We corresponded regularly when we were both in the service in World War II, and maintained some contact throughout the years. He looked after my parents and even brought them from Minnesota to my wedding in Rochester, New York. He always seemed interested in me and my family. Of course I knew enough not to attempt to disagree with his early 18th century Calvinism nor to point out what I saw as inconsistencies in his beliefs.

His inflexibility must have made him a less than perfect father to his four children. His only daughter and oldest child, Joellen, is a nursing professor and author of books on nursing history. She was as strong willed as her father, and between her renouncing Christianity for Unitarianism and getting a divorce, she and her father were totally alienated. Charlie and Gertie also had three sons and two of them have been divorced. At least one of them was reported to have suffered his father's wrath as his sister had. The third divorce may have happened after either Alzheimer's disease or death had softened Charlie's tongue.

I don't really know whether he approved of a career for his daughter, although he must have been proud of her success. I do know that he expected great things of his sons, and seemed satisfied that one became a lawyer and one a neurosurgeon. I heard from some family source (not necessarily reliable) that he had expressed at least slight disappointment when his other son became only a pharmacist.

Charlie had a good (if narrow) sense of humor, was generous, charitable, and for those of us who had no inclination to want to be like him nor to worry about whether he wanted us to, he was a good guy whose bark was worse than his bite. I don't think he really practiced the bigotry that he thought he believed. But he must have been difficult to live with.

It was not difficult for him to diagnose the onset of Alzheimer's disease in himself and he faced his retirement years with misgivings. He died, mercifully, before he had to be confined in a nursing home.

The youngest member of my father's family was my Uncle Roland who was nineteen years younger than my father and only eleven years older than I. Like Charlie, he was more like an older brother than an uncle to me, and was a major role model.

It was conceded by his siblings that Roland was the most intelligent of the seven intelligent Beck children. His distinguished career did nothing to refute that opinion.

Roland was always pleasant, kind, even-tempered, sensitive, and a clear and mostly objective thinker. He always seemed to have goals and the ability to stay on track to achieve them. He graduated from high school in 1929 just ahead of the depression. Even before the depression his family had no money, so he knew he was facing tough times to get an education.

He and his brother Charles went to Virginia Junior College for the same two years (1929-1931). Roland then hitchhiked to the least expensive college he could find, Marysville, Tennessee, to get a bachelor's degree in chemistry and education. He married Jean Coombe, a Virginia, Minnesota, girl whom he met in a church choir when he was going to junior college. He taught high school chemistry in a rural school at Cotton, Minnesota. In a year or two he found a better teaching job in Stillwater, Minnesota, near enough to the University of Minnesota so he could work toward and get his master's degree in chemistry while he was teaching.

That led to a job doing research on synthetic fuels at Texaco's research labs in Beacon, New York. He became a specialist in coal technology and ammonia production and later managed a laboratory in Montebello, California for Texaco.

He eventually moved back to Beacon to a higher level job, and when the U. S. government established a Department of Energy he was so well known for his expertise on coal technology that the scientist forming the DOE in 1975 asked him to retire from Texaco and join the government, so he and Jean moved to Washington for a few years. When he decided that he had had enough of that and had reached retirement age they moved back to their home in Whittier, California. But the DOE decided they still needed him so they set him up with an office in Los Angeles where he continued to work until he finally retired in 1981.

Be impressed by this: He was a consultant in coal technology to the government of Indonesia, and twice a visiting lecturer on coal technology and synthetic fuels at the University of Edinburgh. He is a Fellow of AIChE and is listed in Engineers of Distinction, American Men of Science, Who's Who in Engineering, and Who's Who in Chemistry. He taught research management part time at Cal Tech and served on the advisory board for chemical engineering at USC. And there are many other only slightly less notable things I omitted that further verify his truly distinguished career as a scientist and as a person.

Roland and Jean had three sons. One died of an aneurysm at age six, which was a tragic experience and which led to their becoming Quakers for a while. They apparently found the Quakers more supportive in their days of need than the Presbyterians, although they returned to the Presbyterian Church because their children preferred it. Roland did request, however, that the memorial service after his death be held in the Quaker Church. The children who survived were Bradley and Brian whose place in this story will come later, along with the others of their generation.

I remained as close to Roland and Jean as geography permitted. They attended the ceremony in New York City at which I was commissioned an ensign in the U. S. Navy late in World War II. They attended our daughter Barbara's showing of her class' films made just before her graduation from the University of Southern California film school. I was able to visit them occasionally when my job at Kodak took me to Hollywood or Whittier, and during my retirement when they were living in a retirement home in Fullerton.

I was a bit disappointed that for all of Roland's brilliance and polish, he still showed signs in his later years that he had not shed the family penchant for anti-

Semitism and racial bigotry. I was even more appalled that he seemed to think favorably of that presidential airhead, Ronald Reagan. I think my uncle was also lobbying to solve the AIDS problem by isolating all of those with the disease on a desert island. I suppose the latter is a perfectly logical scientific solution to a social problem—but totally ridiculous in a world that should try to provide reasonable rights for all humans, and even more ridiculous considering the magnitude of the epidemic.

Roland lived to be 88 years old. He suffered a couple of strokes in his last six or seven years, but fortunately these did not seriously affect his speech or his mental processes, so he was able to continue living a life of awareness and social interaction even though his mobility was impaired. He died on December 30, 2001, when his heart could not cope with treatment to repair a broken hip.

The children of John and Hulda Beck were in general strong and good. They believed in themselves and in the American dream—at least for white northern Europeans. While they pursued that dream with mixed success, you will see in future chapters that the momentum they imparted to the next generation really made that dream come true for their families.

The children of John and Hulda were intelligent, and had the great good sense to select mates at least as intelligent as themselves, which helped insure the success of the next generation. John and Hulda were obviously highly successful parents.

The flaws of the seven children were not as equally distributed among them as were their strengths. And they and you may disagree with at least some of what I consider flaws: unquestioning acceptance of Christianity; ultra-conservative Republicanism; varying degrees of intolerance and bigotry; smug self-righteousness; somewhat blind patriotism.

During the Mountain Iron, Minnesota, centennial celebration in 1990, the Beck family had a private gathering of those direct descendants of John and Hulda who attended the event. The only two surviving children, Aunt Tommy and Uncle Roland, attended and were, of course, honored. The seven children of John and Hulda had 15 surviving children and 11 of those grandchildren attended and spoke at this event.

It was interesting that of the 11, I remember that only one cited a father or mother as the main Beck influence in their lives. The others credited their uncles or aunt for being major role models from the Beck side of the family. This confirmed my opinion that the Becks (probably like others in many families) were better as uncles or aunt than as parents, at least in the eyes of their children.

I must be careful to amend that generalization by saying that Roland's sons were not in attendance and that based on relatively limited observations my generalization would not apply here. He was a good uncle—but I also think he was most likely an excellent father and that his sons would have said so if they had been at that gathering. I don't believe that his sons had as much contact with their aunt and uncles as the rest of us did.

The Becks were remarkable family, probably not untypical first generation American-born children of immigrants. In many different ways they all made contributions to my life and how I lived it. I am grateful to all of them for what they were and what they did. None were perfect—they were human; but on the whole, outstanding humans.

7

MY MOTHER'S SIBLINGS—My Aunts and Uncles

The Hanson Family—Children of Bans and Bertha

There were eight children born to Bans and Bertha. The source of this information is a copy of a handwritten record on the flyleaf of a Bible, a common way in years past of keeping family records.

Three of these children I never knew because they died long before I was born. Having described Mabel, my mother, in Chapter V, in this chapter I will tell here about the four others I knew: Harry, Orville, Ethel and Benjamin.

Harry Albert Hanson was born in Duluth, Minnesota, on February 5, 1891. Uncle Harry led an exciting, adventurous life, especially during his first forty years. This is covered in detail in his memoirs published by his family and titled: *My Adventure—The First Forty Years.* I will not repeat much of it here, but I highly recommend your reading it.

Harry grew up in Mountain Iron, but because the high school had not yet been built he had to go to high school four miles away in Virginia, Minnesota. He was the valedictorian of his class.

After adventures in mining, surveying, machining, at sea, in the wilds of Alaska, and perhaps others, Harry settled down to marriage and a career of fish management. He earned his bachelor's degree from the University of Washington and an MA from the University of Minnesota. He was always an avid student and continued to work toward a doctorate at the University of Washington even after his marriage. (He did not complete his doctorate. A family and the depression made this more of luxury than he felt he could afford.)

I knew Uncle Harry quite well because he and his family spent some months living in Mountain Iron during the depths of the depression, and in later years they returned occasionally to visit. Also when I was 12 we traveled from Minnesota to the state of Washington and visited them when they lived on Puget Sound near Seattle. And since Harry lived in California during at least 25 of the years I worked and lived there, we saw Harry and Grace more often than I saw most of my other uncles and aunts.

Harry was always pleasant, interested and interesting. He seemed to know everything about almost anything and loved to talk. He was not at all arrogant about his broad knowledge, and you had to pay close attention to detect how smart he really was. I believe, also, that he not only subscribed to but lived up to the highest possible ethical and moral principles. I think it was not an exaggeration to report that Harry had broken a lot of new ground in the science of fish technology and there are a number of unbiased reports from non-family sources that suggest that his contributions and discoveries were highly innovative and significant.

He married Grace Cummins in 1927. She was 13 years younger than he, even though they had been classmates at the University of Washington. Grace, like Harry and also like most of my aunts, was a refined, educated lady and a most welcome addition to the Hanson family. Harry, fortunately, lived a long and healthy life so their marriage lasted almost 60 years in spite of the age difference. They had two children, Gwen and Harry, Jr.

Harry failed to show for his scheduled wedding with Grace. Unknown to her and the wedding party, he had been shipwrecked in Alaska and was delayed. Fortunately for all concerned he was forgiven and the wedding was rescheduled.

When I was young, I got the impression that Aunt Grace had come from a very wealthy family. I learned later that she was born and raised on a South Dakota farm in a family who had previously lived in a sod house, so if there was wealth in the family it must have been acquired later. In any case, that wealth was probably mythical and certainly unimportant, but Aunt Grace always had the presence that goes with class, which may explain why our family thought her family must have been rich.

If Harry had a fault it may have been a tendency to see his children, their spouses, and his nephews (like me) as being as nearly faultless as humans could be. In this respect he was much like his mother, even though Harry had lived an infinitely more sophisticated life than his mother had. Of course, that was only a fault when it annoyed other members of the family. And to those of us who were considered nearly perfect it made us work hard to live up to Uncle Harry's expectations. I am sure that seeing only good in the people around him made Harry's life happier, too, and made us all love him more.

We visited Uncle Harry and Aunt Grace several times when they lived in a retirement community near Santa Rosa. We attended Harry's memorial service, and later often visited Aunt Grace when she lived in a retirement facility in Walnut Creek. We were privileged to live near enough to stay in touch with this really wonderful aunt and uncle for the last twenty or thirty years of their long and happy lives.

Harry died in 1985 at age 93, and Grace died the day after Christmas in 1999 at age 95.

Orvil Christian Hanson was born in Mountain Iron, Minnesota on December 28, 1899. I always knew him as Orville, which even appears on his high school records, so I suspect that Orvil which appears in the family Bible record was changed early in his life. I knew Uncle Orville less well than I knew his siblings since he rarely returned to Mountain Iron. He was reputed to be the brain of the family. If this were really true he must have been greatly endowed, since his siblings were extremely bright. He was the valedictorian of the Mountain Iron High School class of 1917. It was surprising, then, that he was the only one of the Hansons who never went to college. I am sure that this was his choice because Bans and Bertha strongly encouraged all of their children to pursue higher education.

I speculate that Orville, having graduated from high school in 1917 just after the United States had entered World War I, felt that he could best contribute to the war effort by going to work in the iron mines. He learned to be a surveyor, and while I was still too young to remember him he left home to go west, to either Washington or Oregon and he lived in those states for the rest of his life, except for a couple of years during World War II when he went to Alaska to build roads for the military.

It was after he had been gone for about 11 years without ever having returned home to visit that my father and mother and Uncle Hap and his wife Ethel (Toots), my mother's sister, decided they had better pack us all into two cars and head out to see Orville before Grandma and Grandpa got any older, or worse. In the caravan were Hap and Toots Forder and their one-year-old son Bill; my mother and father and my brother, age five-and-a-half, and me, age 12; and Grandma and Grandpa Hanson.

Harry and Grace and their two children were living near Seattle at that time so we visited there for a while and then all of us including the Harry Hanson family headed out to visit Orville. Orville and his wife Celia and her two children by a previous marriage lived in northern Washington in a place called Glacier on Mount Baker. They always lived at the end of a road, because Orville worked for the Bureau of Public Roads and his job was road building. My impression was that he had progressed beyond doing surveying to doing civil engineering. It was obvious that being somewhat transient and always living in remote places suited him just fine.

Celia was pleasant, intelligent but with limited education, rather plain looking, and a skilled homemaker no matter how primitive the living conditions were. She had no difficulty being accepted and liked by this family that liked everybody, and this first meeting on the edge of an icy glacier was a very warm one.

That was the only time I saw her children, Leola and Robert. Leola died quite young, but last I heard, Robert was still alive and flying a homemade airplane. Both of them were slightly older than I. They adopted Orville as their father and took his name, but Orville never fathered any children of his own.

I only remember seeing Orville three more times before he died. Once was when he visited in Mountain Iron, probably in 1940 during the town's 50th anniversary celebration. He came to Mountain Iron again in 1949 for a Hanson family reunion when I was home from Rochester, New York, on vacation. The last time was in 1955 when I was working in Palo Alto. My father came to visit us here, and we all met at Harry's house in Red Bluff. Orville and Celia came down from Oregon where they were then living to join in this small reunion.

A few years after Orville died I saw Celia once more when she came to Uncle Harry's 80th birthday party in Hillsborough, California.

Unlike his brothers Harry and Ben, Orville was quiet and introverted. Orville was apparently a heavy drinker all of his life, which probably explains why he died at the early age (for this family) of 61. I never heard his being called a drunk and he didn't have any problems keeping a job, so as far as I can tell he kept his alcohol consumption under reasonable control.

Celia outlived Orville by about 12 to 15 years. They both died, I believe, in Coos Bay, Oregon, and Celia had the distinction of being the only member of the family to have become a Jehovah's Witness. This deviation from the accepted traditional Presbyterian and Lutheran main line beliefs did not seem to alter her very friendly relationship with any of the Hansons, who were very tolerant.

The next member of the family, born December 22, 1901, was Ethel Martha Ragnild Hanson. Martha and Ragnild were the names of her two grandmothers, and it is a mystery that these names were not assigned to the two older daughters, Alice and Mabel. There was an Aunt Ethel by marriage to Uncle Otto Johnson, but I think she was not yet in the family. In any case, and perhaps because there was another Ethel, Ethel Hanson was always known within the family and to close family friends as Toots, a childhood endearment bestowed upon her by her father.

Aunt Toots went to the University of Minnesota and became a registered nurse. She worked in hospitals, mostly one in Buhl, Minnesota, until she retired to become a mother.

Toots was a happy, friendly, gregarious person. She was interested in people and had a wonderful memory, so she was able to talk non-stop about the comings and goings and health and welfare of the seemingly hundreds of people she kept track of. This was totally non-malicious reporting, but the problem was that most of the people she talked to were acquainted with only a small percentage of those she talked about. If she had done much reading or pursued abstract ideas or had thoughts about politics, philosophy, religion or the like, she didn't share these with the outside world. She did appear to be a totally unquestioning Presbyterian Christian.

I always enjoyed being with Aunt Toots, from the time she was my maiden aunt baby-sitter. I liked her tales even about people I knew barely if at all. She and my mother were close friends as well as sisters and never seemed to run out of conversation when they were together.

Toots went through at least her first eighty-five years at a high energy level. She was the type of person who rarely sat down in her own home and when she came to visit she tended to take over in the kitchen or laundry or wherever. In her early 90s she had to slow down because of knee and arm problems, but her mind and her memory remained clear until after her 95th birthday. Her memory dimmed in her later years and on October 5, 1999, two months before her 98th birthday, she was the last of the Hanson siblings to die.

At the late age of 30 she married Milton H. Forder, a man about five years younger than she. Milton was known almost exclusively as Hap, and I suspect that few people knew his real name. Hap Forder was tall and handsome with a degree in forestry and without money or a job in 1932, the depth of the depression. So Toots kept on working until the Roosevelt administration formed the Civilian Conservation Corps and there was a new demand for foresters to manage that program.

Toots had been linked closely to a man named Cy (Cyrus?) Gamel when Hap met her. Hap said, I want to marry you. Toots said, I have a boyfriend (or fiancé, or whatever). That didn't deter Hap and whatever may have followed, Hap was the one who met her at the altar. I was about seven years old and theirs was the first wedding I remember attending.

The wedding was held just after dark at the home of Grandma and Grandpa Hanson. It was not a pretentious home, but served the purpose. My mother and grandmother and probably Toots had decorated the house with ferns and pine boughs and whatever else they could find in the woods. As I remember, the bride came down the stairs into the living room, and the groom appeared out of the kitchen. They were married by a woman preacher from a mainstream church in Calumet or Bovey (Methodist, possibly), the Rev. Miss Resor, who was a friend of theirs.

Toots, being a nurse and an inveterate workhorse, had the unpleasant duty of caring for the sick and dying members of the family. She invariably tended all members who were hospitalized for whatever reason as well as those who were at home terminally ill. This included her husband's family as well as her own, but she accepted this assignment without complaint and Hap never complained about her leaving home to do this. This continued at least until Uncle Harry's last illness in 1984. After that she was old enough to avoid that duty, but she has probably not been given the credit she deserved for this lifetime of unselfish service in an unpleasant task. Living far from medical help or even emergency police or fire departments, she was called on by neighbors as well. She told me of a time when she was summoned after a friend and neighbor had without warning blown his brains out with a gun. This sort of help was expected from a nurse, and Toots (like nurse Aunt Tommy on the Beck side) had the emotional strength she needed to handle these situations.

Like his brother-in-law Orville, Hap disliked cities, so he was happy living most of his life in the Minnesota woods. Toots was happy, too, as long as there were one or two other people to talk to, although I think that at times she tired of the rustic accommodations in the earlier days. There were times when she had only a dog to talk to, but they usually had a dog who seemed to understand the conversation. Toots and Hap usually lived in nice enough places and all of their few neighbors in those remote places became lifelong friends.

Their only son, Bill, was born in 1935 and he grew up in the woods and went to rural schools until he got to high school. By that time they lived in the relatively large town of Ely, Minnesota, where Hap was a ranger in one of the wilderness areas of the Superior National Forest. My mother and father were very close to the Forders, and Bill and my brother Gerry have been close friends for all of their lives.

Hap and Toots had a good marriage for just over 40 years until Hap died suddenly in the early 1970s.

I liked Uncle Hap. I remember him as one who almost always brought me some treasure such as a pocket knife or a hunting knife or a compass or binoculars. These things were rarely new, but Hap and his father were collectors of everything. He gave me a new .22 rifle for Christmas when I was only eight years old. (I wonder now whether or how he got my mother to approve of that!) When I was older he tried to teach me how to shoot some pistols from his extensive gun collection. Even when I was much older and had taken up smoking a pipe he gave me some of his slightly used pipes.

But it was really not his gifts that made me like him. He was a living Paul Bunyan who knew and understood and appreciated the forests and the lakes and the animals that inhabited them. I admired what he knew and what he did at least partly because I felt it was something that I would not be likely to succeed at even if I were inclined to try.

Grandma's favorite among her children, because he was her youngest, was Benjamin, whom she always called Benny and who to the rest of us became Ben as he grew and matured beyond the diminutive nickname. Uncle Ben was a favorite of mine, too. He was still going to junior college and living at home for a couple of years after I was born. He drove Uncle Otto's car, and that alone made him a hero to me. He was also a frequent visitor at our house and being young and friendly and gentle he established a favorable image in my infant brain that survives to this day.

Ben followed a much more straightforward life than his brothers had. After he graduated from Mountain Iron High School in 1923 he went to Virginia Junior College for two years and then to Ohio State University for two years and graduated with a B. S. in chemistry. He immediately went to work for Lowe Brothers Paint Company in Dayton, Ohio, and stayed with them until he retired. Late in his career, Lowe Brothers became part of Sherwin-Williams, and Ben retired as a vice-president of Sherwin-Williams.

He never talked much about his work, but his wife Louise liked to brag about him, and even if she had exaggerated it was apparent that he was very successful and had accumulated a large number of patents related to the paint business. I know that he was deeply involved in developing latex-based paints as early as the 1930s when they were first marketed.

He married Louise Lairson whom he met at Ohio State where she was a secretary. Louise was a non-stop talker and smoker. I found her entertaining as well as friendly. I suspect that she especially liked me because I was a receptive audience. Some other members of the family such as Uncle Hap preferred some silence now and then and found her a bit wearing after she had been around for a few days.

Ben and Louise had their first child in 1930, the same year that my parents and Harry and Grace also had sons. This turned out to be especially unfortunate because Ben-Boy as they called him turned up with a Wilms' tumor, a not-uncommon kidney cancer in children that in those days was incurable.

Ben-Boy was a beautiful child with blond, curly hair and brown eyes who was obviously also endowed with brilliance to go with his beauty. When he died at age 4 it was a major family tragedy. It was probably especially painful to Ben and Louise that my brother Gerry and cousin Harry, Jr., also handsome and bright and born the same year, were around to remind them of their loss.

It was even more devastating to Ben and Louise to be told that because Louise had not been shielded from X-rays during Ben-Boy's treatment she would proba-bly be infertile. Luckily, that was incorrect and they later had two healthy, nor-mal children—a girl, Karen, and a boy, Ted.

Ben and Louise were beyond 55 years of marriage when Louise was very sud-denly stricken with leukemia and died. This was several years after Ben had retired and they had left Dayton and moved into a Harlingen, Texas retirement community.

Ben and Louise had become friendly with Ed Kerola, whose family had lived a few doors from us in Mountain Iron. Ed's late older brother Ted had been a boy-hood friend of Ben's and either that or an accidental meeting in Texas may have inspired the friendship with Ed. Ed's mother had a brother named Matt Rautiola. Matt Rautiola's wife was Minnie, a sister of my Grandfather Beck. Therefore the Rautiola children were first cousins not only to Ed Kerola, but also to my father and his siblings. One of those Rautiola cousins, Alma, had been recently wid-owed. Ed recognized that Ben needed a wife and that Alma needed a husband, so he managed to get them together. That was how my mother's brother Ben mar-ried my father's first cousin, so my first cousin once removed became my aunt.

Ben had not known Alma in Mountain Iron, although they both lived there. Alma had been in the class of 1931 which was eight years later than Ben's class, and they had lived on opposite sides of town. I was in the class of 1941, so I knew Alma only very vaguely as one of my father's rarely mentioned country cousins.

Alma was unusually warm and loving, which is supposed to be uncharacteris-tic of a Finn, and it appears to me that Ben had two excellent marriages.

Ben and Alma moved into a house in Alamo, Texas, where they lived happily for several years. We visited them there early in 1993, a couple of months before Ben's doctors discovered that he had inoperable liver cancer and he died in October of 1993 six days short of his 88th birthday. Alma's health deteriorated after Ben died, and she died from liver failure and related complications on Christmas day, 1995.

The members of the Hanson family as I saw them ranged from highly intelligent to brilliant, and were without exception highly moral, ethical, friendly, courteous, kind and with a bare minimum of human weaknesses. They seemed happy with themselves and their lives. They succeeded in rising above their humble beginnings. What's more, they all married spouses who were equally outstanding. We can be thankful that the gene pools that produced Bans and Bertha were passed on without dilution.

8

MY HANSON COUSINS

Five of the children of Bans and Bertha Hanson survived to adulthood and four of them had children of their own and the fifth had two adopted stepchildren:

Harry Albert Hanson married Grace Cummins and their children were:
Gwen Harriet Hanson, born March 27, 1928
Harry Albert Hanson, Jr., born August 12, 1930

Mabel Leila Hanson married John Lennart Beck and their children were:
John Robert Beck, born July 16, 1924
Roderick Gerald Beck, born November 26, 1930

Orville Hanson married Cecilia Custis whose children from a previous marriage were:
Robert
Leola
(These children adopted Orville as their father and took his name.)

Ethel Hanson married Milton H. Forder and they had one child:
William Robert Forder, born April 20, 1935

Benjamin Raymond Hanson married Louise Lairsen and they had three children. The first died at age four. The other two were:
Karen Louise Hanson, born September 15, 1936
Theodore Hanson, born October 31, 1938

I have only seven cousins on the Hanson side. I cannot include Orville's step-children in this chapter because I know almost nothing about them so this will leave only five: Gwen, Harry Jr., Bill Forder, and Karen and Ted to write about. I will include my brother and me in later chapters.

This surprised me because I always thought I knew my mother's family well. You will find that I know some of them even less well than I know my first cousins on the Beck side.

Harry's children, Gwen and Harry Jr., are an exception. They have lived near us in California and we regularly see each other at family weddings, funerals, birthdays, anniversaries, and other occasions.

Gwen went to high school in Red Bluff, California, and then went to the University of California in Berkeley. She graduated from Cal and it was there she met Don Reichert, whom she married. They have lived in Lafayette, California, ever since their marriage.

As a credentialed teacher, Gwen worked as a Special Education Resource Specialist with children with learning disabilities. She got her Master's Degree in Special Education from St. Mary's College in Moraga, California. Don was an engineer with the Upright Scaffold Company and achieved a high level executive position before he retired. In retirement he travels around the country as an expert witness in accident trials involving scaffolds and related equipment.

They tend to lean toward UC Berkeley where they went to school and we toward Stanford which is near where we live, although at least one of their daughters graduated from Stanford (the same year as our son Steve did), and one of our sons graduated from UC Berkeley. Gwen and Don have a son, Douglas, an international lawyer whom we have visited at his home in Geneva, Switzerland; and a daughter Ann Croll, whose daughter Sara attends the same private high school in Palo Alto, California, as our two granddaughters. Gwen and Don have another daughter, Sue Reichert.

Douglas is married to Laurence Courvoisier, and they and their children, Christopher and Natalia live in Geneva, Switzerland. Sue is married to Robert Thomas and lives in Seattle with their three children, Galen, Jared and Grace. The boys are children of Rob and Sue, but Grace was an abandoned Chinese baby they adopted. Ann is married to John Croll and they live in Cupertino, California, with their two children, Sara and Robert.

Harry Hanson, Jr., also graduated from Red Bluff High School where he was valedictorian and from UC Berkeley with a BA in political science. He got his JD degree from the Boalt School of Law at UC Berkeley and has become a highly successful lawyer. He spent some time as an officer in the U. S. Navy just after law school where he met and married Terry Ponvert, the child of a family who had been prominent in the Cuban sugar industry before the days of Fidel Castro.

They live in upscale Hillsborough, California, in what I would call a mansion, and they also have an elegant ranch between Santa Cruz and Monterey. Harry is a partner in the Hanson Family Law Group along with his daughter Belinda, and I suspect it is no coincidence that his success has come not only from his great skill as a lawyer, but also from practicing in one of the nation's wealthiest counties with one of the highest divorce rates. His great skill as a lawyer is verified by his listing in *The Best Lawyers in America* and his election to Northern California SuperLawyers, a title given to 5% of attorneys selected by their peers. Belinda has also earned these honors, so they are obviously a great team.

Harry and Terry have never seemed to come close to adding to that high divorce rate. They seem very compatible even though it does sometimes appear that Terry was attracted to Harry to help her escape from the high society life of her family on Long Island and that Harry was attracted to her because she represented a contrast from the backwoods life in which he had been raised. They still enjoy the outdoors and Harry describes himself as a nut about fly fishing and Terry as crazy about horses, so they have not abandoned the joys of nature.

We have seen Harry and Terry mostly at major family gatherings, either theirs or ours. As with Gwen and Don, we always enjoy being with them and admire them and their families and are always delighted to be included in weddings and birthdays and other family events they invite us to and to have them attend ours.

Harry and Terry have three children: Harry A. Hanson III, a lawyer married to Anne Hollingsworth and living in Massachusetts with their three children, Sam, Tom, and Louisa; Bradley Hanson, an investment councilor who lives in San Diego; and Belinda, also a lawyer and married to a lawyer, Rob Thomas, living in Woodside, California, with daughters Leigh and Katharine.

William Robert Forder was the only child of my mother's sister, Ethel (Toots) and her husband Milton Forder. Since his father was a forest ranger, Bill spent most of his school years in the Minnesota woods going to very small, remote schools. When Bill was in high school they lived in Ely, a fairly big city for Minnesota (population about 6,000).

Bill was a good enough football player in Ely High School to get a scholarship to one of the Dakota colleges to play football. He found, however, that he was not good enough to play much. In spite of that, the demands of the football team were preventing his getting the education he wanted, so he transferred to the University of Minnesota, gave up football and got a degree in Mechanical Engineering.

Bill was tall, thin, and handsome like his father. He married Barbara Beise, the daughter of a man who was a football star at the University of Minnesota in the mid-30s and one of my childhood heroes. Unfortunately Sheldon Beise was killed in an automobile accident a few months before the wedding, so I never did get to meet him.

Bill established a very successful air conditioning contracting business in the Twin Cities. (It really does get that hot in Minnesota in the summertime.) He and Barbara had two children, Robert and Nancee. Nancee is married to William Bray and has twin daughters and a son. Robert is a writer.

Bill is a registered professional engineer and was in several professional associations related to the heating, air conditioning, refrigeration, sheet metal and roofing trades that he used in his business. He designed the mechanical systems in many large buildings including the Methodist Hospital in Rochester, Minnesota, and the University of Notre Dame Athletic and Convocation Center. He was often an officer and director of trade associations, and received the Sheet Metal and Roofing Contractors Association of Minnesota Outstanding Contractor Award in 1987. He even served as a director of the Minnesota Chamber of Commerce from 1981-1989.

After about 20 or 25 years his business and his marriage both had problems, but he bounced back, establishing a consulting business and remarrying after his divorce from Barbara. He is now retired. I have not seen much of Bill since attending his first wedding in the early 1960's, but the times I have he has appeared to be the same pleasant, even-tempered and unflappable person he had always been in spite of what appears to have been a busy, productive, and somewhat stressful career.

I first met Bill's second wife, Felicia, at Gerry's wife Ardelle's memorial service and again a year or two later at Gerry's place at Clear Lake, Minnesota. She and Bill seem to be a good match and it appears that they are headed for many good years together. Now retired, they have a home on a lake near Aitkin, Minnesota.

Karen was the older of the two surviving children of Ben, the youngest member of the Hanson family, and his wife Louise. (Their first child, Ben Junior, had died from a form of cancer at age 4.) About all I know of Karen and Ted has come from their parents, since I have seen nothing of Karen and little of Ted in the past fifty years.

Karen was a bright, good-looking child, and apparently highly motivated through high school. She decided to become a lawyer and entered Ohio State University with that goal. She was doing well until she fell in love. She married, abandoned law school, and had two children, Katherine Louise Inman and Deanne Marie Inman. Karen's marriage did not survive and she became a single mother.

While she didn't pursue law school, she did get a degree from Ohio State and worked as a legal secretary for most of her life.

Karen had two more marriages that ended in divorce. Karen's daughter Katherine was married and divorced after having had a son. She has a degree in accounting and works dealing poker hands at a casino in Las Vegas, I have heard. Deanne Inman has not married and is pursuing a Ph.D. in Anthropology and a Masters in Dispute Resolution at Syracuse University.

Karen is now retired and lives in Arizona.

Ted, the other child of Ben and Louise, studied chemical engineering (at Ohio State, of course) and worked for the Dow Chemical company. That career was successful and satisfying, and Ted made significant contributions both to his company and to improving the environment upon which his company had a major impact, not always favorable.

Ted and his wife Kay lived in Midland, Michigan, for most of his career with Dow, and they have two children. In his latter years with Dow he worked in Ludington, Michigan. He is now retired and spends winters in Arizona and summers in Michigan. I have seen them only once that I can remember and that was in Midland in 1975 when I spent a month attending the University of Michigan graduate school of business.

Ted and Kay's two children are Eric, a computer scientist, whose wife is Michelle, and an unmarried daughter Sharon Kristen who is a veterinarian in Texas.

9

MY BECK COUSINS

It is a bit surprising to realize that on the whole I know the members of my own generation less well than I knew their parents. This may be because I made my analysis of my aunts and uncles when I was endowed with the vast wisdom of youth; or it may only reflect the social and geographical dispersion that occurs in families as the generations proliferate.

The seven children of John and Hulda Beck had 18 children. The fifteen grandchildren who reached adulthood were:

John Robert Beck, born July 16, 1924
Roderick Gerald Beck, born November 26, 1930
(to John Lennart and Mabel Hanson Beck)

Leland Whitcomb Beck, born June 29, 1926, died April 26, 1997
(to Leo and Josephine Whitcomb Beck)

Faith Fuller, born September 28, 1930
Bruce Beck Fuller, born November 29, 1932
(to Lillian Beck and Leland S. Fuller)

Mary Ellen Beck, born August 4, 1943
Joyce Elizabeth Beck, born March 18,1947
(to Clarence Royal and Ellen Linval Beck)

Beverly Jean Beck, born June 3, 1933
Gary Laurence Beck, born September 15, 1936
(to Laurence Randolf and Esther Carlson Beck)

Joellen Margaret Beck, born December 15, 1941
Bruce Lennart Beck, born December 11, 1946
Douglas Charles Beck, born July 15, 1950
David Wallace Beck, born December 28, 1951
(to Dr. Charles Joel and Mrs. Gertrude Waite Beck)

Bradley Beck, born September 11,1940
Brian Arthur Beck, born May 31, 1943
(to Roland Arthur and Jean Coombe Beck)

While I know a fair amount about these cousins, I don't really *know* many of them, even including my own brother. I suspect this is because typically relatives of the same generation tend to interact by trying to impress each other with their careers, wealth, intelligence, children, etc., rather than by sharing ideas. Uncles and aunts, on the other hand, were always trying to make sure that you knew their goals and behaved and believed according to their standards, which, of course, were improved versions of what your own parent—their siblings—were teaching.

With the understanding that I am proceeding largely from ignorance, I will discuss each of these cousins. I plead ignorance because in spite of family reunions and other contacts, I have never (with a couple of exceptions) really gotten to know much about their philosophies or standards and it is probably in the best interest of harmony that we never seriously compared political or religious beliefs.

I will start with my brother Gerry. I am surprised that our parents came up with the name Roderick Gerald for him after having named me just plain John Robert. I don't know how much anguish this has caused him, but I am glad they hadn't been so creative in 1924.

Gerry was six years and four months younger than I. I think we got along very well during the few years that our lives overlapped. I left home when he was still a child of less than thirteen years. He was precocious enough so that we were competitive in most games and were therefore surprisingly close in many ways you would not expect of siblings so far apart in age. I helped somewhat by resisting maturity in some minor respects. We have rarely had communication, however, about anything that might be considered serious in life such as religious, philosophical, or political beliefs, although I have no reason to believe that we are far apart.

Like several uncles and me, Gerry went to Virginia Junior College. (Unlike any of the rest of us, though, he captained the football team. Except for possibly Uncle Ben Hanson, we others were not athletes.) He got his degree in chemical engineering from the University of Minnesota in 1953. He first went to work for a nuclear energy business in Georgia, then to General Mills in Minneapolis, then to Phillips Petroleum in atomic energy in Idaho, and then back to the food business—the American Potato Company—in Blackfoot, Idaho. When he invented the process for making Betty Crocker Potato Buds his career seemed to be set and he was rewarded for this by being made the vice-president of research for American Potato.

In 1956 he had married Ardelle Kosola, who had gone to high school in Buhl, Minnesota. Ardelle had Finnish parents, although her father (probably jokingly) claimed to be from Lapland. She was very attractive with a somewhat exotic hint of the orient in her high cheekbones and coloring. She was intelligent, a professional in home economics with a degree from the University of Minnesota, an excellent homemaker, very personable, and a dedicated non-feminist. Her Finnish roots made our father accept her and her parents into the family with great enthusiasm. They had three children, John, Karen, and William.

When American Potato merged with Basic Vegetables (because the brothers who owned those two companies were approaching retirement) Gerry became an executive vice-president of the merged company in Vacaville, California, and his interests expanded from potatoes to onions and garlic. Either management was not his thing or he was not compatible with the new management, and his health gave out. He was given an early medical retirement. (Gerry had become diabetic in his early middle age, which was probably a factor.)

On retirement, he and Ardelle moved to Jackson, Wyoming, and first bought a frozen yogurt shop, and later a buffalo sausage company. By that time their oldest son, John, had finished college so John became the manager of the sausage factory and Gerry provided money and technical expertise. The products included a delicious salami and other related products made from buffalo meat. Unfortunately the cost was higher than they dared pass on to customers and they decided to get out of the business.

Even though several years had passed, Basic Vegetables was happy to rehire Gerry for his very valuable technical skills, so Gerry and Ardelle moved back to Blackfoot to a lesser job than he had previously. Gerry was soon moved to a more interesting job in King City, California, but still with less pay and freedom than he felt he deserved.

In late 1990 or early 1991, a rich, young potato farmer he knew in Blackfoot, Idaho, offered him a lucrative contract. When Basic failed to counter the offer, he and Ardelle moved back to Blackfoot until his retirement in 1998.

Gerry has demonstrated his great talent as a technical expert in the food processing business and is still making contributions as a consultant. I think that he has enjoyed a happy, satisfying career in which he has excelled and established a worldwide reputation.

We were all shocked when Ardelle died suddenly of a pulmonary embolism on August 30, 1999, at age 66. They were at their summer home in Clear Lake in northern Minnesota and had been enjoying golfing, fishing, and playing bridge and to all appearances she was in good health. Ardelle had every reason to expect another twenty years or so of life since her mother had died less than a year before. Gerry has adapted but with difficulty to living without Ardelle.

Their son John is an accountant and CFO of Lutheran Community Services in Spokane WA; daughter Karen is a travel consultant in Idaho; and son Bill is the manager/teaching pro of a small golf course in American Falls, Idaho.

Leland Whitcomb Beck was the only son of Leo and Josephine. Leland, known more commonly as Lee, was the closest to my age of any of the Beck cousins. He grew up in Dearborn, Michigan, and every summer between his 12th and 15th years he spent a few weeks in Minnesota with our family. He was there for our annual family camping trip and he joined me at our Boy Scout camp. Uncle Leo was a notorious bargain hunter, so I think my assumption that this was a move to get his son some wonderful benefits for next to nothing was absolutely correct. Lee and I were intellectually compatible and had many common interests, so we both welcomed his visits.

Lee was looked upon by the rest of the family as a spoiled child of a bad mother. Actually, while she was not a likable person, Jo was probably a much better mother than she was a daughter-in-law, sister-in-law or mother-in-law.

Considering that Lee was an only child and that his mother was a minor psycho, he turned out pretty well. He attended the University of Michigan during World War II as a Navy V-12 ROTC student and got his degree in mechanical engineering after the war. He went to work for Lincoln-Mercury (Ford) where he made some important inventions, and then went to work for Ingersoll-Rand. I believe that he was an exceptionally good mechanical engineer who fully deserved his career success.

I went to his wedding in June 1949, in Dearborn when he married Frances Hodel. Her family must have had some good connections because the wedding was held in the Martha-Mary Chapel in the Ford Greenfield Village Museum and the wedding, or at least the reception, was attended by the widow of Henry Ford.

Frances was a nice-looking, pleasant, intelligent woman. To all appearances this was a good match. In due time they had a son they named Charles Leland. Within a year or two after that, Frances suddenly left Leland for another man, but she left the baby, Charles, with Leland, although she did retain some visitation rights.

Naturally his relatives wondered why she left him. He had a good job and a promising career. We knew that Leland was useless around the house, but so are many men. He later became a heavy drinker, but that did not seem to have reached problem proportions yet. He was probably too self-centered to be a world-class lover, but he had fathered a child, which put him in the range of normal male achievement. We mostly concluded that the problem was Leland's mother Josephine, who called often on the telephone and dropped in for unannounced inspections and generally harassed Fran. I think I remember correctly that Fran once told us that Leland never referred to Jo as his mother but only as "your mother-in-law."

For whatever reason, the marriage had failed and Leland became a single father. He recovered fairly quickly through his sports car club. He met a glamorous Czech woman named Inka, and married her. The family was delighted—at least most of his uncles and his father who saw Inka as Zsa Zsa or Eva. (My father had reservations, he told me, but he wisely said nothing to others.)

Mountain Iron had a 75th anniversary celebration during the early years of that marriage and Leland's father Leo was the general chairman of the event. He arranged for his new daughter-in-law to be the Grand Marshal and to lead the parade riding on her white horse. This was a bit ridiculous since Inka had no connection with Mountain Iron, the town had no Czech population, and no one had seen a white horse around since at least 1910. Even Leo had only been around for a couple of years, having lived in Michigan for about forty years before returning to Mountain Iron to retire.

By now Leland had moved his career to Ingersoll-Rand, had fathered two more children by Inka, Tom and Anne, and was soon to be transferred to Milan, Italy. By the time his kids became fluent in Italian he was transferred to Stockholm so they were able now to speak Swedish, too. Inka had found a way to thwart her mother-in-law. She became a live snake collector and kept cages of snakes in the entry to her houses. This kept Josephine at bay, thinking, perhaps, that if she snooped in drawers she might very well find a snake or two lounging there. Since she didn't like snakes, she kept her distance.

Leland came back to Ingersoll-Rand headquarters in New Jersey as a vice-president of the power tool division and chief of all their Far Eastern (Asian) operations. Both he and Inka drank more and more. He traveled a lot to Asia. As long as they were either separated or drunk their marriage remained tolerable to them. When we visited them when their children were early teenagers it was obvious that the marriage was not going well, but they didn't discover this until Inka found she had cirrhosis and had to stop drinking. As soon as she sobered up they were divorced.

Leland found a third wife, Jeane, and this worked out fairly well. He never did give up drinking and Jeane hinted that the first couple of years were difficult until she was able to keep him tolerably sober.

In his retirement he became an officer in the Navy League and belonged to a Country Club and a Yacht Club (which probably defines him as being pretty conservative) when he and Jeane lived in Oxford, Maryland. He was the organizer of four Beck family reunions and was much interested in following the fortunes of the descendants of John and Hulda. He died in 1997 after having had non-Hodgkins lymphoma for a couple of years.

Charles, the son of Fran and Leland, eventually married and Leland and all three of the women to whom Leland had been married attended the wedding. This did not disrupt the proceedings as far as I know.

Charles is the program manager for National Public Radio in Maine; Leland and Inka's son Tom is a geologist and fisherman in Alaska; and Anne with a degree in animal science did scientific research in genetics and ecology, has been married and divorced and is now managing a bonded warehouse for a customs broker.

If I have had a close adult relationship with anyone in this generation it is with my cousin Faith. She has always been more interested than my other cousins in sharing her views with me. This does not mean that we have common beliefs, but it does mean that we have been able to discuss our differences as well as our similarities calmly and amicably.

Her mother dismissed her father when Faith was only two or three years old, so she never knew him. Her mother, Aunt Tommy, turned her over to her mother, our grandmother, to raise while Tommy worked to support both her parents and her children. Tommy did encourage Faith to be a performer, probably because she enjoyed performing herself. At family gatherings, Faith was always presented to do acrobatic dancing, or tap dancing, to play the piano, or whatever she was into at the time. This seemed to bore the adults and make the other children jealous; it did not make Faith a popular child within the family.

The absence of a father also encouraged her uncles to attempt to enhance her upbringing by attempting to bend her to their standards. This may have confused her, but it certainly didn't change her. She was probably lucky that her bossiest uncles, Charlie and Phoxey, were off to war when she was a middle teenager.

Faith was only about thirteen and I was almost nineteen when our grandmother died. I think she looked upon me then as a major male figure in her life, although I was about to leave for my wartime service in the Navy.

Mostly, of course, we exchanged letters and visited when I came home on leave. I may have helped her a little in her dealings with her many boyfriends, but the truth was that my experience with girls at that time was next to worthless.

A horrible thing happened to Faith while I was still in the Navy. When a high school gym class was demonstrating track and field equipment, an errant discus caught her in the jaw and shattered it. It was lucky she was not killed. They brought her to the school nurse, who happened to be her mother! Miraculously, she not only survived but the University of Minnesota Hospital put her back together well enough so that there was no surviving external evidence of the accident, and she matured into the attractive woman her childhood had promised with no noticeable effects of the accident.

Faith married Melvin Wick and they had four children: Timothy, Kimberly, Jonathan and Heidi. Stable, calm and dependable Mel was a steady worker in an iron mine, and early in their marriage they also had a tourist attraction called Fairyland. This allowed Faith, who had been trained as a teacher but who was basically an artist, to pursue her interest in figurative art. This is a good description of what she did, one of the definitions of figurative being relating to the representation of form or figure through the medium of drawing, painting, or sculpture.

I remember the scorn many members of our pragmatic and pedantic family heaped upon Faith and her Fairyland and her dolls. In time they realized that she had great talent and was a successful artist making small, dressed art figures not to be confused with toys or dolls.

Melvin was tolerant and easy-going and adapted well to the life of his artist-wife. After he retired he helped in the financial management of her business. Faith has had a happy, creative life. Her creations have been outstanding, and she has earned national and even world recognition.

Faith and Mel's four children are all pursuing successful and varied careers. Tim is a musician whose day job is as a computer software engineer for a legal publication service and is also the only one of his generation to be a grandfather. Jon's degree is in accounting; he is a CPA and works as the chief financial officer and senior vice president of a privately owned bank. Kimberly has a B.S. in Civil Engineering and worked as an engineer for five years before becoming a mother and homemaker. Heidi has a PhD in music, specializing in the natural horn to back up her math and physics degrees.

Bruce Fuller, about two years younger than Faith, was a rather pretty child with blond, curly hair and large blue eyes. He was a good but not exceptional student in school. Because his father—whom he does not remember—was a doctor, his mother a nurse, and his Uncle Charles Beck a doctor, it was decided that Bruce should become a doctor. He got through pre-med and into medical school before he decided that he was not interested.

Bruce enlisted in the Navy, became an officer and a pilot, and after he was discharged he became an airline pilot, captain of 747s. He first worked for Pan Am and later for United Airlines. He is now retired.

Bruce married Marilyn Bystrom and they have one child, a daughter Gretchen. Gretchen is a highly successful senior graphic designer, and Marilyn is a pharmacist. Bruce is a pleasant person who likes to have money, spends it very carefully but also enjoys the good things it can buy. In his retirement he has also found satisfaction in community volunteer work. And he and Marilyn organized a Beck family reunion in Washington (state) in 2004.

Mary Ellen Beck was the first daughter of Clarence and Ellen, who were married in their mid-thirties. Mary was born when Clarence (Phoxey) was in the South Pacific, a Navy Seabee during World War II.

Mary Ellen was an attractive blonde, intelligent and personable. I have scarcely known her since she was an infant cousin I could hold when I arrived home on leave during my military service. When the war ended I went my way and our paths rarely crossed. When I saw her in 1990 at a memorial service for her late father, she thought I was my brother and I was unable to identify her until we got each other sorted out.

She seems happily married to Robert Ganzer, her high school sweetheart, and they have two children, Christine and Karen. Robert is a television producer and Mary works for the United Way. They have lived in Wisconsin, the state of Virginia, Colorado, Montana, Kansas, and now Ohio near Robert's job in West Virginia. Television requires moving around, apparently.

Their daughters both attended Northern Michigan University. Christine works as a Director of Marketing and Karen works as a Customer Service Relations Manager.

The second daughter of Clarence and Ellen was Joyce Elizabeth. Joyce struggled a bit to get established in life and a job and eventually ended up as a nursing helper in a mental hospital in Brainerd, Minnesota.

Joyce has not kept in close touch with the family and moved from Minnesota to Texas and then to Florida. The last I heard she was working as a practical nurse in Mississippi and has never married.

Beverly Jean Beck was the daughter of Laurence and Esther. She and her husband Hal visited us briefly a couple of times as they passed through California, and they have attended several Beck family reunions. She was a schoolteacher, school librarian, and legal assistant and later a mother and grandmother. She married Harold Hatherly, a school administrator. They lived in Rochester, Michigan, until they retired to North Carolina. They have three children, all sons, Mark, Kirk, and Todd. Mark and Todd have technical backgrounds and MBA degrees and work and live in Minnesota. Kirk is a minister in the United Methodist Church at a church in North Carolina.

Laurence and Esther's son, Gary, was handsome and bright and also athletic—an all-state high school football player in Michigan. He became a teacher, but soon had enough of that and he joined the U. S. Navy to become a career officer. He earned an MS degree in aeronautical engineering at the Navy Postgraduate School and eventually as a Navy captain he became the skipper of the U. S. S. Eisenhower—an amazing accomplishment for a non-Annapolis man. He was a shoo-in to become an admiral but when the Eisenhower pulled into port at Norfolk, Virginia, after more than a year at sea, it was bumped by some rusty tub.

Even though Gary was most likely in no way negligent, that ended his upward mobility in the Navy and he was assigned to command the ROTC at the University of Wisconsin in Madison. As I learned in 1943, there is the right way, the wrong way and the Navy way—and only the Navy way counts.

When Gary retired from the Navy he worked for a few years for the University of Wisconsin at Madison as their engineering and maintenance manager. He has now fully retired and he and his wife Louise live in North Carolina, where they organized a Beck family reunion in 2002.

Their son Steven is a professional engineer in California with a degree in civil engineering, and their daughter Karen Sue Painter is a senior vice-president of Time Warner.

Joellen Margaret Beck was the first child of Charles and Gertrude. She was born a week and a day after the attack on Pearl Harbor. Her father was 31 years old, just finishing medical school, and he very soon left to be a doctor in the Army for the rest of the war.

Her father returned to first know his daughter as a relatively grown-up four-year-old. To hear her tell it, he was a male chauvinist who believed that her place for the next sixteen years was to baby-sit her three brothers and help her mother keep house. All of the brothers were born after the war, of course, so were five to ten years younger than Joellen.

Joellen was as strong-willed as her father and apparently disagreed with him in every way. They clashed on feminism, racism, politics, and religion.

She has a very impressive academic record, having attended Oberlin College, getting a BSN from Northwestern University and a Diploma in Nursing from Chicago Wesley School of Nursing. From Boston College she got an MS in nursing and a PhD in higher and special education. She is a nursing professor at Boston College and has a practice as a women's health nurse practitioner. She has served on the faculties of Salve Regina College, the University of Connecticut, and Boston College.

She is the author of 33 books and has published over 100 articles in professional journals.

She married John Watson by whom she had two sons, John and Andrew. She and Watson became friendly with another couple, David Hawkins and his wife. Eventually David Hawkins and Joellen and Mr. Watson and Mrs. Hawkins decided that a realignment of their marriages would be a good idea. Thus they switched husbands and wives (much to Uncle Charlie's chagrin) and have lived happily ever after.

Joellen and David are Unitarian Universalists and members of the American Association of Nude Recreation. With David came two stepsons, Glen and Marshall Hawkins, and now a step-grandchild, Helen May Hawkins, the daughter of Glen.

Joellen's son John is a night auditor and technical assistant, and her son Andrew is a physical therapy assistant.

I did not meet the adult Joellen until she was in her mid-forties and married to David Hawkins. I admire her and her husband. I think that her liberal political and religious beliefs may be more nearly like mine than are those of any of my other cousins, although I don't know that much about most of the others.

The next child and oldest son in Uncle Charlie's family is Bruce Lennart, born in 1946. I don't know him well, but Bruce had the reputation of being an obnoxious child. My only contact in his earlier years was when he came to visit us in California with the entire Charles Beck family. He was about 11 or 12 years old and somehow inspired a rock fight with the children of our neighbors, the Connollys. We ended up with some broken windows.

Bruce became a lawyer and practices in St. Paul, Minnesota. In his now middle age he greatly resembles his father in speech and appearance, and probably religion and politics. He is active in local politics and is an avid bicyclist. He arranged a Beck family reunion in 2000 in conjunction with his daughter Emily's wedding.

He and his wife, Lynn, have three children: Emily, Brian, and Lauren. Emily is a research librarian in Louisiana; Brian is nearing graduation from college and becoming an officer in the U. S. Army; and Lauren will graduate from Cornell College in May 2005.

The third child in Uncle Charlie's family was Douglas, a pharmacist. This seems to fit in a family that is generally inclined toward medicine.

Douglas has been married, divorced, and has remarried. Fortunately his father died before the divorce so he was spared yet another failure. His second wife Linda teaches special education in an elementary school. Douglas is a pleasant person and appears to have a successful career and family. He has two children, Katherine and Kristie. Katherine is married and working toward a Ph.D. in Journalism. Kristie is an accountant and is scheduled to be married in 2005.

The youngest of the Charles Beck family and of this generation of Becks is David. He graduated from Cornell College, went to medical school at the University of Iowa followed there by a neurosurgery residency and four years on the faculty. He went into private practice in neurosurgery in Mason City, Iowa, where he says he is now at the zenith of his career. After a brief and unsuccessful marriage to another neurosurgeon, he married Cathy. (I understand his inflexible father, Charlie, again loudly expressed his displeasure at having another divorced offspring.) David and his second wife adopted three children, Ashley, Grant, and Madelaine. Two of them turned out to be black—or at least half black, since they had accepted the yet unborn children of a white mother.

David says: "As for my family, I could not be more proud." Their daughter Ashley attends the University of Minnesota, son Grant is about to enter Cornell College, and Madelaine is in high school.

The color of these children did not seem to bother Aunt Gertie (their grandmother) nor David's siblings. In fact his brother Douglas also has a non-white stepchild. I find it very interesting and highly commendable that our other cousins range from neutral to positive toward having non-white relatives. I wonder how easily Uncle Charlie or any of his siblings would have adapted to having non-white grandchildren or nieces or nephews.

About his career David writes: "Like my father, medicine is my mistress, and what defines me. I see vast changes in medicine in this country, almost all bad. It is becoming more and more corporate driven, and more and more corrupt. I am sad to think that my career in the wonderful field of neurosurgery will wind down in the next 10 years, but at the same time I will be relieved to get out of it."

The last two members of our generation are the sons of Roland Beck and his wife Jean. (They had three sons, but their youngest died of a brain aneurysm at age six.)

Bradley, their oldest child, got a BS in Aeronautical Engineering at the Air Force Academy in Colorado and became a career Air Force officer. He was in the third graduating class of the Academy in 1962. In the early 1960s he was flying a large Air Force plane similar to a 747 over Greenland when the window popped out. He was sucked out of the plane into minus-100 degree air, but luckily caught a foot in his seat belt. His copilot pulled him back in, but he suffered severe burns from the freezing on all of his exposed skin including his eyelids.

At the Houston burn center where he was sent for repairs he met Gail Dawn Fox, who had recovered from cancer after having had one leg amputated, and they were married. Both of them survived their health problems and Bradley continued in the Air Force until he qualified for early retirement. Their only child, Eric, was born in 1969, is married and a father, and works as a truck driver.

Brad returned to active duty and flew KC-135 air-to-air refueling tankers for the Strategic Air Command until he reached retirement age.

After he retired from the Air Force he worked as Test Director, B1-B program, at North American Rockwell. They lived in Riverside, California until he retired fully and moved to northern Idaho where their son, daughter-in-law and grandson live.

Bradley has recently had surgery for cancer of his mouth and tongue, but seems to be recovering well, although it is a slow process.

The other child in this family is Brian. He went to Stanford and got a BS degree in electrical engineering, and then got an MSEE from the University of Southern California in 1968. While working for Hughes Aircraft he developed an interest in medical electronics, and decided that he should get an M. D. degree, which he did in 1972 from the University of California in Irvine. He practices medicine as a neurologist in Whittier, California, where he grew up, and has served as a clinical Professor of Neurology at USC. Brian and his wife Pat's children are Jason, Jeffrey, and Diane, who appear to be as talented and as academically inclined as their father and mother.

Jason works as an electrical engineer in the San Diego area; Jeffrey is a mathematician doing Post Doctoral research in Neural Networks at the University of

Rochester, and Diane is working toward a Ph.D. in English Literature at Cambridge University in England.

Although I will go into my own career in more detail later, I will insert a bit about my family here. I married my first and only wife, Mary Jane Herby, in Rochester, New York, in 1949, two years after I had arrived there to work for Kodak. She was a newspaper reporter for the Rochester Times-Union. We had two children, Bryan and Stephen, in Rochester, then I was transferred to Palo Alto, California, where we had two more, David and Barbara, and then I was moved back to Rochester where our fifth child, Thomas, was born in 1963. All five are now married, but only Steve has produced grandchildren, our two granddaughters (named Baxterbeck, since their mother is Jane Baxter.)

Bryan has a degree in architecture from the University of California in Berkeley, but has worked mostly as a computer programmer and consultant for various companies. He worked for several years at Syntex and published a book on clinical trials in the pharmaceutical industry. He now works with a small biotech company organizing clinical trials. Steve, with a degree in mathematics from Stanford, has also worked in computer businesses, including several years with Apple and is now organizing training programs around the world for Cisco Corp. David, a graduate of Humboldt State University (California), was once a ships' chandler, but is now working as a technician for a branch of Philips Electronics manufacturing medical ultrasound equipment. Barbara is a graduate of the USC film school and has worked producing informational films and TV for ESL, TRW, and NASA and is now freelancing writing screenplays. Tom, a graduate of the University of California in Davis, has worked for Lockheed and spin-off companies programming and directing flights of satellites for the last 20 years. Bryan lives in Redwood City, CA, Steve in Menlo Park CA, David in Seattle, Barbara in Tucson, and Tom near Boulder CO.

In the last two chapters we have looked at the members of my generation, and even had a peek at the next generations. There are 20 grandchildren of John and Hulda Beck and Ben and Bertha Hanson. None of the four grandparents had any more than a sixth or seventh grade education, mostly less. At least 17 of these grandchildren graduated from college and several of them went beyond a bachelor's degree. What's more important, they all lived productive, successful lives and it appears that most of the great-grandchildren are doing the same.

Those four grandparents who were justly proud of the accomplishments of their children would be overwhelmed at how well their grandchildren achieved the American Dream.

The next generations have given strong indications that this trend will continue, but given that in the Beck line alone there are 34 spread over 31 years in the next generation, reporting on them is beyond the scope of this book.

10

MOUNTAIN IRON, MINNESOTA
My Home Town as I Saw It

My life was shaped by my parents and other relatives, of course, but also by the town we lived in. In the 1930s Mountain Iron, Minnesota, was a small village of about 1,400 people. The first iron ore discovery on the Mesabi Range was made there in 1890. It is about 65 miles north of Duluth, 200 miles north of Minneapolis, and 98 miles south of the Canadian border.

It was a compact village. The town had been laid out with very small lots and most of the houses were built using only one lot each. There were no really big houses in town.

Even though the town was only a little over 30 years old when I was born, the main streets and the schoolyard were pleasantly landscaped with large shrubs and shade trees (much of it by my Grandfather Beck). Not many of the streets were paved in the 1920s, but by 1940 almost all of them were. I remember mostly wooden sidewalks when I was small, but they had been replaced with concrete by the time I finished elementary school.

I remember five significant buildings in town, all made of yellow brick. The two largest were schools, which served all grades from kindergarten through high school. The school district included all of the village and an almost equal population in rural areas surrounding the village.

About a block away, the village hall, a sturdy but undistinguished yellow box, housed the clerk's office, the jail, the fire department, and a meeting room used for elections, council meetings, and municipal band rehearsals. Its smell emanated from the numerous cuspidors filled with the juice of used Copenhagen snuff. Most of the cuspidors were in its public card room where men chewed snuff, smoked, and played games, mostly cribbage. I never got closer than the doorway, but I suspect they insulted each other, cussed their wives, and told dirty jokes. Pat Hagen was a bachelor, the co-owner of the Mountain Iron Store—a general store that sold meats, groceries, and all other necessities. Pat also owned several homes, and the rent from these along with the profits from the store made him one of the wealthier men in town. The Mountain Iron Store charged relatively high prices but had a very generous credit policy. At least half of the town was in debt to Pat Hagen either for groceries or rent, but in spite of his generosity Pat never seemed in danger of going bankrupt.

Being a bachelor and a non-drinker he spent a lot of his time in the village hall card room, so when he died they laid him out there for an all-night wake. I heard that before the night was over his corpse was propped up in one corner of the room so he could better pursue his usual kibitzing.

A fourth yellow brick building was the library, across the street from the village hall. It had been designed with some attempt at elegance with white marble framing around the doors and windows. The windows had rounded tops with panes of clear glass leaded into a symmetrical pattern. The word Carnegie was engraved over the entrance. Andrew Carnegie salved his robber baron conscience by building libraries, at least in towns where he had made some money. There was a meeting room and a kitchen in the basement of the library known as the Parlors where the women's Study Club gathered to drink coffee and sometimes discuss books.

The fifth yellow brick building was on another corner of the same intersection as the library and the village hall. It housed the First State Bank, which I thought was an imposing and impressive building when I went there to deposit my rare pennies in an account that probably never got as rich as $10. When I returned many years later I was amazed to find that the bank was really tiny. It still has a special smell that came from currency mixed with cheap tobacco.

The school was the center of civilization, the library a major satellite, and for most of the people in town one of the three churches completed the trio of important places in their lives. There were three churches: the Presbyterian which provided services in English and which our family attended; a Lutheran with services in Finnish; and a Roman Catholic whose congregation was mainly Italians and Croats.

After the repeal of prohibition, (and probably also before prohibition) bars were important social centers for some of the men in town and even a few women, but they were not significant to my family. Mac's Bar was on the fourth corner of the main intersection that had the village hall, the library and the bank on the other three. It has a stuffed timber wolf overlooking the intersection from a glass case over the entrance. The Bon Air Lounge was across the street less than a block away. (It burned down in about 2003, possibly from arson. It was then about 100 years old and maybe the oldest building in town.) The American Legion bar is a few doors from the library. They are all rather dingy, smelly dives, but thrive in good times and bad in this frontier town where hard drinking is a well-established tradition.

The village was threatened and constricted by iron mines. A gigantic open pit iron mine owned by U. S. Steel blocked the town on the north. Another large open pit mine owned by Wheeling Steel blocked the town on the east. An inactive and deep pit known as the Iroquois Mine blocked the town on the southeast side. Since the mines owned the mineral rights under the entire town, they had the right to buy the homes or other buildings and make the owners move them elsewhere or tear them down. Sometimes several blocks were moved and replaced by a hole in the ground.

In return, the mines employed a small percentage of the population and paid taxes, which supported almost all of the local village and school budgets.

When I was born in 1924, the economy of the United States was in the midst of several very prosperous years, but Mountain Iron and the other communities on the Mesabi Iron Range were already in a depression and sliding slowly into the ghost town status that is the usual fate of mining towns. This slide was briefly interrupted by World War II, but has otherwise continued until now.

There was a lot of good, high-grade iron ore still under the ground in the Mesabi Range in 1924. Through World War II, two-thirds of the entire world's iron and steel supply came from the Mesabi Range. So it should have been a wealthy place.

But it wasn't. When ore was first discovered, it took a lot of human back work to dig it out, so many Europeans were recruited or otherwise attracted to the Mesabi First the Cornish, then the Finns. The Cornish bossed and the Finns worked. But the pay was not very good, so the Finns looked to the Western Federation of Miners, a radical union supporting socialism, for help. This insulted Andrew Carnegie and John D. Rockefeller and the other mine owners, so they recruited replacements for the Finns, mostly from newly arrived Montenegrins and Croatians. Many Italians also joined the work force and Finns were generally blackballed from working in the mines for several years, as all Finns were pre-judged to be anti-American socialists even though probably less than half of them were political radicals. In 1908 a St. Paul district attorney even held up some citizenship papers of several Finns on the basis of the Oriental Exclusion Act, which did not allow citizenship for Orientals, basing his action on his contention that

Finns are Mongolians and therefore not white persons. A district judge over-turned this shortly afterward.

Then came World War I and the demands for iron ore grew so rapidly that machines such as steam shovels were developed to dig the ore more efficiently than men. When the many men who had left to fight the war came home, there were fewer jobs since hundreds had been replaced by machines. There were few alternative jobs on the Mesabi, so the unemployment rate was higher than in most of the rest of the country. Logically, the people put out of work by mecha-nization and reduced demand would have moved to a place where there were bet-ter opportunities to get jobs.

Logic was aborted on the Mesabi, however, because some wise politician thought about property taxes and made an assessment of the value of the unmined iron ore owned by the steel companies. The mining companies were horrified at the tax bill and offered a counter proposal. They said that rather than pay a tax on the ore, the value of which was (they claimed) suspect, they would pay a *per capita* tax on the population—so much a head, in other words. The pol-iticians and the mine owners came to an agreement, which appeared very gener-ous to the cities and villages, and very cheap to the steel magnates.

It became important for the towns on the Range to prevent the unemployed from leaving, because their tax income from the mining companies depended only on population. The municipalities used this tax money for public works projects that employed those who could no longer find work in the mines. They created a large number of low-paying jobs, which helped keep people from mov-ing away and preserved their tax income.

Many people stayed because they believed they had found the true Eden and disdained even Duluth to say nothing of Minneapolis-St. Paul or Chicago as places with horrible climates, pollution, and crime. They would rather live on $55 a month supplemented with hunting, fishing, and backyard gardening and stay in God's Country than work for Henry Ford at $5 a day and have to live in Detroit.

(God's Country: where winter lasted seven to nine months a year with tem-peratures as low as minus 40 F and snow up to one's armpits; where summers were rainy, humid and had giant mosquitoes and vicious deer flies. But those who stayed were able to beat the winter cold with a small fire, especially when in the nearby woods you could get all the firewood you needed free if you were will-ing to work for it. And the summers were tolerable with usually cool nights, and much lower temperatures than the Twin Cities or Chicago and other Midwestern and eastern places. And there were very few officials around to enforce game laws, prohibition, or anything else that stifled personal freedom. And there were almost no taxes since they were paid by the steel companies.)

So the towns hired its otherwise unemployed and paid them with tax money from the steel companies. Pay was low in order to spread the money to as many people as possible. Most people on the Range became public employees long before the WPA and other depression-driven national public works.

On the Mesabi local governments did wonderful things with this tax money and cheap labor. Even small towns were able to build the best schools in the state of Minnesota or maybe the U. S. with gymnasiums, swimming pools, shops, auditoriums, music facilities, and playing fields. They built parks, zoos, libraries, town halls, power plants, and water and sewage systems. Five of the first seven public junior colleges in Minnesota were built on the Iron Ranges in the 1920s.

When the building was done they manned the schools with all the teachers needed for regular and special classes. The schools even had doctors, dentists, and nurses to care for the kids. The bands and orchestras had not only instructors and conductors but also instruments. The athletic teams had coaching staffs and uniforms. All students were furnished with everything—books, pencils, paper, pens, even jockstraps, and iodine pills to combat a deficiency in the local water which was known to cause a thyroid problem.

Under these conditions, parents had only the minimum need to provide food and clothing and shelter, so low pay was not a serious problem. The school and the village hired people to shovel snow, empty garbage, and as janitors, firemen, policemen, librarians, cow punchers, hydrant checkers. Elected officials generally did a good job of redistributing the public money, although there were a few who were convicted for having stolen from the public trough.

In spite of minor imperfections, this system worked! Almost everyone was poor, but nobody felt poor just because they had little money. They ate well, had shelter, and their kids were getting a good education and opportunity. For most of us, opportunity meant moving away when we reached adulthood, although a few stayed on and still live there, enjoying poverty in what they still consider the best of all possible places to live.

I was born into and lived under this social system for my first 19 years. Many of those years had passed before I had even a vague notion that this was not the wonderful American Way Of Life enjoyed by all. I didn't fully appreciate until years later how well off the low-income people of the Mesabi were compared with poor people elsewhere.

Mountain Iron had three sections—a hill to the east where mostly Slavs lived, a hill to the west largely populated with Finns and Italians, and a valley between with a somewhat more mixed population along with the business section, the library, the village hall, and the school. Our house was in the valley as was the house of my father's parents. My mother's parents (who were Norwegian) lived on the edge of the Slavic hill. That hill was referred to either as the Grivich Ranch after the large families of the three Grivich brothers, or Hunkie Hill since the Slavs were generally referred to as Bohunks. In those days there was much less sensitivity to using mildly derisive terms for ethnic groups and these terms were commonly used by people even to describe themselves.

Many people in town were immigrants, so we heard a lot of foreign languages. These immigrants were anxious to learn English, however, and the school provided night classes to help them as long as there was a demand.

The mines had to do their work in the summertime. The frozen winters made it difficult to dig the ore and the frozen Great Lakes made it expensive to ship. In summer during days, evenings, and especially late at night I enjoyed the sound of train whistles, the banging of ore cars being coupled, and the dynamite exploding in the mines to loosen the iron-laden rocks. The demand for steel fell off so badly in the 1930s that the mines only needed to work about 3 or 4 months a year. Even when I was very young, however, I sensed the importance of the activity and was enthralled by the clangor that signified the beginning of a process that would end as automobiles and refrigerators and locomotives and steamships.

Autumn, too, was magical. Even at dusk it seemed as if the sun were out because the bright yellow and red leaves glowed in the twilight. But the fall season was brief. It was frosty in September and freezing and snowing in October.

Most of the year was winter. This was the really enchanted time for living in northern Minnesota. I remember cold, clear winter nights when it seemed you could hear a whisper from a mile away, and when the only blemish in the crystal-clear air was the cloud your own breath formed when you exhaled. The clean, white snow crunched when you walked on it. Each year we had a blizzard or two, and it was really a challenge to walk the three or four blocks downtown to get the mail at the post office or a loaf of bread from the grocery. You couldn't see more than two or three feet ahead, so it was like being blind, I suppose. Schools were closed. Of course there was no hazard, because no cars and not even snowplows were out on the streets. More often than not you didn't see other people, either because of poor visibility or more likely because most people didn't venture out.

During the long northern winter nights when the mines and the railroads had shut down, everything was absolutely quiet unless someone was walking and crunching the deep-frozen snow. On cold, clear nights you felt you could reach out and harvest the stars. When the moon was full on the clean snow there was no need for streetlights. There was a magical beauty to being out in the still starlight or moonlight when the temperature was below zero and having a cloud move in, dropping sparkling, gently falling, tiny and almost dry snowflakes. It may have been the nearest I have ever been to having a religious experience.

One of features of this village was that about half of the people had cows, and those who did used about half of the milk they produced and sold the rest to those who didn't have cows. I was glad we were buyers rather than sellers of milk because I was terrified of the cows when I was a child. Since the residential lots in town were only 25 to 50 feet wide and maybe 100 feet deep, cow owners milked their cows and turned them out to graze on their own initiative. Everyone had a fence to keep the cows out, but there were vacant lots available to the cows. We kid also used the vacant lots for playing baseball and football, and the dry cow patties were handy as bases.

Eventually the village became a bit embarrassed to have cows wandering its main streets and blocking traffic as well as producing deposits of unneeded manure, so it created the paid position of Village Cow Puncher. The village fenced off a few acres of land owned by a mining company about half a mile out of town. The job description for the cowpuncher specified that he was to round up all the stray cows on the streets after the morning milking and get them into this pasture, and then to return them to town and distribute them to their owners for evening milking. It was easy to identify the cowpuncher as the only older man in town carrying a stick that had no fishing line attached. He was probably multi-lingual, too, since the cows were not.

The roaming cows required another feature of the town landscape, which we all accepted. The schoolyard was fenced with elegant wrought iron fencing. It had, however, no gates. Instead it had openings that were gate-sized. In those openings were 3-inch iron pipes mounted vertically in concrete bases in sort of a maze pattern which allowed humans (except very fat ones) to get into the schoolyard, but effectively kept the cows out. I don't think it ever occurred to me during the many years I navigated those mazes what their function was. I just assumed it was some kind of a challenge to achieve passage to higher education.

Mountain Iron's being a cow town ended in the early 1940s when pasteurization and homogenization reached the hinterlands. It was not difficult for the large dairies to take over supplying milk when it was realized that the incidence of tuberculosis in our town was alarmingly high, and that avoiding raw milk could easily solve the problem.

The Mountain Iron Store was a general store and the main local shopping center. It was a large wooden building not too well constructed and by the time I was in high school the south wall of the store had bellied out and appeared to be on the verge of spilling some of the store's contents onto the north wall of Mac's Bar. If that south wall with its chicken feed and fertilizer and snow shovels had collapsed it would have been the end of both the Mountain Iron Store and Mac's Bar. Luckily this was not earthquake country and someone shored up the pregnant-appearing wall with steel I-beams in time to save Mac's Bar.

The Mountain Iron Store is long gone, but in its day it was a major economic force. When my father was young he worked for the store as an order taker as his father had done before him. There were few telephones, so he went around town from door to door before school in the morning taking orders that he delivered to the store. After school he returned to the store and picked up and delivered the orders that had been bagged during the day.

In later years the schoolboy order takers were replaced by telephones, but the store still made deliveries to its customers. I don't think my grandmothers ever set foot in the store, and yet they bought most of their groceries there. My mother did not believe in this—she made me go to the store and bring home the groceries.

There was another service the Mountain Iron Store reportedly had. It had a couple of rooms—maybe more—upstairs. I think that Pat Hagen lived in one of them until he died. The others were for rent. Sometimes they had tenants who were relatively legitimate flop house seekers, but it was rumored that they were also used by the local prostitutes.

In a small town like that no one believed in prostitution. Those women who sold their services were married and sometimes even mothers, but times were tough and this was a way to get money at least to slake their and their husbands' thirsts. Especially their husbands', who seemed to be directly involved in their activities. Gilbert, about ten miles away, was the sin city of the Range, and having a hotel of sorts could have prostitution. Mountain Iron was pure, with no hotel and only three taverns. You could hardly call the local grocery store a whorehouse, so activities there were mostly ignored. I am surprised, however, that even modest activity on its upper floor did not cause the fragile, bulging walls of the store to collapse.

My uncle Ben Hanson told me about an event that he was involved in while he still lived at home in Mountain Iron. I must have been about three months old when this happened.

It was the fall of 1924. Grandpa Hanson was sixty-five years old. He was not only unable to work in the iron mines because of his age, but also because automation even then had eliminated some 80% of the jobs. Besides, he had fallen down a mineshaft and hurt his back some years before and this limited his ability to do heavy labor.

In Mountain Iron there wasn't much need for policemen. This was prohibition, so there weren't even saloons to patrol. The few Model T Fords couldn't go very fast, so there were no traffic problems. Murders, if any, were discreet family matters. Everyone was poor, so there was nothing to steal. So it was logical for the village politicians, in assigning jobs to those who needed them, to appoint the least physically able men to the police force. That's how Grandpa, at age 65 with a bad back and no other income, became one of the three or four members of Mountain Iron's sterling staff of law enforcement officers.

Grandpa often manned a small kiosk where an unpaved street ended a cutoff from the main highway coming in from Buhl, a neighboring town to the west. Italians, who were, of course, Catholics, mostly inhabited this section of town. Their priest visited the houses of his parishioners on a bicycle. Bicycles and cars entering the main street through town from the unpaved cutoff were required by signs to stop. The priest usually ignored the stop sign. Grandpa had a running feud with the priest, almost daily citing him for running the stop sign, but getting nowhere with Catholic justices and other officials. I think Grandpa and the priest enjoyed this game. After all, what else did they have to play?

The priest was a minor power in that small town. He would go into the library and remove books from the shelves he thought were not suitable and no one ever brought legal action against him, although there was a bit of grumbling about his highhandedness.

One frosty October evening, Grandpa was, as usual, the only officer on the usually quiet four-to-midnight shift. His son, my Uncle Ben, had come home after dark from his football practice at Virginia Junior College four miles away and was doing his homework. About nine thirty or ten o'clock he got a telephone call from his father. Grandpa said: There's some trouble up on the hill. I want you to come with me. I'll pick you up. (Grandpa had no desire to be a dead hero and much preferred to be a live chicken. Or at least he wanted to face danger with the help of his able-bodied son.)

The hill was less than half a mile from the police station. The Hanson house where Ben was then the only child still living at home with Grandpa and Grandma Hanson was about two-thirds of the way up, and on the top of the hill was a settlement of largely Slavic people—mostly Croats. These were not normally troublemakers any more than the Italians and Finns who lived in their own enclaves in other sections of the small village. Ben was probably more annoyed at having his homework interrupted than frightened by the assignment.

Grandpa puffed up the hill and stopped by his house. There was no patrol car for Mountain Iron policemen. The town was easily patrolled by foot, and none of the policemen could drive a car, anyhow. Ben put on a sweater and they headed up the road. Grandpa looked stern and official in his blue serge police uniform with his badge shining over his left breast pocket, clutching his billy club, and wearing his stiff round hat with a shiny, hard black visor that looked just like those the streetcar conductors wore, except that the emblem on the front said M.I.P.D.

There's trouble at Kaiser's house, he said. I hope we can handle it. Kaiser—no one ever supplied a first name—was a fairly young widower with a couple of small kids. I never knew whether his name was given him because he looked like Kaiser Wilhelm or because it was as close as someone could come to a Slavic name, or even whether it was a first or last name.

They got to Kaiser's house, knocked on the door and entered the kitchen. There, bent over the sink, was Joe Novak, bleeding profusely from a scalp wound. Novak was a Czech, a recent immigrant who had left a young wife in Europe and was hoping to have her join him soon. He was probably about 25. "Don't put me in jail, Mr. Ben." he said to Grandpa. Uncle Ben answered for his father: I don't think you need jail, but we had better get you to the doctor.

The only doctor in town was Dr. McDaniel, who was about a half mile away. No cars were available, so poor Joe had to walk to the doctor. Ben got all the clean rags Kaiser could find and they pressed them on Novak's head to stem the flow of blood and walked him to Doc McDaniel. Doc shaved his head, sewed him up, and sent him walking home.

Since this was a police call, it had to be reported and referred to a Mr. Foss, the local justice of the peace. Life was not very exciting for the justice, so he called for a hearing. There was probably no legal need for this since it did not appear that any laws had been broken and no charges had been filed. However, the recently European immigrants, and especially the Slavs from the Austro-Hungarian Empire, seemed to accept without question the right of authorities to invade their lives.

Uncle Ben and Grandpa attended the hearing with eagerness, I am sure, and got the full story: Joe Novak was lonesome that frosty night and Vic Ruth and his wife had invited him over to their house to share some bootleg hooch. The Ruths were Finnish (the name was probably shortened from something like Ruotalainnen) even though they lived in the Slavic section of town. Vic and his wife were still young, but already well established in their careers of becoming two of the more celebrated town drunks, not in the least thwarted by the recent amendment which prohibited the sale of alcohol in the United States.

As the evening wore on, Joe, and Vic, and Mrs. Ruth approached some happy state of drunkenness. When the night got colder and the fire in the pot-bellied stove in their living room dwindled they needed more than the booze to keep them warm, so Vic decided it was time to go outside and fetch some more wood for the fire.

Mrs. Ruth was not exactly Miss America or even Miss Ore Dump of 1921. But apparently through the haze of the bootleg liquor she became attractive to Joe, in whom the booze had also revived enough memories of his wedding night in Czechoslovakia to get his youthful hormones flowing.

As soon as Vic shut the door on his way to the woodpile, Joe made a move on Vic's wife. But Vic was an experienced drinker and, drunk as he may have been, made a fast trip in the frosty night to the woodpile and back. When he returned and saw what was going on he dropped the wood, picked up a poker and hit Joe on the head. Joe ran bleeding to his friend Kaiser's house. Kaiser told him to stop bleeding on the goddam floor and then called the police.

Justice Foss listened to this story with interest. You have to expect a bit of voyeurism from small town judges whose lives are normally dull, so he asked, somewhat haltingly, "Mmm, Joe—ah—tell the court—ah—just how far did you get?"

Joe's answer was quick: Justa one-a button, judge, justa one-a button! (Pants did not have zippers under their flies in 1924.)

Justice Foss: You are fined $2 court fees. Case dismissed.

◆   ◆   ◆

Some things in the Mountain Iron of my youth may be typical of that time and some were probably unique to that part of the world. I mean, of course, the mechanics of life, not the people.

Mountain Iron, like some other Mesabi towns and cities, had its own coal-burning power plant to generate electricity for the town. This electricity generally did what it needed to do like lighting lights, running refrigerators, etc., but it apparently didn't have a consistent cycle because the electric clock which my father had proudly given my mother as a gift for her kitchen ran inconsistently and was useless.

A by-product of this generation plant was heat. Steam that was left over from the electrical generators was piped to the village buildings first, then the school, and then to businesses and homes within range of the power plant. The lucky home and business owners had to pay for this service, but enjoyed clean and reliable heat and were saved space and work. My parents were able to get this service only after I left home, so I was never able to enjoy the luxury of not having to feed fuel into a stove.

While the garbage dump was a sort of social center for some of us in our elementary school years, sewage disposal was a mystery to me. I don't know what sort of sewage disposal plant the village had, but our house was served by one. Not everyone in town was, however, because the village provided another service called the gold wagon which circulated in the dead of night emptying outhouses in sections of town not served by the sewer.

The village provided other services such as water. In Minnesota that was not a big problem since the water table was near the surface and there were springs everywhere. I think that the water we drank came from abandoned mine pits filled with water from springs. There was always a definite taste of iron in our water, but it was always cold, fresh, and apparently pure.

Since the village or the school provided income to many through a somewhat socialistic structure, it was not surprising that these governments were expected to and did provide a lot of non-essential services. The village paid for janitorial services at all three of the local churches. Both the school and the village supported Santa Clauses at Christmas to deliver candy and nuts. Independence Day was financed from the village treasury with money for prizes in races, treasure hunts, baseball games and in some years parades and fireworks.

The Fourth of July Parade down Mountain Iron's Main Street in 1914. All of the Becks and Hansons lived there at that time and probably most of them are in this picture. Orville Hanson is probably one of the trombonists in the band. Mabel Hanson is probably one of the girls in white on the float just in front of the flag with the white cross.

People on the Mesabi Range expected to be taken care of by the local governments. There was no feeling of guilt. The mining companies were exploiting the land and were responsible for having brought more people there than they needed. It seemed only fair to those whose jobs had been made obsolete that the companies who had brought them there should, through the taxes they paid, continue to support them.

This idea was rarely questioned. Of course the mining companies were not being altruistic. It was only to avoid even higher taxes that put them in the position of supporting the former or potential employees who had been replaced first by strikebreakers and later by mechanization.

The Mesabi Range into which I was born and where I grew up was not operating under the rules of a free capitalist economy. There was probably nothing else like it in the world. It was not exactly socialist; it was a bit paternalistic, but with a looseness that allowed the paters (politicians) to be tyrannical and self-serving graft takers if they were so inclined.

With limited opportunities for even a modest income, the citizens of the Mesabi through this arrangement and a very low cost of living were provided a much higher standard of living than their meager earnings would have given them anywhere else. It was probably this that made the inhabitants of the Mesabi Range in the 1930s far happier than one would expect.

This background makes me less inclined than most of my successful business executive colleagues to look on government or corporate largess toward the unfortunate poor as an evil. It was not until I became a manager with bottom line responsibility that I questioned Eastman Kodak's unusual altruistic practice (during most of my career there) of keeping a significant percentage of employees who were sub marginal producers on the payroll. Nevertheless, I believe that my peers from the Mesabi, whose parents might not have survived without that unique subsidy, have made more than average significant contributions to improve the United States economy, professions, government, and arts. I suppose this is why I support so-called liberals who believe that subsidizing the poor can be a good investment for the future. I have seen it work, and work well. (Twice, actually, but more later about the second example.)

There were some other events that happened in Mountain Iron that I remember or heard about that might be worth mentioning. In 1894 when the town was only about four years old there had been a lynching there. A young French itinerant who spoke little or no English was impolitely urged to get on his way. It appears that he may have stopped a couple of miles out of town to relieve himself and a couple of young girls from the town observed him through the bushes. They reported this in a way that made him sound like a potential rapist, so a group of hotheaded vigilantes took off and captured him. He spoke too little English to defend himself and since he was French and thus assumed to be oversexed, they immediately convicted and hanged him without a trial. The girls' stories later seemed to indicate strongly that he was innocent, but that was too late to save him. He was buried in a small local cemetery of a dozen graves including one that housed a Hanson uncle of mine who had died in infancy.

It was another man of French ancestry, I think, who made local headlines in the mid-1930s. Jack Loushin (or Luchine, or something we pronounced Loosheen) was a sort of local ne'er do well who apparently needed some gasoline one winter night. John Anderson, the local Chevrolet dealer, rented empty space in his heated showroom on winter nights for locals who wanted to keep their cars from freezing. One cold night, Jack broke into Anderson's showroom and siphoned out a few gallons of gas from one of the cars. He made the mistake of lighting a cigarette during the process and started his stolen gas and himself on fire. It was apparently a spectacular sight for men from the fire department (only half a block away) and other observers to see a man in flames in the show window of the garage. Jack died, but amazingly there was very little other damage. I remember one of my schoolmates reporting that they had seen what they thought was a glove near the site, and was later appalled to realize that it was really one of Jack's burned hands.

There was probably a normal quota of sexual activity outside of marriages, but I knew of very little. It was a fairly open secret, however, that one man was spending a lot of time in the bed of a woman whose husband was in a tuberculosis sanitarium. This philandering man was my scoutmaster, the superintendent of my Sunday school, and a principal, teacher, and, at the time of my graduation, the school superintendent. His reputation did nothing to encourage me to believe that the Boy Scouts, the Sunday school, or the high school were bastions of morality. It appears that his two daughters survived his scandalous behavior, and I believe that one became a highly respected mayor of Mountain Iron in her later years. One of my high school classmates mentioned, as we celebrated the 50th anniversary of our graduation, that this sanctimonious lecher had once physically accosted her in a secluded area of the school when she was about 15 or 16. She successfully fended him off by telling him that her father would kill him if she reported it—and she was probably right! I have to wonder what some of the teachers might have had to put up with to keep their jobs. And I am amazed that his suitability for the jobs he held was never challenged. I expect that this was more typical of the times than of the place, and that perhaps today even in Mountain Iron someone would object to this kind of sexual harassment.

I have not described Main Street, U.S.A.—or have I? Every struggling little town has its problems, and while they are unique they are also universal—only the details are different. Iron miners are probably not as different from cowboys or farmers or oil well roustabouts as we may have thought. The struggling people on the Mesabi Range I knew in my childhood had two goals: a reasonable life for themselves, and better lives for their children. For those I knew I would rate them as having been at least 90% successful. It was only getting there that may have been a little different.

11

GROWING UP IN MOUNTAIN IRON

In the first ten chapters I told all I know about the people and the place that prepared me for adulthood. This chapter will tell you how I fit into this picture.

When I was born, my father's parents still had four sons living at home and going to school and my mother's parents had one. Even though I was the first of my generation on both sides, I was born into a large and close family who were a significant part of our small town. My father was the respected postmaster; my mother had been a schoolteacher, a job highly regarded in a town of immigrants who saw the opportunity for their children to get an education they had been denied. My father's father was leaving his mark as a landscape gardener and my mother's father was one of the town's three or four policemen.

My two sets of grandparents owned houses in Mountain Iron. My parents lived in a flat until I was two years old when they bought the small house they lived in for the rest of their lives.

My goal in this and succeeding chapters is to tell you what my life has been like during my time on earth.

My parents, Mabel Leila Hanson Beck and John Lennart Beck lived in Mountain Iron, Minnesota, where my mother had been born and where they had both gone to school through high school. I was born in Eveleth, Minnesota only because it was a nearby town that had a hospital.

One of my early memories is of my third birthday—July 16, 1927. I liked the cake with the white frosting, but not the small hard candies that had been sprinkled on it. Being the center of attention was not new to me, since I was the first child of my generation and was at that time the only grandchild and nephew who lived in the vicinity of four grandparents, ten aunts and uncles, and a very attentive great-aunt and uncle who were childless and looked on me as a surrogate grandchild.

The birthday party was held in the small kitchen-dining room of the small house I grew up in, the only house my parents ever had. I vaguely remember that my parents and at least one grandmother were there, and I clearly remember two of my uncles. They seemed grown up to me, but they were only about 11 and 14 when I was born so they treated me like their little brother, a relationship that lasted all of their lives.

I suppose I got some other gifts, but the one I remember was a rag doll effigy of Red Grange. Red Grange was the football star of the nineteen twenties, and possibly the first professional football player who was paid enough so that he didn't need a second job. I had the doll for a couple of years until it wore out and I buried it in the vacant lot next door.

Of course I was not aware of the message the gift conveyed. In the rough, raw mining town where we lived almost everyone had to do hard physical labor to survive. Men were men, and often so were the women. Little boys were taught that strength was the essence of survival. Football offered one of the first chances to test their masculinity. Even though on both sides of my family there was a high regard for intellectual achievement, athletics and physical strength were also highly regarded.

In its 100 years of existence, Mountain Iron has produced more than its share of moderately successful men and women, but only one who achieved even modest national recognition. It is amusingly ironic that from a village that raised its boys to be macho he-men the most famous native son is a somewhat effeminate, allegedly homosexual Hollywood dancer and choreographer. It is even more surprising that he is accepted as the village hero with as much enthusiasm and pride as if he had been a professional football star.

I remember having my tonsils removed when I was about five in Dr. McDaniel's office in downtown Mountain Iron. This was about four or five blocks from our house, so we walked there. I remember going under ether, being revived, and stopping by my father's store for a little ice cream on the walk home. I was accompanied by my mother at least, and probably Aunt Toots, a nurse, who always attended family medical events.

When I was about four years old a new child arrived in our neighborhood and stopped by to play. He was within a few days of being the same age as I, but he spoke only Finnish and I spoke only English, so our first encounter was not exactly smooth. It turned out that he had moved into a newly built house a few doors from ours with his mother and his sister. His father had been killed in a mine accident, and apparently the new house (very minimum, of course) was part of the settlement. Sulo Lundgren soon learned to speak English, and we were friends through our school years, and with limited contact until he died in the late 1980s. His father's was the only fatal mine accident I remember hearing about. The mining company was obviously not very generous to his survivors, and his widow was not prepared to fight the system, so she raised her two kids by running the school laundry until she retired. Sulo became a school principal in northern Minnesota, and on weekends traveled to small colleges in Minnesota and the Dakotas to referee football and basketball games.

I remember going to kindergarten already knowing how to read when several of my classmates couldn't even speak English. I carefully hid my reading ability and hoped that it wouldn't be discovered, and I was either successful or the teachers preferred not to deal with it.

In the first grade, however, I was only given a week before the teacher and the school administration decided that something should be done about me and I was moved to the second grade. This was not a happy day and I remember crying and running home. The next day I reported to the second grade and from then on never looked back.

My remaining years in the Mountain Iron school system were relatively happy. I became a classroom leader even though I was always the youngest member. It may be that my age was forgotten because I was usually also the biggest member of the class.

My classmates didn't seem to resent me, probably because my leadership was in non-athletic things—academics, writing, speaking, and politics. In our frontier town, the things that counted most were physical. I was definitely not a leader in anything physical (except size and weight). I did not avoid participation in baseball, basketball and football, but I was always nearly the last one chosen by captains picking sides, and for good reason: I was slow and awkward. I found this painful and I would gladly have exchanged a few I.Q. points for more athletic ability.

I remember summers as being long and rather lazy times, very pleasant, undemanding, good for reading books. Of course we played some baseball. Our baseball was self-organized—no Little League, no parents, no fans. We seldom had a full team of nine so we played with whatever matching numbers of players our opponents and we could muster.

We always spent a couple of weeks at a lake every summer. Our family combined with the Henderson family (that made four adults and six kids, or often seven when cousin Leland Beck from Michigan joined us) to qualify for two weeks at the American Legion cabin on Lake Leander. Then I had another week of Boy Scout camp at Perch Lake.

Some summers we even took an automobile trip for a week or two.

But I still remember summers as mostly free time and I especially enjoyed those days when I was able to have time to myself, not only for reading but catching and studying ants, grasshoppers and other insects, or even trying to learn Latin and algebra from textbooks my uncles had left behind.

There were enough risks in the world so that when we left school in June we always wondered who wouldn't return in September. It seemed that at least one student in our school, usually a junior or senior high student, would die during the summer. The causes were such things as polio myelitis (then called infantile paralysis, later polio), spinal meningitis, appendicitis, and, rarely, accidents. I remember all of these things as summer tragedies, although I do remember one sixth-grader being killed by a car during the school year as he was crossing the highway after being let out of a school bus.

Since we knew everybody in school, all of these deaths were personal tragedies, and I especially remember one that touched me closely. The summer after I had finished the third grade a close friend of mine who had finished the fourth grade went swimming in the local swimming hole, an abandoned mine pit, and drowned after he struck his head on a rock. I was not there because I was not permitted to go near the treacherous place. Even after I learned to swim I never went near the pit and, in fact, never learned where the swimming hole was.

In later years the school opened up its pool for summer swimming, which probably kept at least the younger kids out of the pit. I don't remember any other drownings there.

Winter was the normal season, the way of life. It was quiet and beautiful. The down side of winter was the clothing we had to wear. It was all heavy and cumbersome, and I always felt clumsy in itchy woolen long underwear, heavy pants, shirts and sweaters, a sheepskin-lined corduroy coat, two or three pairs of woolen socks, and heavy boots. The boots we most commonly wore were known as Pike River Oxfords—Pike River being a rural Finnish community a few miles away. They were made of heavy rubber (like automobile tires) covering the feet and sewed to leather tops that went almost to the knees. Mine were always very heavy since they had to be big enough to cover at least a couple of pairs of knitted woolen socks.

I always felt I moved at about half speed in the wintertime. However, I never did get frozen toes. I can't say the same for some of my nattier peers who switched to fancy and tighter all-leather boots with a knife pocket on one side. I envied them until they had to undergo treatment for frostbite.

How cold was it? We saw forty below zero (Fahrenheit) at least briefly every year, and 15 to 20 below was normal for four to six weeks between December and February. Ten above was a heat wave during the winter months. This was not a big problem, and the people who lived there were no more impressed nor handicapped by it than people in California who face normal winters of temperatures between 25 and 50 degrees.

The first twelve years of my life were dominated by my large family (parents, grandparents, aunts and uncles), by the school, the band, the Presbyterian Church, and the public library. My friends were all boys from the neighborhood with whom I played football, baseball, basketball and built shacks in backyards or in the woods. We experimented with cigarettes some, but were otherwise disgustingly innocent, being much too naive to be more sinful.

I began playing in the high school band when I was in the fifth grade. I played the mellophone for two years. (That was an alto horn that looked like a right-handed French horn but was much easier to blow than a French horn.) Then I switched to the baritone horn which had much more interesting music to play.

This was a small school and the band had competition from other activities, so it was common to start potential musicians early and get them into the band and orchestra as soon as they were minimally qualified.

The village had a band, too, and paid its players. Here, too, the number of available players was small and not particularly skilled, so I was introduced into this by the time I was in the sixth grade. The pool of players was even smaller than for the school band because only males were allowed to play in the village band. The sex barrier was broken when I was in high school: the daughter of the band director played the saxophone and she and her father decided that she was just as well qualified as the men and boys to share in the village money. That opened the door for all the girls and upgraded the quality of the band's music considerably.

You might say I became a professional musician at age 11. The municipal band paid a starting rate of ten cents a rehearsal and one dollar a concert or parade. The top pay, which I reached in two or three years, was 25 cents a rehearsal and two dollars a concert. This sounds insignificant now, but in those days it kept me with a very generous supply of pocket money, and even paid for some of my clothes. I never had an allowance, never even considered asking for one, and I don't remember ever being broke.

The band performed on a gazebo (bandstand) in our small village park. These concerts were major events for the townspeople. There was no television, the town had no movie house, and summer radio attracted very little interest. There were probably 6 or 8 concerts a year on those Friday evenings in the summer when it didn't rain. Older people would bring chairs or sit in parked cars on the park road. Kids and dogs would play, often noisily, around the bandstand. There was very little, if any, criticism of the quality of the music and it is not likely that anyone paid close attention. People near the bandstand would clap and those in cars would blow their horns whenever the music stopped. Those in cars too far away to hear soft passages would occasionally blow their horns while we were still playing.

When I first joined the band we provided our own uniforms of white shirt, white pants, dark jacket, and a black bow tie. In 1940, however, Mountain Iron had its 50th anniversary celebration, so the village bought us very fancy uniforms. The pants were gray whipcord with a wide red-orange stripe down the side. The jacket was the same red-orange and had gold braid loops coming down from one shoulder and gold buttons. We wore a brown Sam Browne belt over the jacket. The hats were gray and red with a gold lyre emblem on the front and they had a metal slot on top in the front just behind the emblem. We had large gold plumes that fit into the slot, and these plumes were part of our parade uniforms but not worn for park concerts.

Probably our major performance was on the Fourth of July. Our pay depended on the budget, but was always at least $1. We started by marching from the western hill of the town and down past the Duluth, Missabe and Northern railroad depot to the school playing field. Rain, snow, or sun—and we really had at least one of those every year—we played and paraded and picked up kids and adults as we went. We looked like the Pied Piper of Hamlin as we led them to the day's activities. When we got to the schoolyard there was a pile of sawdust full of pennies for the little kids to dig in. Then there were sack races, three-legged races, and dashes for married women, single women, married men, single men, and whatever categories were needed for everyone to have a fair chance at the cash prizes available. My parents did not participate in those events, nor did I. I got paid my dollar or two for blowing a horn. My mother avoided such competition. My father was waiting to play in the afternoon baseball game against a team from a neighboring village where he would collect maybe as much as $2 to $5 for his efforts, so he eschewed the juvenile activities of the morning. Most years there were two games—one seven-inning game at each of the home fields of the two village teams. And there were sometimes softball games between the married women and the single women. The Mountain Iron budget did not usually include fireworks, but Virginia, a city only about four miles away, always had them along with an evening band concert by the very good Virginia Municipal

Band. Some of our Mountain Iron band members also played in the Virginia Band, but if I had been good enough for that I would have had to displace the director of our Mountain Iron band who also played the baritone.

By the time I was sixteen I was the town's best stenographer. I learned how because I knew that I would need some earning power to pay my way through college. I recognized my limitations in music and athletics—both of which I had pursued with great pleasure and little talent—so I decided to develop marketable skills in some other area. It turned out that I was able to make my fat fingers operate a typewriter and take shorthand faster than anyone else in Mountain Iron High School had ever done.

This got me assignments to type theses for teachers, records for a teachers' association, and other requests. I am sure I was underpaid for these jobs, but they did pay something and did hone my skills. This was dreadfully dull and I remember having great difficulty, even at age 16, resisting the temptation to edit and improve the turgid prose of those teachers aspiring to masters' degrees. Even in 1940 teachers were rewarded for being dull and unimaginative.

I got other assignments. George Orcutt, the local butcher and a partner in the Mountain Iron Store needed a confidential typist. So did the North East Minnesota Education Association.

For obscure reasons, secrecy always seemed to be important and I was always totally trustworthy as a stenographer or typist. I was not only well able to produce the required documents when sworn to secrecy but they were also so boring that they were easy to forget. But I was grateful for the experience, which led to better similar jobs.

What did all this do for me, and why would I not have been as well off in Emporia, Kansas, or Syracuse, New York? It might, of course, not have been any different. But I feel indebted to Mountain Iron for several things:

A good basic education in a small school, which was well-equipped and attracted good teachers. Teachers were, in fact, the highest paid people in town and were regarded so highly that this was rarely resented.

The opportunity in school to try everything. Most small schools had limitations, but in the well-funded Mesabi Range schools they offered music, dramatics, speech, journalism, football—everything. I did almost all, usually badly, but I left with the firm conviction that if a thing is worth doing it is worth doing badly as long as you do your best and have fun.

The recognition that even people who are doing low level jobs do them well. Since the village and school provided 75% or more of the jobs, people (mostly men in those days) didn't take off in the morning to work in a closed plant or mine. They came down your street with a snow shovel or a snowplow, or down your alley with a garbage truck. Or they swept the floor at the school, or mowed the public lawns. They often didn't speak much English, they never got much money, but they always worked hard and well and seemed grateful for the opportunity.

A conviction that ethnic differences are non-existent. This was difficult to grasp at first because my father and his family believed that southern Europeans and Catholics were inferior. (Of course in our town the southern Europeans—Italians and Croats—were the Catholics.) Our town was so small that it was impossible not to know the Italians, the Slavs, the Finns, and the Others very well. In the normal course of these associations it was obvious to me early in my life that we were all alike. The only differences were that I had to tune my ear to somewhat different accents when I was listening to the parents of my schoolmates. But I had more trouble understanding my own grandfather speaking English with his Finnish accent than I had with the Italian or Croat immigrants.

Some differences were important to the immigrants. They nurtured the special cultural differences they were proud of and I hope these have survived through subsequent generations.

In my and the two or three generations following, ethnic intermarriage among those who stayed on the Mesabi has been so common that there is probably almost no child there today who can claim unmixed ancestry back to a single European country. The American melting pot, as usual, has easily prevailed over petty bigotry.

I was graduated from Mountain Iron High School in June 1941. I was a valedictorian of my class—one of three. This had never happened before, but apparently there were three of us who had earned nothing but A's in our high school years, so all of us were selected. Our teachers must have had a few years of lenient grading, but I thought it was nice to share the wealth, and as far as I know the others thought so, too.

I continued to live in Mountain Iron for two more years while I went to Virginia Junior College. The high school bus was routed to give us free transportation. The tuition was very small, so it was easily affordable. These were, surprisingly, the most efficient years I ever spent in college with better teaching than I had later in a number of supposedly prestigious universities. Even though Virginia J. C. was not the choice I would have made if I could have afforded anything else, I have no regrets.

I managed to get a job in a local service station just after my high school graduation. Jobs were really scarce, but when the incumbent cut off a couple of fingers in a wood shop accident, his job opened up. I got 25 cents an hour for part time work there, and was able to enter college with $75 in the bank, which easily carried me through my first year. (The guy who lost his fingers was able to come back to work when I had to leave for college in the fall. Unfortunately he was never able to resume pitching for the baseball team, and I was totally incapable of replacing him in that capacity.)

Pearl Harbor and the U. S. involvement in World War II occurred about three months after I started junior college, and life changed drastically for everybody. I signed up with the Navy for their college training program, and the Navy allowed me to finish my two full years at Virginia J.C. Most of my male classmates departed one by one during those years, some of them to their deaths.

The war opened up jobs in the mines and related industries and I was able to get a job as a stenographer with the Great Northern Railway in their Mesabi (ore transporting) division. That required a daily commute of about 50 or 60 miles round trip at the 35 miles-per-hour wartime speed limit. (The pay was $5.05 per day for six days a week, which made me comfortably well off.) Putting that on top of a full academic load made for long, hard days during the four or five months I was doing both. But I survived, found the job interesting, and still got good grades and graduated in 1943 near the top of my class (a close third, I believe) with an AA degree. I even found time to be editor of the college newspaper and be a sports correspondent for the St. Paul Pioneer Press.

12

COLLEGE AND THE NAVY

Finishing college and even some graduate school was interwoven with my being in the Navy, so I will not try to separate them here. My first two years of college were, as noted, at Virginia (Minn.) J. C.

I had committed to the Navy in 1942, but since I was already in college and the Navy V-12 program had started slowly it was not until November 1943, that I was called to active duty. This was fine with me. I was not eager to see or feel the shooting war, nor did I have an urgent need for a uniform and a life of regimentation. Of course, I would not have admitted this to anyone as World War II was raging and all able-bodied red-blooded American men were rallying to the colors to put their lives on the line. I was in no hurry, even though I was prepared to serve when my time came.

I had been ready to leave the nest for a couple of years. Not that living at home was bad. I got along well with my parents and my younger brother. My mother was a good cook even with wartime food rationing, and my father was as generous with the family car as wartime gasoline and tire rationing allowed. It was just that there was a great big world out there and I felt stifled in the very small town I had come to realize was not very close to the real world.

Leaving was different from what I had visualized. It was wartime, 1943, and I was leaving for military service. Already some of my schoolmates were missing or dead.

I was not afraid. With typical youthful confidence in my own immortality I did not expect to die in battle. I was much too naive to even begin to visualize the utter horror and carnage of even the most minor military skirmish. I was off to war, like almost all the boys I had ever known. Only those few very unlucky ones with physical problems were being left behind.

My mother said goodbye at home and my father drove me to the railroad station in Virginia. Mother did not like to have anyone, even me, see her cry, but I knew she would as soon as we drove away. Mother did not believe in war and especially not for her son. I don't think she approved of violence of any kind; she had never even attended a football game I played in.

She was not unprepared for my leaving, however. For many years she had been telling me in many different ways: You *must* leave this place when you grow up. You don't *have to* work so hard for so little as your father and grandfathers. See how well your uncles are doing by having left this town.

My father was a World War I veteran, an American Legionnaire, and a staunch patriot. For all I could tell, he put me on the train with nothing but pride in his offering his son to his country. I am sure now that he had other emotions, but he did not believe, at least in those days, in showing any emotion he considered soft.

He shook my hand firmly. I know you'll behave yourself, was all he said, and I accepted this as a vote of confidence. I knew he meant that he felt I was ready to face the world and whatever challenges and temptations it offered.

The steam locomotive blew its whistle and the only passenger train on the Duluth, Missabe, and Iron Range Railway puffed out of the station and headed for Duluth.

I knew I would be back. But I also knew that I would be back only to visit. It was home—and still is, more than sixty years later—but I had known for several years that there was no life there for me. I knew this train was taking me to my future. In spite of the war I was confident that my future would be long, but I knew that it would not be near where I had gotten on that train.

I felt a little sad to realize that this really was the end of my life there and I was leaving my home and family for good. But mostly I felt relieved to be freed at last from a part of the world that had no place for me.

A few hours later I reported to the Navy and found another temporary world. I did not find this new world intolerable and the experiences were more often fun than not, but there was no time when I considered the Navy more than temporary. I was highly adaptable and willing to subordinate my natural inclination to question and resist often illogical authority as long as there was a war on, but like most of my peers in all branches of the service I looked forward only to peace and freedom from military life.

I cannot deny that the Navy made a highly significant and positive contribution to my career. I was in its V-12 program, and they kept me at the University of Minnesota until I earned a Bachelor of Chemical Engineering degree. Not only was my tuition paid, but I was paid $50 a month for going there.

There were a few hundred of us at Minnesota studying chemical, electrical, aeronautical, civil, or mechanical engineering, or dentistry or medicine. Other schools offered Naval Science plus a less technical curriculum. Nationwide, there were some 60,000 in this program. We were selected on the basis of test scores and physical examinations. African-Americans were accepted on orders from President Roosevelt, and since race was not specified on tests and applications they were admitted on the same basis as white applicants. Only a few dozen blacks were commissioned because apparently only a few applied, but this was a major breakthrough since up to 1942 the Navy allowed blacks to serve only as steward's mates or Seabees (construction battalion).

Fifty years later I went to a reunion of my V-12 group. I was surprised, but I should not have been, that the lifetime contributions of my V-12 shipmates to the growth and health of the United States through technological and management skills was far beyond what is normally expected from college graduates. I am really convinced that for once the government had invested its money and got a return far better than it expected.

I suppose it took a war to make this possible. There were no exceptions to the rules. No one got into the V-12 program with political pull or influence. Family wealth was of no use. My colleagues who were later so successful came from Minnesota pig farms, mink breeding ranches, Dakota wheat farms, city low-cost housing areas, families of Seattle fishermen, of Texas college professors, and of rich Kansas City meat packers. No one cared who your father was; only test scores and performance counted.

I am sure that in World War II there were ways that money could buy safe havens the same way that Dan Quayle bought his way out of Viet Nam. But the Navy V-12 program was not for sale and appeared to be incorruptible.

It was not an attractive program for someone seeking an easy way out of the war. It was tough, demanding, and unforgiving. My classmates washed out for low grades, suspected cheating, changes in their physical condition (such as eyesight, hearing, or blood pressure), or for failure to live up to expected military behavior. There was no appeals process. The Dan Quayles and George W. Bushes of the day would never have asked their rich or influential fathers to buy their way into that tough a program even if it had been possible.

The Navy did not give me many choices. The question was "Which engineering," so I selected chemical. I had been considering careers in journalism or mathematics but these were not now options. In junior college I had discovered an interest in chemistry, so I made what seemed to be the best choice for me.

It turned out that I did very well. I managed to get a lot of A's in the critical courses and I even understood some of them. By the time I graduated I had earned good enough grades to be awarded a degree in chemical engineering with distinction and to be elected to Tau Beta Pi (an honorary engineering society) and Phi Lambda Upsilon (an honorary chemistry society).

This was pretty good for someone who might rather have been a sports reporter or a math professor. So I left Minnesota with a ticket for a career in chemical engineering and a train ticket to New York City to join the Navy's midshipmen's school and the chance to become a Naval officer.

I was assigned to the U. S. S. Prairie State. The Prairie State had been the battleship U. S. S. Illinois, flagship of Theodore Roosevelt's Great White Fleet and decommissioned in 1920. In 1924 it was renamed the USS Prairie State and became the nation's largest floating armory docked at Manhattan's 135th St. Pier on the Hudson River. It had been modified with a superstructure that made it look like Noah's Ark. It became a midshipmen's training ship early in World War II. I was in the 24th class, and by that time only engineering graduates were trained on the Prairie State. The rest of the midshipmen in our class were housed on the campus of Columbia University about fifteen blocks to the south. On the Prairie State we slept in bunks attached to poles and stacked one above the other down in the bowels of the ship. We must have had at least two hundred human roommates in addition to the thousands of cockroaches that swished among us in the dark of night.

A man named Alan Ford slept in the bunk next to mine. He was a Yale graduate and had recently broken Johnny Weismuller's swimming records and had his picture in *Life* magazine. I never got to know him well because there was no time for idle chitchat between bunkmates and besides the epidemic for this class happened to be mumps and he was a victim and disappeared for some time during our stay there. It is only worthy of mention to illustrate what you may find when you leave the hinterlands and go out into the big world. Alan Ford, by the way, seemed to be quite shy and not at all impressed with himself or his swimming.

I really liked being in New York. We were given weekend tickets to the major Broadway shows and plays, invitations to socialize with the women at Barnard College, events at the New York Yacht Club and other things that made me feel I was at last touching the glamour I had yearned for but never thought reachable from Mountain Iron. At one event I met Rube Goldberg, whom I had always admired and who may in fact be the most creative cartoonist who ever lived. I wanted to stay there forever and get to see and know all those things and people I thought were the most important in the world. I loved New York before I left Mountain Iron, I loved it when I got there, and I still love it 60 years later.

Midshipmen's school was something else, however. It was the only school I ever have gone to where I was not at or near the academic top. I was, in fact, always on the edge of being booted out. I never caught on to their system. The Navy apparently thought it was necessary for engineering officers to memorize the systems of pipes and valves and discharges and wiring in all kinds of ships, but I was either incapable of or unmotivated to memorize the details of these for destroyers, destroyer escorts, cruisers, battleships, etc., etc. I really suspect that when our class arrived someone decided that they only needed about 250 of our 400 to be officers so they devised some really stupid ways to screen out the surplus. Many of the brightest members of our class were bilged and I could easily have been included.

Nevertheless, I enjoyed New York, and made the cut (very near the bottom of my class) and became an ensign in the United States Navy.

I was then assigned to Naval Intelligence to study the Japanese language. This assignment was reserved for those judged to have really superior intelligence and aptitude. I made it because I had been elected to Tau Beta Pi in college. (It was obvious that the Navy was not the least bit concerned that I was a dummy as a midshipman, confirming my suspicions that no one seriously considered midshipmen's school performance much of a test of intelligence or aptitude but more of an exercise in survival.)

I was very happy with my assignment. The Japanese language course was a guarantee that I could avoid being shot at for another 14 months.

The atomic bomb and the end of the war with Japan came only a little over a month after I entered the 14-month program so none of my classmates faced battle.

I really enjoyed studying Japanese and was happy that the inertia of the military kept me there for 12 months even though the war had ended in the first six weeks. I learned the language so well I was dreaming in it (and did for five years after I left the Navy) and could still speak it passably fifty years later after a little review.

The language school was in Stillwater, Oklahoma, at what was then Oklahoma A & M College and is now Oklahoma State. Even though Stillwater was a racially segregated town and A & M a redneck college, I liked it there. Our lives were not much in conflict with the natives and they seemed to tolerate us. Our Japanese instructors who had been recruited from the relocation (concentration) camps of the west were less well tolerated. Stillwater, like all of Oklahoma at that time, was southern Jim Crow. It had two high schools—one white and one black. The black school was inferior to put it politely. The natives decreed that the children of our Japanese-American instructors should go to the black school. The Navy decreed otherwise. The Navy won. Not surprisingly, during the time we were there the Japanese-American students won most of the academic awards in the white high school.

I expect that the citizens of Stillwater were very happy to see us leave along with the non-white academic competition in their white schools.

Oklahoma was a dry state in 1945. The sale of 3.2 percent beer was allowed (except within 100 feet of where people danced), but nothing stronger. That meant that bootleggers were able to make out well. Any taxi driver was selling whatever anyone wanted, and there were other sources of booze. We Navy officers were not often customers, however, because our C. O., a captain and survivor of the Bataan death march or some other Pacific horror, felt that access to booze at less than black market prices was a privilege that those of us who were being trained to face the Japanese monsters should have if we wanted it. So he regularly sent the Navy station wagon to Joplin, Missouri, to fill orders for liquor. The good captain probably consumed more than any of the rest of us because he wasn't studying Japanese, and he was probably working on forgetting some of the real horrors of war that, it turned out, none of the rest of us would see, except maybe those who were recalled for the Korean War.

He was obviously a great and unusual C. O. His personality and his wartime experiences made him able to put the trivia of military procedures into their proper perspective, so he let us live as nearly like civilians as possible.

After almost a year of this life, the Navy seemed to remember we were there and we got orders to proceed to the base nearest our homes for discharge. In my case it was the Great Lakes Naval Training Station near Chicago. I bought a car, a 1937 Oldsmobile, and drove to Chicago with a couple of close friends whose homes were in Chicago. The car was in terrible shape and we barely made it. We managed to get separated from the Navy in June 1946, and I took off alone toward home in Minnesota. With some major stops for repairs I finally made it and returned to civilian life and my old job on the Great Northern Railway.

Less than three months later, in September 1946, I was back in the graduate school of chemical engineering at the University of Minnesota. I knew I had forgotten a lot of the engineering and also needed to pick up some courses that weren't offered during the war. The government picked up the cost under the GI Bill without question, even though they had paid for my undergraduate studies in V-12. The world is not fair and I am a prize example of one who benefited greatly from its unfairness.

I joined a number of my former undergraduate classmates in graduate school enjoying the benefits of that same unfairness, so I had a great year working on a master's degree, which I never did get. I ran out of patience and money (the GI

Bill was not *that* good!) and with several good job offers at the end of the summer of 1947 I knew it was time to go to work. The job offer I accepted was from Eastman Kodak Company, a decision I never regretted.

13

MY CAREER AT KODAK

I started work at Eastman Kodak's Kodak Park Works in Rochester, New York, in November 1947, and retired from the Kodak Processing Laboratories in Palo Alto and Hollywood, California in June 1986. That means that we will be covering 38 years and seven months in two chapters, so hang on!

I decided that I had had enough of graduate school and was ready to leave without an advanced degree to go to work as a chemical engineer. In 1947 the demand for engineers was great and the supply almost zero, so I had job offers from every company I smiled at. Among those I remember passing up for Eastman Kodak were duPont, Standard Oil, Goodrich Tire, and eve my Uncle Ben's Lowe Brothers Paint Co. All of the offers were competitive (Kodak's being somewhat on the low side), but the chance to get in on almost the beginning of the color photographic print business was an attraction I couldn't refuse. It was a good choice.

Rochester turned out to be a good choice for another reason, too. It was there in 1949 that I met and married Mary Jane Herby, a newspaper reporter for the Rochester Times-Union. We have now been married for 55 years, have five children and two grandchildren, and have been fortunate to have had good health and so far few bumps in the road we have traveled,

Not only was Kodak a good company to work for, the work was challenging, it fit my interests, and provided technical growth and a never-ending supply of problems. In a very short time I had pretty much a free hand to tackle problems with a minimum of supervision and a broad access to a wealth of resources in the company's research, development, manufacturing and testing divisions. The division I worked in first was Color Technology, headed by Ralph Evans. We did mainly development, coordination, and quality control and Evans nurtured innovation, spurned regimentation, and encouraged us to stick our noses into any corner of the company where we might find help with the problems we were working on. It was surprising that we didn't get into serious territorial disputes.

I had to learn a lot more about physics, optics, color, electronics and mathematics as well as photographic chemistry and the then rather new practice of statistical quality control. I was glad I had not wasted any more time in college, because I was learning more in a month on the job than I had in a year in college. The company never refused my requests to be sent to training courses, seminars, and conferences; in fact they often suggested some I should attend.

I was happy with my job, which remained relatively unchanged for about five years. The color print business survived because there were several of us making both individual and joint contributions in all of the problem areas—film manufacturing, paper manufacturing, film processing, color printing, and paper processing. My own contributions were in all of these areas, but the most significant were in improving the control of the electronic color printers; using internegatives to produce prints from slides; and some chemical engineering improvements in processing.

One function of the group I was part of was to run experiments and make measurements of the variability of each element and analyze those measurements. Our goal was to find where solving a problem would yield the greatest gains, and to help solve them, Contacts with film testing, film manufacturing, paper manufacturing, the film process, the paper process, the printing operation, and research and development gave me a chance to learn every technical facet of the business and to interact with people in all of the divisions involved,

I specialized in designing and planning experiments and analyzing results. The actual work of carrying out the experiments was usually done by technicians, When the design or analysis got too complex, we had statisticians available to help with calculations and make sure that we separated random results from significant differences.

My job as an engineer was challenging, interesting, and greatly satisfying. It required very little of what I had studied in college. I had to keep studying and learning new things constantly.

Eventually the processing of color films and making color prints became successful enough so that the company felt justified in establishing color processing as a separate division instead of a minor branch of the film manufacturing division, I became a quality control supervisor in the new organization. Management soon decided we were ready to make color prints out of Rochester and Palo Alto, California, was selected to be our first away-from-home site. I helped lay out the Palo Alto laboratory (which was really a manufacturing plant) and later accepted an offer to move to Palo Alto to be the leader of the technical group serving the color print manufacturing departments there. We were so successful the U. S.

Government decided we were in restraint of trade and forced the company to teach competitors how to process color films and compete with us.

That consent decree (of 1955) with the government required that by 1958 we had to give away half of our business to competitors. Half of our employees in all Kodak U. S. labs including Palo Alto either left the company or transferred to other divisions. I chose to stay with the processing organization even though the future looked bleak.

The business survived and by the end of 1959 I was offered a promotion to return to Rochester as a staff supervisor on the headquarters staff of the processing organization. So we moved back, by this time with four children, the oldest being 8 years old.

My responsibilities in Rochester included managing a technical group, one of whose many duties included measuring the quality of color print operations throughout the world. This was very interesting and did get me to Europe and New Zealand and Australia once and very often to the U. S. labs in Chicago and Palo Alto.

After eight years of this, I accepted the job as assistant manager of the Palo Alto lab. Five years later I became manager and held that job for the last fourteen years of my career. During the last few months of that career I was also the manager of the Hollywood lab since the manager there had retired and my boss thought (at my suggestion) that I could handle managing both labs, since Hollywood was a very small operation.

I was a pretty good engineer and supervisor of engineers; that's why I was selected to be a manager. My colleagues in other laboratories had also been successful engineers. It turned out that I was probably even better as a manager than I had been an engineer. Unfortunately many of my colleagues were not, so some of our labs were not well managed. Palo Alto became the star performer and during my years as manager we were the most profitable, had the best quality and service, and were also leaders in most ways including productivity, controlling pollution, recycling, safety and equal opportunity. I believe that Palo Alto was the best Kodak processing laboratory in the world and, by the time I retired, the biggest. Hollywood may not have been the worst, but it was a challenge. Unfortunately or fortunately, I chose to retire with a golden handshake before I was able to have any influence on the Hollywood lab.

I am not claiming any personal responsibility for the excellence of the Palo Alto lab. The main reason was that it was located in an excellent labor market from which we could assemble a topnotch work force. A secondary reason was that the lab had been well designed and equipped. All I had to do as manager was to see to it that our people had the tools and staff and budget to do their jobs and to resist the temptation to over manage.

The Hollywood lab had a poor labor market to draw from and the plant had been cobbled together from old buildings which had been warehouses and a brassiere factory, There was no way it could have been efficient as a processing lab.

My life at Kodak had been everything I expected of it and more, and it was probably merciful that I didn't end it by failing to solve the problems of the Hollywood lab.

Management at Kodak

When I arrived in 1947 the CEO (then called the company president) was a fairly recently acquired lawyer who was one of Rochester's celebrated drunks. It was not clear who ran the company. Not all of the vice presidents were also alcoholics, although I have heard from a reliable inside source that at least a few were. As I remember things and look at them now, it was amazing that Kodak was rated by *Forbes* or *Fortune* magazine in the 1950s as one of the five best-managed U. S. companies. Since I was getting adequate pay and wonderful benefits I agreed heartily with this evaluation. Apparently one of the bases at that time for judging management was how well the company was using and treating its employees. By the 1990s this was no longer considered an important factor in evaluating the management of a company; only the treatment of shareholders seemed to count.

Kodak and similar companies depending on technology hired graduates with technical skills. (*Time* reported that Kodak hired a higher percentage of chemical engineering graduates in the top 10% of their classes than any other company in the U. S. during the 1930s through the 1960s). This provided their pool of management candidates, especially at Kodak where its practice was to promote from within the company. Since there is no better formula for selecting successful managers, the best engineers were selected for promotion. Since the best engineers seemed to succeed as managers only about half of the time, Kodak covered this by doubling its middle management, having both a superintendent and an assistant superintendent hoping that at least one could run things. I heard about assistants who got more pay than their superintendents because someone recognized who was really running things. Kodak appeared to have a practice of never demoting or firing anyone who had been selected to be a superintendent, assistant superintendent, manager or assistant manager no matter how incompetent he was. I think that Kodak paid its managers less than companies who fired or demoted those who didn't succeed, but the pay was adequate and the Kodak system was humane and face-saving.

This was good management? I suppose if the company made money and paid good dividends it was. I will not attempt to describe the Kodak pricing system and profit structure since it was a tightly kept secret from those at my level in the company, but it worked in those days.

In those days, too, Kodak was dedicated to humane treatment of all employees, not just inferior managers. The company considered hiring a lifetime commitment. One result was that some 5 to 10% of the hourly work force was not productive enough to earn their salaries. This never bothered me much until I became a manager and had to take responsibility for the profitability of my division. It seemed unfair for the company to ask managers for better profits on the one hand and on the other to refuse to permit managers to weed out unproductive employees. Being a benevolent employer first and profitable second was a practice that Kodak, out of necessity, was in the process of changing by the time I retired.

Technology

My working career spanned about half a century of remarkable technological changes everywhere. Making color prints from color negatives may be one of the less important. When I began, color negative film (Kodacolor) was only available as a six-exposure roll film for large format box and folding cameras. (Kodachrome film was the only color film for 35 mm cameras.) After processing, the rolls of Kodacolor film were cut into individual negatives. An operator wearing white cotton gloves put each negative individually into a densitometer which made red, green and blue light transmission measurements. Based on these readings, the operator punched a code of holes in the border of the negative. The printer had a file of color filters which could be inserted between the light source and the negative, and the printer operator pulled what looked like organ stops to select the color filters indicated by these holes. The printer modulated the light further with a neutral filter of graduated density, and when everything was balanced properly the operator opened a shutter and made the exposure of the negative on color paper. After the paper was processed and the prints inspected, those that were unacceptable were sent back to the printer for another try with instructions from an inspector on how to improve the printing conditions. Printer operators and inspectors needed to be highly skilled.

The yield of acceptable quality on first printing was about 30-40%, and on second printing about 80%. All of this took a lot of time and labor, and it sometimes took a couple of weeks and many printings to pass an order. The cost to customers for these prints was high (37 cents each, when $10 a day was considered very good pay). Nevertheless, this operation was a major loser for Kodak.

I arrived about the same time as the first of a new generation of printers which were able to read the negatives and balance the exposures semi-automatically. This was a big step toward improving quality as well as productivity. My first assignment was to improve the quality yield of those new printers by finding ways to improve how they were controlled and used.

By 1951 company management was looking at color print and processing as their next great profit center. Except for the government anti-trust action in 1955, it would have been. (I think the government was right, by the way, and customers have been better off as a result of opening competition in color print manufacture.)

As the years went on everything had been improved—film, paper, processes and printers—and by the time I retired we had very smart printers using computer technology and yielding high quality with low waste. Better film, cameras, and paper also helped. When I first went to work I felt that we were lucky to produce really good quality 5% of the time. By the time I retired, we were approaching 95% good quality on first printing, only some of which had resulted from improved cameras and smarter customers. So I felt I had participated in the life of a product almost from its birth to its highly successful maturity.

Random observations on a changing world

When I first went to work performance appraisals judged workers mostly on attributes such as shoeshines, neckties, haircuts, and maybe tardiness and attendance. This gradually evolved into judging productivity, creativeness and things more closely related to the value of an employee's contributions to the company's business. While I was never convinced that performance appraisals were very useful, at least the later ones were asking the right questions, and maybe some day will elicit useful answers.

Eastman Kodak Company was pretty much like most other Fortune 500 companies when I joined them. Some attitudes and practices were like the Great Northern Railway where I had worked, and appeared to be like those of other companies where I had had job interviews.

Top management was 100% WASP. Italians and Jews were significant percentages of the Rochester population, but were rarely included in Kodak management in 1947. I suspected that there was an unwritten quota system in hiring these minorities, and it appeared that very few blacks were hired and then only as janitors. You could find most of the members of the board of directors and company vice-presidents on the lists of elders of the large downtown Presbyterian and Episcopalian churches. I don't think any were Catholics.

The processing lab managers held an annual conference/retreat to share problems and to get acquainted. This was a good idea, since they were scattered and needed to be reminded that they were not as alone and isolated as it sometimes appeared. One of the early favorite meeting places was a stuffy resort at Skytop, Pennsylvania, in the Poconos. The New York City laboratory manager was named Everett Moses. When the managers were registered for the meeting, the Skytop resort made a discreet call to Kodak's Rochester management to inquire whether Mr. Moses was Jewish (he was not), implying that if he were the group would not be welcome. Rather than being offended by the question, it was my impression that the general manager who was arranging the event felt reassured that his managers were being shielded from undesirables.

Things changed a great deal during my working career. Several vice-presidents have had Italian names. At least one CEO in the 70s was a Roman Catholic. A later CEO was a Mormon. Women appear at all levels of management. Jews and African-Americans are no longer excluded, although they are not common in Kodak top management. And the processing lab managers who met at Skytop at the time I was one of them included the Korean-American manager of our Honolulu lab.

Our memories may make us think we would like to be living in the good old days, but even though we have times of crooked corporate management and stupid politicians and pockets of tragedies in all parts of the world, things seem to be improving in the long run. Unfortunately we find that our short lives leave us frustrated by our barely measurable contributions.

14

INTO EACH REIGN SOME LIFE MUST FALL

After you read Chapter XIII about my nearly forty years at Kodak, you probably concluded that it must have been a nice but dull career. Technical successes can be a little exciting, of course, for those who launched spacecraft and made landings on the moon.

For me there were hundreds of human events that added interest and challenges to the satisfying but humdrum technical successes.

I don't mean the traditional challenges of management. A successful manager merely has to pick the best available candidate for a job to be done and to see to it that subordinates do likewise. This only requires an ability to judge talent and the guts to make decisions that will make enemies of friends who expected the appointment. Managers without guts made promotions strictly on seniority which were easy to explain, but the teams they assembled were seldom winners. I became a successful manager, but I lost more than a few friends.

Much went on in my realm that I never knew about and didn't want to. With as many as 500 employees, most of whom worked at night, a manager is better off not knowing about adulterous affairs in the parking lot on the midnight shift lunch break, for example, or who left an empty whiskey bottle in the basement rat proofing. It was more productive for the manager to focus on quality, service and cost than on morality. I was usually brought in for midnight bomb threats and major catastrophes, but I tried to let most problems be solved at the lowest possible level in the organization.

Fruit Flies

Not all memorable things happened while I was a manager, however. In my early days I had a boss whose goal was to be the president of the company. Being bright and articulate, he had a good chance to make it. He worked hard to be as

visible as possible and to arrange presentations to people in higher management—the higher the better. These presentations included graphs and charts
which had to be perfect and our staff included some talented artists to keep them
looking good. I was often his chart carrier and shared in his presentations, which
gave me good visibility, too.

Our group was made up mostly of young veterans of the recent war who liked
to spice things up a bit with various attempts at low-grade humor and other fun
and games. One of the members of the group was an attractive woman, Marge,
who had gone to high school with a couple of our engineers. They liked to bait or
needle her in ways that these days would probably be considered harassment, but
in those days was part of the normal daily give and take. One day one of the guys,
Dick, was needling Marge while she was eating a banana in the office during her
afternoon break. About the time I picked up a two-foot by three-foot chart and
stood up on my way to the boss's office to join him for our weekly meeting with
a division superintendent, Marge had reached the limit of her patience and threw
the remains of her banana at Dick. He ducked and the banana splattered all over
my chart. We may have been a little late for that meeting, and I wonder if the
boss wondered why our chart smelled like a fruit stand. (The ambitious boss, by
the way, didn't quite make it to the top, but he did get close.)

Wrong Way Ralph

Ralph was an artist/photographer assigned to our group in Rochester. He was
quite talented in drawing and lettering and we depended on him to make us look
good when we took our messages to other divisions. I worked with Ralph in my
first years in Rochester and he was a member of the group I supervised when I
returned from Palo Alto in 1959. Ralph had a talent for being in the wrong place
at the wrong time. When he went out in the field to take pictures, he took models
with him. The models were usually young women who could be spared that day
from their jobs—not professional models, and not necessarily photogenic. He
would normally be accompanied by another man or woman so there would be a
witness to insure the propriety of their activities. But one time on a rush job he
could find only one woman available and no witnesses. She seemed sufficiently
proper and safe for the short assignment. When she turned up pregnant shortly
thereafter she accused Ralph. I felt sure that Ralph was innocent—he and I had a
relationship of mutual trust I counted on—and she did eventually admit that he
had not even hinted at doing anything but take her picture.

Another somewhat windy day Ralph was out taking pictures of a model holding a brightly colored beach ball (a test of the film's color reproduction qualities,

of course) when the ball got away from the model and blew into a shallow pond in the park where they were working. Ralph took off his shoes to retrieve the ball and stepped on a broken bottle. This required some stitching and several days off.

There was a large, refrigerated storage room for color paper and film in our building. One day Ralph went down to get some paper out of storage. Much later, I got a panic call from Ralph that he was locked in cold storage. I sent someone down to help him out and it turned out that he wasn't locked in. He just was trying to pull the door open when it only needed to be pushed. And it was far from the first time he had been in the cold room.

Our building also had a built-in vacuum system, which janitors used when they cleaned the floors. Ralph's cameras got a lot of use and accumulated dust from the miles of film and backing paper that went through them so he got the bright idea that the vacuum system would be an easy way to clean his equipment. When the vacuum sucked the lens right out of one of his cameras, Ralph spent some time sifting through the dust bins in the sub-basement until he found it.

Danny Boy

In Palo Alto we had a man named Danny, who had started out in Rochester the same year I had. Even though he started and ended his career on the bottom rung of the ladder, he somehow managed to get transferred to Palo Alto in 1955. He was homosexual, and his partner was also a color print employee, so maybe someone thought that two for the price of one was a good bargain. (Or, from the sending side, good riddance. Gays, open or suspected then as now made many people uncomfortable.) The partner left the company in a few years but Danny stayed on until he reached retirement age.

Danny was also an alcoholic, but our Palo Alto medical department was able to steer him into a life of sobriety. His job for most of his career was to handle orders whose subject matter was such that we wanted to shield other operators from it. This included pornography, medical pictures, and police crime pictures. I guess someone thought this was a good assignment for a homosexual, although I never could see the connection. Danny apparently had the stomach for it since I don't remember he ever complained.

Over his career, Danny used bad judgment often enough so that he ended up in the front office (mine) with some regularity. One time he went into a dark printing room to help the female operator load an enlarger with a new roll of paper. Danny thought it would be fun to stick a banana in his pants as an imitation erection and goose the operator with it. The operator didn't think so and filed a complaint.

Another time a highly qualified and intelligent enlargement inspector with a Japanese name was inspecting an order that Danny had some interest in, and for some reason he called her a dumb Chink. I don't remember whether her complaint was that he called her dumb, or that he implied she was Chinese.

The strangest complaint I remember about Danny came from a male employee who had suddenly been stricken with some paranoia about Danny's coming on to him. This man was married, but before his marriage eighteen or twenty years earlier Danny had apparently made a real or imagined pass at him. He was now imagining that Danny was stalking him and he wanted me to fire Danny or otherwise protect him. I was convinced when we confronted Danny that he hadn't spoken to nor even thought about this man for years.

The last time I saw Danny in his post-retirement, he was showing pictures of his new home in the Sacramento area. It was a nice place with a swimming pool, and not surprisingly the swimming pool appeared to be well furnished with young male studs and Danny looked and acted as if he had gone to heaven without dying.

Only Murder

Rudy was a black man about 30 years old who worked on our day shift janitorial staff. He commonly wore a broad-brimmed black hat, which I was told was the uniform for pimps in the black community. One morning I got a call from a woman informing us that Rudy would not be in to work today because he had some trouble with the PO-lice. It turned out that Rudy had killed another black man, apparently another pimp, in a jurisdictional dispute. It further turned out that unknown to us, Rudy had worked at Stanford Hospital some years before and had killed a medical resident student in a parking lot after a Christmas party. He was convicted of that and served a prison sentence. We followed his trial for the second killing and were not happy that he got a lighter sentence than we would have expected because the jury was not allowed to know that he had a record as a convicted killer. I was always afraid that Rudy would show up some day looking for his job back and might be inclined to kill one of us (me?) if he didn't get it.

(S)he was a problem

A young black man working in Palo Alto as a print inspector announced that he was planning to have a sex change operation. His name change and some noticeable effects of hormonal treatments provided good gossip but was no big deal until (s)he thought it was time to begin using the women's rather than the men's locker room and toilet. The women didn't much go for this idea and there was a threat of rebellion. Luckily there were a couple of unisex toilets in the medical department, so our nurse solved the problem by letting him/her use that. The last I heard (s)he was having second thoughts about the genital operation and (s)he quit Kodak and moved to Las Vegas.

Watch those nuts!

While I was still the assistant manager in Palo Alto we built a major addition to the building. Business was by that time growing again, mainly because we seemed to be the favorite laboratory for the soldiers in Viet Nam, so we needed more space. The addition was a full bay all along the back wall of the building which amounted to something like 10,000 square feet. For stability in an earthquake the steel I-beams of the new addition were bolted with very large bolts to the I-beams of the original building. At least we thought so, until a couple of years later one of our engineers took a good look and discovered that the subcontractor hadn't bothered to drill the holes necessary for the bolting. He had merely glued the heads to one I-beam and the nuts to the other. (We did get the contractor to fix it.)

Roofscaping

When our Palo Alto building was built in the Stanford Industrial Park there were many unusual aesthetic requirements laid down by both Stanford, which owned the land, and the City of Palo Alto, in whose domain it was. One of the requirements was that the tar and gravel roof be finished with an artistic pattern of colored gravel, I suppose so that it would be a pleasing sight to passing airplanes. Nobody else was expected to see it. Twenty years or so later, a high rise office building was built next door. By that time I was the manager, so when the president of Kodak got a letter from a lawyer tenant in the high rise complaining about our ugly roof, it was passed on to me along with a copy of Kodak's rejection of the complaint.

Nothing but the truth

We were Kodak, so any business with the company in the vicinity of Palo Alto came to us. We were surprised one day to be served with papers announcing that Kodak was being sued for false advertising. A San Jose State student had read the label on some Kodak black and white developer chemicals labeled poison, assumed they were deadly and tried to commit suicide by ingesting them. He was suing Kodak because he was still alive. We referred this one to regional headquarters.

A Toothless Gift Horse

The Kodak Sales Division hired the graduate of a black college who had played football briefly for the New England Patriots. They decided he was not doing the job they wanted in Chicago, but instead of facing the problem as they should have, they tidied up his performance appraisal and got our Chicago lab manager to talk us into accepting him in Palo Alto. Under affirmative action, we were short of qualified minorities in higher-level jobs, so we were happy to have him, and assumed from what we were told (by other Kodak people) that he was qualified. He was a nice enough person and he and I got to be pretty good friends as we often rode the bus together to and from work. Unfortunately, he had no knowledge of nor interest in learning about photography, he was unable to write a decent letter, and he was just not suited to do anything we had to offer. He told me he wanted my job (the manager), because I suppose he figured I just sat there all day and watched other people do the work and he knew the equal opportunity people would be delighted to see a black face in the front office. I counseled him about learning the business and sent him to school to learn how to write letters, but nothing took. Eventually I gave up and somehow managed to separate him from the company with no noticeable hard feelings and to my surprise no subsequent legal action. My technique, by the way, was to take him to a farewell lunch with as many of our top management people in the Palo Alto lab as I could assemble and try to make him feel that we were saying goodbye to a valued friend. In my case that was true—he had become a good friend but was a useless employee. He apparently found a job that fit his talents at the neighboring Hewlett-Packard plant.

No Nonsense with Clarence

Clarence Braden, an elderly black man, was on duty one Friday night as the gate guard whose job was to admit employees with passes into the plant to work and keep out those who didn't have passes. (The gate guard job was later eliminated and replaced by an electronic system.) Clarence worked for Walt Horwege who was the general shop foreman. Walt showed up on Saturday morning as he usually did to make sure everything was in order for the weekend shutdown. He met Clarence about the time that Clarence was completing his shift, and asked how things were going. Clarence casually mentioned that he had received a call early in his shift from someone who said he was going to set off a bomb in the plant shortly after midnight. Walt, much alarmed, said, "Why didn't you call me? Did you call someone else?" Clarence said calmly, "No, I just told him, 'You show up here with a bomb and I'll shoot you!'"

Walt searched the entire lab and found neither a bomb nor a body, and then he called me to report that Clarence had saved us from a midnight evacuation by not exactly following the standard prescribed procedure.

Detective Work

I didn't have enough to do when I was the assistant manager, so I took on a project of finding lost customers. We had a customer service department and they did a great job, but there were some very tough problems that we couldn't really afford to pay them to spend time on. I spent some of my spare time with whatever tools I needed to look for clues in the pictures which might lead us to a customer. I was especially interested in what appeared to be once-in-a-lifetime events. One order I remember was someone's 100th birthday party. It was obviously a picnic somewhere in an eastern state, possibly Maryland. With a microscope I was able to read a license plate and its color told me what states it could have been from. I contacted those states and with the description of the car was able to find someone who was at the picnic who led me to the owner of the order. (The customer was in Florida and had sent us a mailer without putting his return address on it.) I think I was cited for performance above and beyond the call of duty in a Florida weekly newspaper.

Ears, for Instants

In the early days of the Pocket Instamatic cameras a very irate woman customer of our Palo Alto lab who insisted that we had given her the wrong pictures accosted us. And not just one, but 400—20 rolls of 20 exposures each. Our system of handling orders was very good, and while on rare occasions we might have misdelivered one picture or even one roll of film, 20 wrong rolls would have been almost impossible, so we did some very serious investigating. The woman had purchased a new camera and had never tried it before she took her trip to Africa where she had taken the pictures she expected us to deliver.

We studied the pictures, all of which had a large, pinkish, out-of-focus blob over most of each frame, but with some distant in-focus landscape in the background. Some of them were identifiable, and on review the customer acknowledged that they seemed to include some of the places she had visited. Finally we spotted some with a metallic object sufficiently in focus to identify. When we asked the customer about it, she said, "Why, that looks like my earring!" That solved the problem: she had looked through the wrong end of the viewfinder, pointed the camera backwards and taken 400 pictures of her ear.

Dirty Pictures

A small but significant percentage of the pictures we processed depicted sex in forms ranging from raunchy to artistic, mostly the former. It is interesting to track the attitude toward this over the years I worked in the business.

At first, all of our deliveries were made by mail, so the Post Office Department visited our laboratories and made a lot of the decisions and trained our employees to make decisions about what was mailable and what violated postal regulations. Many of these government inspectors were very prudish and might forbid us to ship a portrait of a woman whose lips were—in their opinion—pursed suggestively. Except for having to communicate with disappointed customers, life was easy for Kodak in those days. We put the blame on the Post Office Department.

When we began making direct deliveries to dealers, this became more of a Kodak decision, although for a few years the postal standards were still dictating policy. Kodak was a conservative company run by men who felt that it was in the best interest of the country to keep the customers pure, so the policy of withholding questionable pictures was kept in force. It was, in fact, also thought that the women who mounted or inspected pictures should be protected from sex, so each lab had a special group of one or two men who handled all of the shady pictures.

Eventually the newsstands were openly selling magazines with pictures far more explicit and pornographic than what we were withholding from our customers. It was obvious to our more enlightened managers that if we shipped everything we could reduce the load on our service department, reduce the cost of handling special orders, and have fewer unhappy customers. That worked for many years until one of our more prudish lab managers decided to hold back some work for Penthouse magazine and some lawsuits followed. Company management, still conservatively puritanical, decided to defend the lawsuit and made those of us who were shipping almost everything once again assume the role of censors in order to be consistent among the Kodak labs.

Over the years I looked at many pictures. I never saw any evidence that there were more than two sexes, so that the pictures revealed very little that was new anatomically. The sex acts may have varied somewhat in position and were flavored by such things as sadism, bestiality and homosexuality, but in all cases seemed to be leading to the usual and invariable climax. Pictures of these visually unattractive events were less offensive to me than pictures of corpses. They all recorded things that I thought were better not recorded. I believed, however, that our customers were recording things that they considered important and that we should not impose my or other Kodak employees' moral or artistic judgments on the results. And our judgments would in no way change our customers' moral standards. From a practical and business point of view not censoring those pictures made the lives of our service department employees much simpler and our business more profitable.

◆   ◆   ◆

So, you see from this small sample, there was more to life in the Kodak processing industrial world than mix tanks and test tubes and big, noisy machines. I found my life there never dull.

15

RETIREMENT

I had always visualized that I would retire with a special party just for me, with all of the 500 lab employees invited, and with a band and dancing making it a really big occasion. This had been the norm for those who had gone before when retirements were relatively rare. When I retired, I was the only one, but it was only a month after some 60 or 70 others had retired and I stayed only long enough to get my replacement established. My retirement, then, was an afterthought, and all I got was a luncheon in the company cafeteria in Palo Alto with no acknowledgement at all from the company management in Rochester. I felt that 39 years of outstanding service might have deserved better and I was a bit bitter for a while, until my retirement checks started arriving.

I had no great blueprint to guide my retirement. It came somewhat suddenly and I fumbled into it. My first impulse was to relandscape our yard, which I spent a lot of the first year doing. Probably one of the best things I did was to quit smoking. I had smoked a pipe for most of my Kodak career, and when I retired I decided not to buy any more tobacco—so when my tobacco ran out I never smoked again. My stinking pipes went into the garbage and my mouth, nose, throat and lungs were relieved of the poisonous onslaught.

I had been diddling around the house and yard for almost a year when I got a call inviting me to help save the San Jose Museum of Art. I hardly knew where the museum was and nothing about their problems. I went to lunch at the invitation of a woman named Charlotte Wendel and was reintroduced to Janet Gray Hayes, a former mayor of San Jose whom I had met once or twice previously, and Albert Dixon, a former museum director. Charlotte was an early 1970s founder of the San Jose Museum of Art and was attempting to resurrect it from the mistakes of its current board of directors by leading a revolt of dissident members. The board was recalled, Janet Gray was recruited as a neutral replacement board chairman, I accepted her invitation to serve as the business manager, and Albert volunteered to be the Executive Director.

I was so overwhelmed by the challenge of the problems that I was unable to resist it even though I really had little interest in whether the museum survived. I accepted the job as unpaid business manager with the title Acting Deputy Director and I think it is close to the truth that the museum, which is today a major success, owes its survival to the efforts of Janet Gray, Albert and me. It is also true that hardly anyone else in San Jose knew this except maybe Charlotte Wendel who has since died. After I had been there two years, we, with much help from the city of San Jose, had built a major new addition to the 1892 post office building, expanded the paid staff from three to about thirty, increased the budget by about three times and balanced it, hired a world class director, and established the museum in its rightful place as a major factor in the ninth largest city in the United States. Even though our world-class director blew it by shacking up with the curator and getting politely run out of town, the museum has continued to become even more successful. I left when I realized that the museum was running well and didn't need me, and was a bit bitter that almost no one in San Jose knew or appreciated what I thought I had done for them. (Sort of like my exit from Kodak.)

My close connection with the San Jose Museum of Art lasted about two years, and at the end of the first year doctors discovered that I had squamous cell cancer (a skin cancer) in one of my ears. The discovery was later than it should have been, so the operation was fairly extensive, but apparently fully successful. It did not slow me down much.

I had done quite a bit of volunteer work for the United Way of Santa Clara County during my working career and this continued during my retirement. I now had time to serve on agency review committees to insure that the United Way was justified in continuing to support its member agencies. The committee I served on put one of the agencies on probation for questionable management, and this led to my serving on a committee which monitored and advised several agencies on probation. Monitoring is too mild a word—we browbeat them, usually into successful recovery.

This experience, combined with my experience at the art museum, made me quite expert at spotting, analyzing, and helping non-profits with problems. There are a lot of them. Non-profit agencies all do good things, usually very well, but often neither the staff nor the volunteers have any interest in managing and naively assume that if they continue to perform good works they will automatically survive. Unfortunately this is not true and the simple advice we usually gave was to improve management. If they could man the board of directors with some people interested in paying attention to such dull things as income, expenditures, fund raising, and long range planning, and if they could hire a good and honest executive director they could probably survive. Agencies that listened and followed that advice generally succeeded and those that didn't generally failed. We managed to save most of the borderline agencies, but I must admit we lost a few.

During my years at the Kodak lab in Palo Alto, customers often brought us old cameras which were no longer useful to them but which they couldn't bring themselves to throw away. We accumulated a couple hundred of these and other photographic antiques which we displayed or stored. A few years after I retired, Kodak had sold the lab and the new owners decided to move it out of Palo Alto. Since the new owners had no interest in moving the collection, I managed to acquire control of it.

I had no interest in keeping the collection for myself, and it would have been unethical for me to do so, so I went on a search for a museum that would accept the collection.

After some searching I discovered the Museum of American Heritage in Palo Alto. It was a new museum (opened in about 1990) dedicated to collecting and storing mechanical and electrical artifacts that predated solid state electronics. They were happy to accept the collection, and I did some volunteer work with the museum along with cataloging the camera collection I was contributing. It was obvious to me from my United Way and San Jose Museum experience that this museum fell into the category of non-profits highly likely to fail, so with some reluctance I joined their board of directors and eventually also took over the job of volunteer executive director, in hopes that I could turn things around. It was essentially an all-volunteer operation with an outstanding exhibition and education program, but with no concept of how to manage it for long-term survival, so I signed on to help. I eventually served three years as chairman of the board. During those years I helped recruit people with money who knew other people with money and we raised about $750,000 to occupy a new location and hire professional management. I think it has moved from having a 99% chance of failure to having a 99% chance of success. The secret was to get support from wealthy people with wealthy friends who were interested in the mission of the museum. That is not as easy as it reads, but with digging it proved to be possible. In the beginning we had some help from the David and Lucile Packard Foundation, too, and some previous connections I had had with David Packard and the executive director of the Foundation probably helped at least a little.

I have found non-profit organizations to be fun to work with because the people are generally outgoing and friendly, probably because they are doing what they do because they like it and because there is no chance for personal financial gain. Even paid staffers don't expect big salaries and are not working only for the money. And the people tend to be stimulating, so these contacts are important in keeping a retiree (me, among others) in touch with the world and avoiding the danger of an early-aging syndrome that comes with isolation.

The other greatest satisfaction of my retirement has been travel. Even though we aren't rich, we have had enough disposable income to allow us also to do such frivolous things as going to Hawaii to see a total eclipse of the sun, and to Calgary for the 1988 winter Olympics, and to Cincinnati in 1987 and Vancouver in 2001 for the world figure skating championships. We went to Tahoe several winters to try to ski, even though I never owned downhill skis until I was over 65 years old. Once we even tried skiing on icy slopes in Killington, Vermont—which was totally impossible for my skill level. I did have fun skiing for a few years at Tahoe on the beginner slopes until one of my knees failed to respond. We balance our crazy whims against the money, time, and stamina we can muster and hope that all three last a long time. I suppose if we get too old for other things we might consider golf and bridge.

The nice thing about retirement is that after working for forty or fifty years you are suddenly free to spend your time as you like within whatever limits your money and mobility dictate. I feel especially lucky to have had the income, the good health, and a wife who is at least as adventurous and as impractical as I so that I feel I am getting everything I can out of these golden (or, as one of my friends puts it, bonus) years. The first eighteen have been great, and we will appreciate whatever more we are privileged to enjoy.

Perhaps our most important discovery was Italy. One year we rented a car in Geneva and traveled across Switzerland to Italy and crisscrossed Italy until we got to Rome. We found on that trip that wherever we stopped in Italy there was a rich treasure of art and history that we could barely sample. From then on, we returned to Italy as often as we could arrange it (without cutting off the rest of the world, that is) and we studied the Italian language to help increase our enjoyment of the Italian culture. We spent two months in an American junior college class in Florence studying art and history (taught in English). We spent a month in Perugia studying the Italian language at the University of Perugia for foreigners and then staying on for another month to travel over much of the country. And we have been back a couple times more to visit other cities and revisit Florence. We have, in fact, spent enough time in Florence so that we feel completely at home there. We also feel at home in Perugia where we had a really crummy apartment for two months. We are far from fluent in the language, but we are not uncomfortable in it, and luckily the Italians are very forgiving.

I like to list countries we have visited: England, Scotland, Belgium, Germany, Norway, Sweden, Finland, Russia (when it was the Soviet Union), Hungary, Czechoslovakia—and later the Czech Republic and Slovakia—Austria, Italy, Greece, Malta, Turkey, France, Spain, Portugal, Egypt, Singapore, China, Japan, Thailand, Hong Kong, Romania, Bulgaria, Yugoslavia (now Slovenia, Croatia, Serbia too), Denmark, The Netherlands, Luxembourg, Liechtenstein, Andorra, Mexico, Canada, San Marino, The Vatican, Australia, New Zealand, India. I may have missed listing some, but we feel lucky to have been around and we hope we are not through yet.

This is a chapter that hasn't yet ended. But no matter how it ends—suddenly or slowly, peacefully or painfully—be assured it is a happy chapter. Retirement has given us the opportunity to serve the community and to see the world. For us, this has been just what we wanted. God (or whatever else we don't believe in) willing, we will continue until we are taken away.

[On that last note I have to add that if I die tomorrow please don't mourn. Celebrate! My life could hardly have been better. I can only wish the same for everyone.]

16

OBSERVATIONS

On Religion

The pursuit of happiness belongs to us, but we must climb around or over the church to get it.—Heywood Broun.

Perhaps the problem with the legacy of Abraham is that all three monotheistic faiths have yet to come to terms with the historical development of their own traditions. If we could see all sacred scriptures as a common record of the universal human search for meaning and not as the revealed word of God, we would recognize that for millenniums we have been reading meaning into these texts instead of getting understanding out of them.—Letter in *Time* from Rabbi Richard Hirsh of Wyncote, Pa.:

God bless those who seek the truth; and God save us from those who think they have found it.—A Georgian monk.

Religion was and still is an important and dynamic part of my mental processes, although I have abandoned hope of finding a viable organized religion that suits me.

I was raised in a climate where Protestant Christianity was an accepted truth and where weekly church attendance was habitual. This did not necessarily include fundamentalist beliefs, and I remember many direct and indirect references by my parents expressing skepticism about the virgin birth, the resurrection, the creation myth, and minor Bible stories such as those about Noah or Jonah.

This skepticism, however, did not reduce the importance of our attending church and Sunday school, nor did it reduce my father's participation in church politics nor my mother's in the Sunday school and the Ladies' Aid Society. The church was their anchor and a major part of their social affiliation with the community, and they never seemed to worry about the theology. I interpreted what they said and did to mean that they believed that the church was important to the morality of the world, not necessarily because of the myths that the church wanted them to believe. They strongly supported the church.

I was an inquisitive child and tended to question the Bible and Christianity. By the time I was sixteen or so, my skepticism had progressed to a degree of agnosticism bordering on atheism.

I did not then, however, consider leaving the church. (For the record it was a Presbyterian church.) I had the habit of attendance, some emotional satisfaction from the rituals, the rewards of belonging and the feeling that I was a partner in a force for good over evil.

With all of this I continued in the Presbyterian Church through my wedding and through the baptisms of four of our five children. I not only attended faithfully along with all of my family, but I also served as an usher and as a fundraiser.

I was close to 40 years old with four children when I was approached by the elders of the church who said they thought I should become an officer—a deacon or trustee, or whatever the title was. So I asked what that entailed. (Such an invitation from the Brick Presbyterian Church of Rochester, New York, was not to be slighted since the officers of the church included a significant number of the top Eastman Kodak Company executives.) They said all you have to do is reaffirm your faith by standing before the congregation and saying that you believe in the Apostle's Creed: I believe in God the Father Almighty, maker of Heaven and Earth and in his son Jesus Christ, born of the Virgin Mary, suffered under Pontius Pilate, was crucified—etc.

I thought about this and had to admit to myself that I really did not believe in the divinity of Jesus, a basic requirement of Christianity, and that I could not in good conscience accept an office in the church. I considered whether continuing our membership would be best for the children. I never considered the possible Kodak benefits worth lying about. (My wife, Mary Jane, was neutral, since her skepticism was fully as deep as mine.) My older children would soon be making decisions about joining the church and I would be facing their questions about my beliefs. How could I tell them I did not believe what I was publicly pretending to believe and encouraging them either to believe or to pretend to do so?

I think that by that time (early 1960s) the mainstream churches had pretty much weeded out the liberal elements like the preachers who served Mountain Iron in the 1920s and 1930s and like Dr. Nicely in Rochester, New York., who married us and whose liberal sermons made his church easy to belong to. The more fundamental interpretations of the church in 1963 gave me little choice but to resign from the Presbyterian Church and from Christianity. I have never regretted that decision. I did not realize until after I made it that living even an unconscious lie had interfered with my enjoyment of life.

We still felt the need to satisfy our Sunday habits so we began attending the Unitarian Church. The Unitarians gave us no problems of dogma and provided a good deal of intellect and even entertainment. It did not wear well, however, and I eventually decided that in the long run the Sunday New York *Times* took care of my Sundays better than either the smug intellectualism of the Unitarians or the Presbyterians' holy righteousness and outmoded beliefs.

I am not saying that I believe that there is no force in the universe or the cosmos more potent than humans. The patterns of nature—the complexity of biological and chemical interrelationships—suggest a phenomenal intelligence and a plan that probably could not have occurred by random chance. Consider the dung beetle: if this seemingly insignificant insect hadn't been included in the complex plans of nature, we would be up to our armpits in you-know-what. It is hard to accept that the dung beetle came about merely by random chance. My problem is that the religions I have studied are not willing to update theology to keep pace even with man's limited scientific discoveries.

Religion to me is an attempt to explain how and why we are here and where we may be going. To do this it must use all the tools available to it. Because the organized religions I have studied are mostly committed to reject all knowledge less than 2,000 years old, and to promote outlandish myths and superstitions, I reject those religions.

It baffles me that many intelligent and educated people are apparently able to insulate their archaic religious beliefs from their intellects. Fortunately, this is usually harmless and may sometimes even make a small contribution toward better behavior. Whatever one believes is shaped by the complex interrelationships of our experiences and is highly individual. We cannot force ourselves to believe what we cannot believe.

I am also turned off by the history of atrocities committed by many religions in the name of righteousness. Sometimes it was for personal or political gain, and sometimes it was merely assuming that if you don't believe what I believe I have the God-given right to torture you until you do, or until you die. It seems that most of the worst things that have happened in the history of mankind and are still happening are committed in the name of one religion or another.

My Grandfather Hanson influenced me at the time in my life when I was still able to establish a pattern of healthy skepticism and I credit him for implanting the habit of questioning dogma of any kind. I wonder if at that age I had instead had a Christian fundamentalist as a mentor I would have different beliefs today. Probably not. When I was in high school our church had a series of very serious fundamentalist preachers (whose beliefs were not much admired by my parents, I must admit) whom I could have followed if I had been so inclined. My beliefs were influenced not only by Grandpa, but also my parents, teachers, Sunday school teachers, preachers, one or two friends of my own age who were deep thinkers, and the sum total of a lot of reading including all of the Judeo-Christian Bible.

I would rather approach the end of life with only unanswered questions than to face it armed with firmly entrenched wrong answers.

I am happy that all of my children are living highly moral and ethical lives without the burden of archaic religious beliefs, and that they have equally liberated spouses.

On Politics

My political beliefs seem to have diverged as much from my parents' as my religious beliefs have.

While on the one hand I feel that the best government is the least government, I tend to support liberal causes that attempt to use government to better the lives of the less fortunate. I strongly support attempts to improve the lives of people who are poor. (This is more government.) I do not favor abortion, but I strongly oppose legislation to make abortion the business of the government. (This is less government.) I favor laws to regulate the ownership of some types of firearms. (This is more government.) So, like those of many others, my political stands are inconsistent.

I do not believe that war is right or necessary. In an ideal world we would have leaders who would work to avoid conflict. Unfortunately, it seems that most of the leaders in world politics see war as expeditious solutions to problems they are not smart enough to solve in other ways; or they see war as an opportunity to increase or maintain their wealth and/or power.

Most of my peers at Kodak and in industrial management in general seemed to have political leanings opposed to mine. They tended to be conservative and seemed to believe that people were poor because they deserved to be. I observed life in Mountain Iron (see Chapter 10), which consisted mostly of immigrants on the dole through no fault of their own. My unscientific observations of their children and grandchildren have convinced me that because of the help the government (local, in that case) gave these immigrants, the succeeding generations made contributions to the culture and economics of the United States proportionally greater than the national average. A second observation was that the Navy V-12 program—a highly selective national educational dole during World War II—was tremendously successful in producing lasting and phenomenal benefits to the nation, which would not have been achieved as easily if at all without the program. The V-12 program identified 60,000 young men regardless of economic status whom they judged, based on the best tests available at the time, to have the potential to be the leaders of the future and underwrote their educations. The experiment—if that is what it was—was successful beyond their most optimistic expectations.[1]

These experiences shaped my feeling that government money can be profitably spent on helping people to the long-term benefit of the country. This tends to influence my voting even though too many candidates who claim to believe as I do seem to miss the point and are only seduced into helping the rich get richer and into getting themselves reelected. Whether they claim to be conservative or liberal, politicians seem not to be smart enough or honorable enough to spend our money wisely by making decisions that would strengthen the nation.

It is likely that the examples I gave of good investments of public money were more blundered into than made out of wisdom. It seems like a stretch to believe that the petty politicians of the Mesabi Range in 1920 were looking at the long-term gains for the nation from taxes on the steel companies which they spent to improve local education. The Navy, on the other hand, was only trying to increase its supply of superior leadership to win the war. The post-war contributions to the nation were a happy by-product probably never thought about in the heat of battle.

---

1.   See: Schneider, James G. *The Navy V-12 Program, Leadership for a Lifetime,*1987, Houghton Mifflin Co.

AFTERWORD

This is not the end. There is no end and no beginning to a family history. I am only declaring it the end of my contribution. I hope each of you will continue to add to this and bring it up-to-date for your children and that they in turn do their part to continue it.

If I should happen to live another ten or twenty years I may reverse this declaration of the end and revise it further.

I have not attempted to include much about the generation following mine. You will have to do that. I have indicated that my feeling toward your generation is very positive, and I am sure that you, my children, and your second cousins, are on track to continue the successful upward movement of the Beck-Hanson line and the lines that have been added.

I have tried to be gentle with my own generation. My first drafts included stories that some might not have wanted published, so I have edited them out. I have been more open about those who are dead—and even in those cases not too brutally so. We are not, after all, describing families who are dysfunctional or criminally inclined. (If I were, this could be a best seller.)

While my main purpose has been to record what I know or have found out about previous generations, I have written a few chapters about my life, my beliefs, and myself, which I hope helps you better understand me and the times I lived in.

To my children: you please me greatly because you seem to be tolerant about differences in race, religion, sex, and sexual preferences; because you are not hung up on any narrow religious beliefs; and because you are politically liberal or at least free thinkers. I hope that we have made it more easily possible for you to move toward tolerance and clear thinking than it was for me or your mother who had to overcome some narrow, bigoted ideas from the well-meaning generations that preceded us.

We love you all—Becks, Hansons, in-laws, whatever. You have made our lives full and enjoyable. I cannot imagine a better family. I hope you feel the same and are able to pass it along to future generations.

Appendix A

NOTES AND ST. URHO

Names of our ancestors were sometimes spelled in more than one way. While I have tried to settle on the same spelling for each person in this book, I am not sure which spelling was correct, so I am listing here the various spellings. The first spelling is the one I have used.

Kjustad—Skjustad
Lexabak—Lexaback, Lexabeck, Lexabaken
Odegaard—Odegaarden
Christian—Kristian
Eriksson—Erickson, Ericksson
Bernt—Berndt

I have not maintained this consistency when the names changed between living in Europe and living in the United States. Hansen became Hanson; Johannesen became Johnson; Johan or Johann or Johannes became John.

NOTES FROM VISIT WITH ROLAND BECK, 7/12/01

(Roland was 88 years old and had suffered from two or three strokes, but he was lucid and could speak, so his memories are probably fairly accurate. He died on December 30, 2001, about five and half months after this interview.)

Q: Is John Wargelin, the high school principal when Roland graduated from Mountain Iron High School (Minnesota) the same as the Rev. John Wargelin who is mentioned several times in a book, The Finn Factor, by Carl Ross? John Wargelin resigned as the president of Suomi College in Hancock, Michigan, because he wanted classes to be taught in English rather than Finnish.

A. From what we were able to put together, the answer is almost certainly yes. It was not clear exactly how he got from Suomi College to Mountain Iron High School, and he was only in Mountain Iron for a year or two.

Q. Did you always live in the same house in Mountain Iron?

A. No. I was born in a house that stood on the corner where the Standard Oil gas station was later built. [This was after the fire mentioned in Chapter 2, page 21ff, Aunt Lillian's account] We then moved to a house near where Rossi's lived, and then to a house in Costin. The house in Costin cost $1200, and that house was moved to its present location near the school, which is where I lived most of the time I was living at home. My father enclosed a porch and made some small additions to the house after it was moved.

Q. Did you ever go to activities at the Socialist or Temperance Halls in Mountain Iron? (His sister, Lillian, about 10 years older, wrote about her going to parties in the Temperance Hall.)

A. I don't remember any. During my childhood there were Christmas parties held in the Village Hall. My father and mother seemed to be important among the organizers of the parties. My father arranged to get a supply of lead, which he melted during the party. Children dropped a small spoonful of lead into cold water that made the lead freeze into various shapes. My mother would then read each child's fortune from the shape of the frozen lead.

Q. Do you remember speakeasies and other results of prohibition in Mountain Iron during the 20s?

A. I was not aware of any effect on Mountain Iron. There was very little drinking among high school students. (He graduated in 1929.)

Q. Were jobs easy to get during the 1920s on the Mesabi Range?

A. Yes, as far as I remember.

Q. How did your father and mother manage to support a large family as well as they did?

A. My father had worked in Michigan, Wisconsin, and Cloquet, Minnesota for the Weyerhaeuser Lumber Company. They did clear cutting and thus moved from one forest to another as the trees were depleted. About the time I was born Weyerhaeuser moved out of Minnesota to the state of Washington. After that my father had a job as the school janitor in the wintertime and the school gardener.

Landscaper when there was no snow on the ground. He never made as much as $150 a month. My mother went around the town taking orders for the Mountain Iron grocery store in exchange for groceries.

Q. Did you ever meet your father's sister Mary Mattson (later Anderson), who lived in Michigan, or her son Matt and his son Dick who lived in Virginia, Minnesota?

A. I do not remember Mary, and we had very little contact with Matt's family or Dick, who was a few years younger than I.

Q. Did you have much contact with the Rautiolas, your cousins who were children of your father's sister Miina?

A. Very little.

Q. Did you know the Bygdens, your mother's family in Michigan?

A. When I was about fourteen my mother and I visited her parents in East Tawas and I met some of them. I remember that Emil had a fruit farm and another brother, probably Joel, had a fox farm where he raised silver foxes for their fur—a venture that was soon abandoned as being unprofitable. I remember seeing or hearing about Emma and Hilma, but I don't remember ever meeting Charles or his family. We had very little contact with the Bygdens over the years.

I remember that for a year or two a cousin Edna Beck (Oscar Beck's daughter) came to live with us and go to school in Mountain Iron. (Oscar, my father's brother, and his family lived in Upper Michigan. They had at least 10 children, all of whom had been given a name beginning with the letter E.)

Q. What do you remember about your mother and father?

A. I remember that my mother was very bright and liked to read a lot. It seems like whenever I came home at night no matter how late she would be reading. She was the chairman of the library board, so all library books came to her before they were put into circulation.

She also did a lot of handwork. She crocheted, knitted, and made rag rugs. Her hands were never idle, except perhaps when she was reading. The products of her hands were mostly for gifts and for charity, rarely for sale.

My father was devoted to my mother and depended on her a great deal. The first thing he said when he arrived at home from work was, Where's Ma? When she and I went to Michigan, my sister had to keep him away from the telephone.

Because she knew that he would tell my mother to hurry home because he needed her.

Q. What else do you remember?

A. I remember once having been arrested by your Grandfather Hanson, a Mountain Iron policeman. About a dozen of us had taken the waste from the journal boxes of railroad cars to make fires to keep us warm after we swam in the cold water of the spring-fed, inactive open iron ore pit. The oily waste was put in the journal boxes to help lubricate the wheels, and the railroad had complained.

We were taken by school bus to the courthouse in Virginia (4 miles away) and with great fear and trepidation faced a judge and the railroad detective. When the judge found out how little the damage and cost to the railroad was he criticized the railroad representative for having wasted the court's time and money on the case. He dismissed us with only a warning not to do this again.

Q. What did you think about Virginia Junior College?

A. The teaching was excellent and the credits and grades I got there were fully accepted in Marysville (Tenn.) College where I went and I understood that they were equally acceptable at colleges and universities throughout the country.

◆   ◆   ◆

REPORT FROM LILLIAN BECK (TOMMY) FULLER, 7/25/1990

On July 25, 1990, the Beck descendants of John and Hulda had their first biennial reunion. At that time only two of the children of John and Hulda were still living, Lillian Beck Fuller, and Roland A. Beck, and they attended the reunion.

Lillian wrote a brief memoir of how she remembered her parents and her childhood and her six brothers as children:

EARLY BECK FAMILY MEMORIES
(Growing up with six brothers)

BY LILLIAN (TOMMY) FULLER
July 1990

PROLOGUE

What a fun family heritage we have...of course not all fun...we had sadness and sorrow as well; but it was our sense of humor which braced us, let come what may.

This is a fun festival being together; but, of course, we miss our loved ones. How we would enjoy having them all here, but we can imagine their spirits are with us.

Now I would like to relate some of our fun times and give a little insight into the family members' characters as I knew them.

GRANDMA BECK

She was a wonderful mother. Although she had only a seventh grade education, she was so brilliant she could associate and converse with college graduates. She was an avid reader; a self-educated woman. Her aim in life was to have her children educated and become good American citizens.

Mother was only seven years old when she arrived in America from Europe. She was of Swedish heritage, but was born and raised in Finland. She spoke both languages fluently, and in later life did much interpreting.

GRANDPA BECK

Dad was 18 years old when he arrived in America and he spoke no English. He later learned English, but as we kids said he mostly spoke Finglish. He had a good sense of humor and was very sociable. There was no language barrier. He used to call for square dancing. One time we asked him to call one set for us. He said, Harness your partner and upset the lady. (Honor your partner and opposite lady) Evidently the dancers understood.

He liked radios and clocks. We had one of the first radios. He also liked calendars. On New Year's Day he'd visit every place of business and get a free calendar which he promptly nailed (and I mean nailed) on the walls. Mother never complained about them. Clocks also were a hobby, but as clocks were expensive we only had an alarm clock and a fancy one on the dining room wall which was wound every night by Dad after he put the cat out.

EARLY DAYS

We moved to Mountain Iron from Cloquet, Minnesota, when I was three. (Editor's note: This would be in 1905.) Clarence (Phoxey) was the baby. While in Cloquet Dad played the snare drums in the band. I remember Mom telling that

Dad took me to band practice, and the next day I lined up my dolls on the sofa and played bandmaster and was swearing like one wouldn't believe. Needless to say I never attended another practice.

When we moved to Mountain Iron we settled in a tarpaper house with two bedrooms, kitchen and living room. There was only one outside door that led out from the kitchen. Dad was working at the mine. Our house was in a settlement near the mine called Costin. At that time Mountain Iron had a jail, two bordellos and several saloons. When Dad was on the night shift Mom would lock the door and pull the sewing machine in front of it.

When I was seven years old our house burned down on the coldest night in January. Dad had driven a team of horses for a sleigh ride party of young people. My brothers Len and Leo were with him. Mother was awakened by the smoke and wrapped my brother Laurence in a blanket and yelled for Phoxey and me to follow. We ran out in the snow to the neighbors. Our home was completely demolished.

We moved many times after our house burned down until finally the folks were able to purchase a home in Costin which was later moved to its present site in Mountain Iron.

We were not affluent, but it wasn't long before we had a piano. Mother was determined that I should learn to plan the piano. How very grateful I am for that, as I have had so much pleasure and rewarding experiences as a result.

I will only reiterate the fun times of the family, as this is a happy time for us to be together. Who knows when another opportunity like this will occur?

How nice it was that Mom and Dad had the boys in pairs: Lennart and Leo, Clarence and Laurence, and then Charles and Roland. I remember that if I was being punished for a misdeed I was sure that I must have been adopted. How could it be, only one girl among so many boys!

LENNART

Lennart, the oldest, had a great sense of humor which I am sure served him well in times of worry and distress. He wrote many Finglish poems and essays and was quite a prankster. He married Mabel Hanson, his high school sweetheart, and they had a happy life.

LEO

Leo was quiet but fun loving. As we were growing up he always felt so responsible for me. If I had a date, he'd check it out carefully. My early recollection of him is when he built a lovely bobsled, and how he loved to don big fur mitts and steer the sled down Costin Hill. Also, he and Lennart built a lovely Eskimo igloo, freezing the water in blocks. It was the size of a real Eskimo Igloo.

Another episode. When Len and Leo were in their teens, on Saturday night they often would go to Virginia on the streetcar to attend a movie. One night Leo came home earlier than Len, so Mom asked where Len was. Leo said, Oh, he took the Fatima kid home. The Fatima kid was a teenage girl who hung around the bus depot. You can imagine that Len got what for when he came home on the next streetcar! The next day Len was mad at Leo and so when they were outdoors Len picked up a rock and pitched it at Leo and hit him in the head. It wasn't a serious injury, but he told Leo not to tell Mom, and he'd give him his camera. That ended the feud.

Speaking of rocks, I tell people I grew up in the stone age. Rocks played a big part in our development. We played house using rocks for dishes. We played jacks with them and many a rock fight we had. I guess we were pretty tough.

CLARENCE (PHOXEY)

Phoxey was not as vigorous and healthy as the rest of the flock. He developed rickets and had to wear glasses at a very early age. His hair was very blond and we teased him and called him Foxey because we said he looked like Foxey Grandpa, who was featured in the Sunday funny papers. He kept the nickname all his life, only changing the spelling after he grew up. He was gentle boy who was very caring of our Mother, and of others as well.

LAURENCE

Laurence was quiet and an in between child, kind, gentle, and a follower. He never seemed to get into trouble like the rest of us. He was always a sociable, caring and lovable soul.

CHARLES

Charles was a cute boy and always had a come-back if apprehended. For example, one time at dinner we had steak and it was rather tough. Charlie took out his jackknife to cut it. I reprimanded him by saying, What if we had company, and you did that. His answer was If we had company, we'd have a roast.

ROLAND

Roland was a lovable little boy. He didn't like to be kissed, but I couldn't resist, as he was so adorable. When he was small our parents had a boarding hotel and

Miss Sarah Edes, who was a missionary for the Range Parish, boarded with us. She lived on the second floor and was taking Italian lessons from the Reverend Terranova, another Range Parish worker. Roland was extremely jealous of him, and one time Mother heard Roland singing at the bottom of the stairs. The words were I go, you go, Sheenee go Dago. Needless to say, he received a paddling.

So ends the saga of me and the six brothers. I was the privileged only sister raised by six wonderful brothers and a patient, loving and caring Mom and Dad.

COUSIN DICK MATTSON AND THE LEGEND OF ST. URHO

The Richard Mattson in the story from the Mesabi Daily News, which follows, is the grandson of Mary (Maria) Keto Mattson, the sister of John (Keto) Beck, which makes him my third cousin.

◆   ◆   ◆

St. Urho Legend's Creator, Richard Mattson, Dies
St. Patrick got fierce competition from Finnish grapes-saver

Linda Tyssen Williams, Mesabi Daily News, Thursday, June 7th, 2001

VIRGINIA—The Irish had their St. Patrick and the wearin' o' the green. So why not the Finns?

Thus the good St. Urho was born nearly 50 years ago at Ketola's Department Store in Virginia, thanks to a fun-loving Finnish-American named Richard L. Mattson, who figured it was time for a saint of the Finns' very own.

Mattson died on Tuesday in a Duluth hospital. He would have turned 88 on the Fourth of July.

The fame of St. Urho, who drove frogs from Finland and saved the grape crop, has spread far and wide, even across the sea to Finland where there's more than one St. Urho's Pub. There's a St. Urho's statue in Menahga, Minn., and one in Finland, Minn., and the Helsinki Bar in Butte, Mont., has a St. Urho's celebration. Mattson's wish that St. Urho and the wearing of the purple and green would live on would be fulfilled.

Mattson, a manager at Ketola's for 42 years, once wrote this about how he created St. Urho: "Winters McCavic, a co-worker at Ketola's Department Store, chided me in 1953 that the Finns did not have saints like St. Patrick. I told her the Irish aren't the only ones with great saints. She asked me to name one for the Finns. So I fabricated a story and thought of St. Eero (Eric), St. Jussi (John), and St. Urho. Urho, a common Finnish named, had a more commanding sound."

So Mattson told McCavic the Finns had a St. Urho. And to save the grape crop, he chased all the poisonous frogs from Finland before the last Ice Age. Never mind that grapes never grew in Finland—this is legend.

The women of the store threw a St. Urho's party in the coffee room, and Mrs. McCavic wrote a poem in "Finglish" dialect (best read aloud). It begins, Ooksie kooksie coolama vee, Saint Urho iss ta poy for me! He sase out ta rogs so pig unt kreen, prafest Finn I effer seen!" The legend had begun.

Clarence Ivonen wrote in the Mesabi Daily News in 1956:

"While the sons and daughters of Erin were paying their respects to St. Patrick, Mattson was loudly praising the feats of 'Saint Urho.'" It was the first known mention of St. Urho ever published, and in the years since, the saint and his holiday have been featured in newspapers across the country. "I was actually there at the start of his legend. That's why he was special to me," Ivonen said in a phone interview.

He was one of a kind, not only for St. Urho, but for the way he greeted everybody at Ketola's Department Store. He always had a smile and a witticism. That's part of the St. Urho legend, always tongue in cheek and a quip. "He had that twinkle in his eye," Ivonen said.

Dave Torrel of Sparta, who also has written St. Urho's poems, said Mattson had a great sense of humor. He thought this was a great thing that it had gotten as far as it did. He started that day just as a fun thing. There should be a lot of Finnish people who have fun over the day, Torrel said.

Mattson's son, Marc Mattson of New York City, said his father got a big kick out of starting a legend. A few years after Mattson spun his tale, a Bemidji college professor named Sulo Havumaki changed the frogs to grasshoppers. Marc Mattson laughed about intellectuals debating something that was made up.

The story of St. Urho is perhaps best told in Richard L. Mattson's own words, as reprinted in *The Legend of St. Urho*, compiled by Joanne Asala.

I have given lectures on this long-neglected saint, explaining to rapt audiences that he was born of peasant stock on the Finnish-Swedish border. After showing promise in schools, he was given a scholarship to a Stockholm seminary and studied in Paris under the humanist Catholic theologians. When Urho returned to Finland, he was given a parish in a rural area...A small creek and bogs created an ideal breeding ground for poisonous frogs...This had a devastating effect on the new young crops. The people appealed to the gods in 'The Kalevala' and then to the Christian God with no results. In desperation they asked their new priest, good Father Urho, to help them.

After studying the problem and the height of a frog jump, Urho built a sluice high enough to contain the frogs. They eventually went to a holding pond. Then the frogs were sailed to France in the holds of ships with ice to preserve them. Thanks to the Finns, this is how the French first acquired their taste for frog legs."

St. Urho's Day was originally to be a May celebration, Mattson wrote, but everyone wanted to have a party in March as the Finnish answer to St. Patrick. The response became phenomenal—going nationwide within a few years with programs, parades, parties, greeting cards and buttons. I have heard there is a movement in the southwestern states to make St. Urho the patron saint of refrigeration, which makes it possible to ship fresh fruits and vegetables to the rest of the nation. Who knows when and where miracles will end?"

Marc Mattson said his father was a "mover and shaker" and "the Mayor of Chestnut Street." He started the Saturday Night Dance Club at the Coates Hotel, a gala affair with formal gowns, tuxedos, big band music—and Mattson and his wife Carolyn gliding across the floor like Fred Astaire and Ginger Rogers.

People would speculate on what Mattson's middle initial "L" stood for, and Mattson would jokingly tell them "Lovable." So in honor, Mattson's grandson, Travis Myers of New York City, gave his own son Lovable" as a middle name.

Richard L. Mattson had numerous health problems over the years, but he used his sense of humor to help him through, sometimes wearing a T-shirt that read "Mayo Clinic Cadaver Society," Marc Mattson said. And Myers said his grandfather went out with a smile on his face.

Richard L. Mattson had said his tombstone epitaph is to be "I finally made it." The truth is, if success can be measured by a legendary saint named Urho, Mattson found it a long time ago.

Appendix B

THE MEMOIRS OF ALEXANDER KETO

Preface

I am a grandnephew of Alexander Keto, and for the first 19 years of my life we both lived in Mountain Iron, Minnesota. This preface reveals my memories of him and my thoughts about the memoir which follows.
John Robert Beck, March, 2004.

Alexander Keto was my grandfather's brother and they lived with their families in Mountain Iron, Minnesota, next door to each other during all of my first 19 years. (At least Alex did—my grandfather died when I was 15.) I lived less than two blocks away from their two houses. My Finnish grandfather, who went by the name of John Beck, hardly ever spoke to me during his lifetime and I am sure that his brother Alex never did. I was baffled by this but now ascribe it to their being Finnish, and perhaps not being comfortable speaking English. I was offended when my grandfather didn't acknowledge me when we met on the streets of our small town. I was not offended when my great uncle Alex—I was not always sure that it was he, I knew him so vaguely—seemed not to know me.

It is apparent from his revealing story of life in Finland and beyond that Alexander Keto, the shoemaker, and his siblings survived great difficulties and lived to follow the American dream of paving the way for their children to succeed in the New World. His descriptions of his mother's and grandparents' lives are also revealing. This is a valuable chapter in understanding what we came from. What makes this memoir especially valuable to us is the description of their lives in Finland from Wilhelmiina's childhood through Alexander's emigration to the United States.

Alex's memoirs were different from what I remember hearing from my father and what Aunt Lillian Beck Fuller had said and recorded. Grandfather John Beck and his siblings were not born in Oulu, but apparently in the town of Inankyla on the shores of Lake Evijärvi. This, incidentally, was only 60 kilometers from Karleby where Hulda Bygden, our grandmother, whom John met and married in Michigan, was born (according to the best information I have). Oulu, where the Ketos moved later, was about 160 kilometers to the north.

Uncle Roland believed that although his father was poor he was well educated in the good schools of Finland. Alex's story indicates that they never saw the inside of a school and what little they learned they were taught at home. Alex could not be confirmed on his first try because he couldn't read well enough. An uncle taught him to read after that while he was learning to become a shoemaker. All of the children of Antti and Wilhelmiina did become literate, but it appears that they were self-taught or home-schooled and had to work such long hours early in life that getting an education was very difficult. An exception was the youngest, Emelia, who came to Michigan when she was about seven years old and was probably educated in the United States.

I had believed (from family reports) that Antti Keto never got to the United States and that Wilhelmiina and Emelia came to Mountain Iron after his death directly from Finland. Alex wrote that Antti came to the U. S. twice and stayed the second time. Wilhelmiina and Emelia joined him in Michigan and they were together there when he died in 1901 when Emelia was nine years old. They moved to Minnesota from Michigan after Alex had arrived from Finland in 1902 and found work in Mountain Iron.

Alex has written the story of his life as you and I might have written our own—not admitting any personal faults. It is not important that his marriage to Hulda may not have been as idyllic as he portrays it. (I remember that I over-heard Aunt Lillian telling my mother that Alex's wife Hulda often made him sleep in a shed in the back yard.) He does not, of course, mention the rumor that he lost his job as a school janitor because it was alleged he had made improper advances to a schoolgirl. He doesn't even mention being a janitor. He doesn't diminish his temperance stance by reporting that he smuggled whiskey to his brother through the bedroom window in medicine bottles as John was lying there during the last weeks of his life. He portrays himself as a nearly perfect Christian without faults with a wonderful marriage and children. I include these bits of unsubstantiated hearsay only to reassure you that Shoemaker Alexander Keto was probably more nearly human and less saintly than he portrayed himself.

I had never known that Alex Keto was a shoemaker. While the original memoir in Finnish showed a picture of his shoe repair shop in Virginia, Minnesota, about 1910, he did not have a shop that I knew of during my lifetime. When our shoes needed to be fixed we took them to a shop in Virginia, not to Uncle Alex. I don't know what he did for a living and he doesn't make this clear in his memoir.

My father's and Aunt Lillian's stories and family photographs suggest that John Beck and his family were the caretakers of mother and grandmother Wilhelmiina and sister Emelia. Alex gives them no credit in his memoir. The only mention of his older brother was Johan's leaving Finland for Michigan with his father Antti. There is no mention in this memoir that Alex and his brother John (Johan) both lived in Mountain Iron and in fact were next-door neighbors. On the other side, my father's version gave Alex no credit; Lennart's memory was that Grandmother Wilhelmiina and Aunt Emelia were Becks and housed and cared for by Becks. It was my understanding from Lennart that both women had taken the name Beck (which was not true). There was no acknowledgement by either family that the two families shared in taking care of their mother/grandmother and sister—both seemed to claim full credit.

For the record, Wilhelmiina died of tuberculosis and Emelia died in childbirth. Wilhelmiina's death certificate, signed by her son John Beck, gave her name as Keto. My father never believed (or wanted to believe) that the true family name was Keto and would have been more authentic than his birth name of Anderson and his father's later adopted name of Beck. Aunt Lillian in her handwritten history of the family suggested that the Finnish family name was Korpi, which apparently has little more basis than that someone named Korpi once owned the house that Antti Keto bought in Oulu and was later lost to a foreclosure.

The Alex Keto children and the John Beck children were first cousins who lived next door to each other. They were friends and schoolmates and kept in touch with each other in later years. They were, however, raised under very different philosophies.

The Alex Ketos were Finnish. Their children learned Finnish as a first language and English second. Their church was the Finnish Lutheran Church and they were confirmed in that church in the Finnish language.

They were brought up to be Finnish first, and American second. I knew all of the Keto children and am sure that they were all loyal American citizens, but Alex and Hulda started them out as Finns.

The John Becks, on the other hand, were determined to be Americans first. My Finnish-born Swedish grandmother (also named Hulda), and her husband John Beck, my grandfather and Alex Keto's older brother, did not believe in putting old world culture first. My father, the oldest Beck child, was sent to a Finnish Lutheran confirmation class but rebelled against the Finnish Lutherans and left and brought his whole family to the English-speaking Presbyterian Church. I was never clear on his reasons. It was not language; he spoke Finnish as well as if he had been born in Finland. But I suspect that he was rebelling against the church's putting Finnish and Finland ahead of the United States and English, and above all my father was to his dying day a super-patriotic American.

The Keto children all learned Finnish as well as English and spoke Finnish at home. Their next-door neighbor cousins, the Becks, did not. The oldest Beck, my father, spoke excellent Finnish and his next brother managed to get by. The next child, a sister, barely made it, and the next brother spoke a kind of pidgin Finnish often referred to as Finglish. The last three children didn't even attempt the language as far as I could tell.

In those days, immigrants were encouraged to be American and to give up their European background. It appeared that Finns were often more reluctant to become fully Americanized than were immigrants from other countries. Alex Keto mentions a traveling Finnish preacher named John Wargelin. John Wargelin lost his job as president of Suomi College, a Finnish school in Hancock, Michigan, because he tried to get Suomi College to teach its classes in English rather than in Finnish. This was in the 1920s. (My source of this information is a book, *The Finn Factor*, by Carl Ross.)

My father Lennart Beck learned Finnish to communicate with his father and grandmother (and because he had an interest and aptitude that made learning languages easy for him.) But my father never considered teaching me Finnish. I think he considered it un-American and unnecessary.

John Beck was ten years older than Alex Keto. Alex Keto was only 11 years old when John's son Lennart was born. Lennart was 12 years old when Helmi Keto, Alex's oldest child, was born. Minerva Keto, Alex's youngest child, was born the same year as I, John Beck's oldest grandchild. Minerva and I were not close as children, but we did go to Mountain Iron schools and even Virginia Junior College at the same time. I was a year ahead of her in school, so we did not take any classes together. We became closer friends after I moved to California in 1955 and discovered that she and her family were living nearby in Palo Alto. Her husband was a school principal in South San Francisco, and they had three sons. We also had two small sons at that time, and we visited back and forth during our first stay here and enjoyed our visits with Min and her husband and their children. I remember that her very personable husband was named Joe Smith and we had much fun kidding about the anonymity of his name.

There was one similarity between the Becks and the Ketos. Both families were against alcohol. I know that Grandma Beck did not allow alcohol in her house, and I feel sure the same was true at the Ketos. Since Grandma Beck was the daughter of the town drunk of East Tawas, Michigan (according to Grandma's niece, Virginia Bygden Fox) it is easy to see her motivation for this. This did not seem to keep subsequent generations away from alcohol, at least among the Becks. I don't know very much about the Ketos' drinking except for Minerva, whose husband Joe Smith eventually took their three sons and left her because she was an alcoholic. That happened shortly after we moved back to Rochester, New York, in 1959. Even though our visits with them included moderate drinking I was not aware that Minerva had a problem with alcohol, but as far as I know she never challenged her husband's allegations.

The Shoemaker's Apprentice has opened up an understanding of our Keto ancestry that appears to have been largely unknown to those descendants who had adopted the name Beck.

I am grateful to Alex and to those who have translated his Finnish memoir into English for having enriched our family history. I hope that we can all do as well by our descendants and I wish that more of our ancestors had done something like this.

The version which follows, is my consolidation of two excellent literal translations from the original Finnish by Verna Risku and Eunice Keljo commissioned by Bruce Fuller and Faith Wick, respectively. I have attempted to present what Alex Keto would (in my opinion) have written if English were his first language and he was writing it in 2003. The Risku and Keljo translations are available upon request. I tried to preserve the strong feelings Alex expressed. I did not, however, change his style of using the third person to mean himself, so when he refers to Alexander or Alex or The Shoemaker he is really referring to himself.

SHOEMAKER'S APPRENTICE
By Alexander Keto

FOREWORD

This memoir was written to satisfy my desire to relate my experiences in life. I survived many difficult experiences with the help of a faith in God, and I hope that readers will be encouraged to turn to God when they face troubles and adversity.

I am thankful to my dear daughter Leah Aallotar Koski who has helped me with this book. Verses quoted are taken from the Finnish Sunday School songbook used in our home devotions, from Wilho Reimanin's book People's Song-book and from the Zion hymnbook.   A.K.

CONTENTS
IT WAS A HARD LIFE
WILHELMIINA'S CHILDHOOD
EVIJARVI
OULU
SEPARATION
CONFIRMATION
THE SHOEMAKER'S APPRENTICE
THE IRON RANGE
HAPPINESS AND SADNESS
CHILDREN
ALEXANDER'S GREAT LOSS
LONELINESS
SEATTLE, WASHINGTON
A MIRACLE
FAITH AND GOD'S WILL
A WONDERFUL TRIP

It Was a Hard Life

In the 1800's Jake Antilla and his wife Anna Katharine lived in Kortesjarvi, Finland, which at that time was part of Russia. They had little income and life was difficult. The cold climate and lack of money often made it necessary to make do with inadequate or poor quality food. When crops were spoiled by frost they had to eat pettuleipää—a bread made from flour made from the inner bark of pine trees.

Finnish men were forced to fight on the battlefront between Russia and Sweden, leaving the heavy farm work to the women. Hunger and poverty were common in the best of times and the wars made things even worse.

Jaakko and Anna Katherine had a daughter named Wilhelmiina. They were very poor, so when she was still a young girl she was sent to live with her uncle Elias Kleimola near Kauhava because Uncle Elias owned a farm and her parents thought that he would be better able to feed and clothe their daughter.

Jaakko and Anna Katherine trusted their God even though he had assigned them hard, oppressed lives. Hard as life was, Jaakko lived to the age of 92 and Anna Katherine to 85. They both passed away on the same day. Their Lord blessed them at last by sending the angel of death to take them together to a peaceful dwelling place to await the miraculous Resurrection morning.

> *Oh, blessedness unparalleled, the Lord's children at home.*
> *No one can imagine the joy they have there.*

Wilhelmiina's Childhood

Wilhelmiina Antilla's mother Anna Katherine was born in Kortesjarvi near the border of Harma. Wilhelmiina's Uncle Elias Kleimola's home became home to her even though as the poor cousin she had to be humble and obedient and willing to do work that the homeowner's daughters (her cousins) wouldn't do. She did not complain, believing that work (no matter how menial) was a command from God—a belief she needed for survival all of her life.

The uncle's home was busily happy. Inside in the evening the large living room (*tupa*) became a workshop. Women wove fabric and spun yarn. Everyone accepted working in the evening, like working outside during the day. Whoever doesn't work shall not eat, was the rule—day and night. Wilhelmiina learned to sew and other women's skills while the men and boys made sleighs, wagons and even furniture out of wood.

Their only light was a burning shingle. It was the job of children to hold the flame to illuminate the work. They were criticized if the light faltered no matter how tired their small hands became. Holding the flame is a thankless job, were the most complimentary words they could expect to hear.

Finns traditionally sang while they worked. This was how children learned folk songs, sacred songs and hymns. The messages from the songs she learned as a child taught Wilhelmiina later to call on God to help her whenever she faced rough times.

Evijärvi

Wilhelmiina became a teenager, and daydreamed of her future. Her uncle's home seemed cramped and she became more aware that she was only a second-class daughter of the household. Wilhelmiina decided to leave and make her own way in the world. She asked her uncle to take her to Evijärvi where she had found a servant's job. While Uncle Elias assured her that she could remain, he bowed to her wishes and hitched his horse to the buggy and delivered her to Evijärvi. Wilhelmiina thanked her uncle and he spoke tenderly to her and left.

At that time the best wages for a servant was 50 marks. Wilhelmiina found that hired hands were treated with even less respect than she had been as the poor cousin. Servants' lives were lived at the convenience of the family who employed them. Their food and their accommodations were very basic. But because Wilhelmiina did her work well she was highly regarded by the mistress of the house.

While the sons and daughters of the homeowners shared some of the same social activities as the maids and hired hands, the homeowners' children did not mingle with the servants. At one of these events Wilhelmiina met a young hired hand named Antti (Andrew) Keto. They eventually were married and went happily, full of zeal and hope, to live in a small cottage under a single ridgepole in Inankyla on the shores of Evijärvi. Over the years they found joy, weariness, sorrow, and the severity of life.

Evijärvi was a beautiful lake with many fish. It is also called the Northern Saimaa. [Saimaa is another beautiful lake in southeastern Finland.] The lovely waters are blue and deciduous trees and pine trees surround the lake, and tasty wild berries grow on the heaths.

Its centuries-old church still stands. Under its cross over turbulent and tranquil times little ones, youth, middle aged, military heroes and elderly were blessed as they were baptized, married and buried during famines, wars and the rare good times. Those buried there rest awaiting the time when the Prince of righteousness, holiness and eternal joy will call them to be His own. That house of the Lord is the sacred rock for the living and its churchyard the gathering place for those awaiting eternity.

Lake Evijärvi abounds in fish and Antti fished to support his family. From Evijärvi the fishermen went as far as Hull on the North Sea and from the Gulf of Finland to Sweden. At that time the seas were still being mapped. Both Antti and Wilhelmiina were lonesome when he was away and she worried when Antti was gone because the rough waters were treacherous. She felt less alone after the children were born, but still looked anxiously for Antti to return from what seemed like very, very long journeys.

While they lived in Inankyla they had eight children, seven of whom survived. The survivors were Johan, Maria, Oscar, Wilhelmiina, Nickolai, Alexander and Emelia.

They were happy to see Father Antti come home and sad to see him leave. Fishing was not always bountiful, and when the catch was small life was difficult. When the oldest children had matured they promised their mother that they would do the chores and care for the younger ones so that Wilhelmiina could look for work.

Wilhelmiina worked as a seamstress, midwife, blood cupper, and masseuse. She worked skillfully with her hands. It is not surprising that some of her grandchildren are nurses and doctors in America. One of the nurses has her grand-mother's cupping horns and she treasures them.

Wilhelmiina's oldest daughter Maria cooked for the family. When Mother returned at night the smaller children were already asleep and the older ones earnestly awaited her footsteps.

Mother told them stories about her day at work. The little ones awakened and Mother took Emelia, the youngest, into her lap and put her arms around Alexander, next youngest, as he sat near her on the bench by the table. The other children crowded around. Mother kissed Emelia and looked at her and Alexander's big blue eyes and smiled at the other children. Together they sang and talked. Before they went to bed they sang *My eyes I lift unto heaven above, and fold my hands together. You, O Lord the children's friend, I thank from my heart....* Then they said an evening prayer. The light from the burning shingle was extinguished and they went to sleep hoping that Father would return from his fishing trip soon. They all said Goodnight, Mother.

Whenever Antti returned home Wilhelmiina and the children were happy. He told them of his trip and experiences during storms. God protected him, as He is the ruler of the sea and the waves.

When Father brought a lot of fish, the family greatly enjoyed a long-awaited feast. Father talked about the power of the sea and its dangers but he said, Yes, we know how small our boat is and how great is The Creator.

> *My strength is grace, grace eternal,*
> *Sea's power can't break it.*
> *My leader is the Lord of heaven and earth,*
> *It was He who once overcame the sea, and*
> *From Him I receive help.*
> *After all, heaven is above the sea and ruler of it.*

Once when Antti came home he had a strange look on his face like he was deep in thought. Wilhelmiina asked him if everything was all right. Antti answered, When I was at sea I heard a lot about America and how the people from Finland are moving there.

Wilhelmiina asked him, "You aren't thinking of going there?"

Antti answered, "I've been thinking of going as they say it is even easy to get gold!"

He made his plans to go to East Tawas, Michigan, where there were several sawmills. Wilhelmiina packed his suitcase and a lunch for him. He promised he would return soon. Wilhelmiina continued to work and the older children also got jobs as household helpers. Father wrote often to his family who rejoiced at his hopeful spirits.

The children grew. Wilhelmiina taught the older ones to read. Because there were so many they had fun together. They used the swings, they played circle games, ran in the sunshine and sang. They went swimming and the boys went fishing sometimes. Summers were more fun since the sun never set. They could run and jump barefooted. The children were sent to pick berries to be preserved for winter. They watched the Northern Lights in the fall and winter.

One day a man came walking down the road with a suitcase. One of the children saw him and said, "That's Father! He has come home from America!"

There was no happier day. Antti came in and hugged his wife and kissed all the children with big tears of joy in his eyes. Then he said, "Greetings from America, but our homeland is the best place." They all waited to hear what Father had to say about America.

Oulu

When Father came from America all of the members of the family were excitedly waiting to hear the news from the ideal land. They listened in amazement when Father said there were virgin forests and newcomers could make a living logging and in the sawmill.

"In the small village there was a general store, a train depot, and several saloons. East Tawas, Michigan, where I worked in a sawmill, was like many other villages. If the times are good one can save a little, as I have. But life was wild with much violence and drunkenness and there is no Finnish Church. But now let's talk about what your mother's brother wrote from Oulu."

Wilhelmiina's brother had written suggesting they move north to Oulu. Houses were inexpensive and the land and forests were good. So Antti went to Oulu and bought a house named Korpi.

The family moved there. Antti, being a skilled carpenter, began to remodel the home and built a barn, a stable and a storehouse. Money ran out so he took a loan and mortgaged the home. Earning enough money in Finland was difficult.

One day Antti told Wilhelmiina that he would go back to America to earn some money and he would take their oldest son Johan with him. The oldest daughter Maria had left earlier for East Tawas, Michigan, to live with Father's friends and was working in a restaurant. They would feel at home with three of us in America and, Antti told Wilhelmiina, "I will send you money to pay the mortgage and when we can look out of our own windows the three of us will return."

So Antti and his son Johan sailed to America on a beautiful ship. Johan was greatly excited. When they arrived in America, Cleveland was President. Democrats were in power and times were bad—later referred to as that famous Democratic time. Unemployment was high and if you were lucky to get work at a logging camp the pay was only $10 to $12 a month. Even when Antti and Johan both worked there was no money left to send to Finland.

The family in Oulu panicked. Wilhelmiina waited for letters and money but Antti just sent bad news. Antii told the family it would be best if they joined him in America. Their greatest comfort was prayer and God's word. But neither Antti nor God provided fare for the trip. And Wilhelmiina's sister's son, who held the mortgage on the house, put pressure on Wilhelmiina to make payments on the mortgage.

One day the village constable drove his horse into the yard in Oulu and knocked on the door. He said to Wilhelmiina, I have come to inform you that your home will be announced for sale in church since you are not paying your mortgage. Wilhelmiina closed the door and dropped to her knees and cried, My God, I have been shamed in your eyes, save me! Where will I go with my children? Help me. Alexander and Emelia ran to their crying mother and asked who that man was. This brought Wilhelmiina to her feet and wiping her tears she said, The Lord will take care of his own even if our home is sold and we are driven out.

There were only a few days to pay the mortgage, but Wilhelmiina went to work at the neighbors. When she quieted the children and had their bedtime prayers she stayed awake by lamplight and prayed earnestly. Even after she extinguished the lamp and went to bed she remained awake until morning. She wondered if Antti had started drinking in America, as she hadn't heard from him. It looked like he didn't care about them. The last letter only stated that both Johan and Maria had married good mates.

Wilhelmiina arose, sighing, and started a fire in the fireplace and started breakfast for the children knowing it was their last meal in this house. The children arose, ate, and said goodbye to their mother as she left for work. They were precious as gold to her. They promised to do their chores and behave.

The calf didn't drink her milk so Alexander suggested to his sister, Let's butcher that calf and we'll hide the meat and the potatoes and the grain so the police chief can't come and sell them.

Yes, you kill the calf and I'll get a container for the blood.

Alexander said, Mother can make blood bread, pancakes and sausage for us.

So they slaughtered the calf, skinned it, and cut up the meat and hid it in the woods along with potatoes and grain. They covered it all with spruce branches.

Their delicate younger sister, Emelia, didn't want to be near them when they killed the calf.

When Mother came home she was shocked at what she saw. But since the calf was killed she started to make blood bread.

In the morning the house and belongings were put up for sale. On the lawn were the sheriff, police, and many landowners from the town. No one had any compassion, everyone was looking only to make himself richer. They bid on the horse, the cow, and the sheep. Mother's sister's son, who had given Father the money to go to America, bought the house. Now nothing was left but the meat, grain and potatoes that the children had hidden in the woods. But they were lost because the new owner ordered them to get out immediately. Wilhelmiina went in and packed their clothes and other personal items. She consoled herself with verse:

No peace is found on earth.
I am a stranger here
But in Saalesies is my homeland
If only I could be there
[Saalesies probably refers to heaven.]

Separation

Mother left in tears with her children and went to the village where she was able to rent one room from a tanner. There they settled down to live. Alexander was ten years old and Emelia was three. Wilhelmiina, age 13, found a job in a home as a maid and planned to go to America as soon as she earned enough money.

Alexander became a hired hand in a home where he was paid 30 marks a year and some clothes. It was hard to leave Mother but being a man of ten years he shed no tears. The master of the home was good but his wife made life miserable for the servants. The master was a Christian man who prayed and read God's word, but his wife was impossible, so Alexander decided to leave. His mother wasn't happy but Alexander said he would never work at that house again and went to look for another job.

The next day he got a job in the sawmill as a machine oiler. The pay was so little he couldn't rent a room and Mother lived too far away for him to live with her. Alexander and another boy, Matti, made themselves living space under the board piles. They made a bed of wood shavings and got a horse blanket from a horseman. Their food consisted of limpuu (rye) bread and lard and a cup of soup from the local restaurant. The boys thought this was great fun.

While Alexander was working here he received word that his mother and young sister Emelia had received tickets to America from their father and Alexander thought he must have gotten a ticket too.

He hadn't, so his dear mother and sister left without him. Evidently Father didn't have enough money for Alexander's passage. Mother knew that God would take care of him. Emelia was so sweet, so small. All three cried on that beautiful summer day when Mother Wilhelmiina and Sister Emelia left Alexander to cross the ocean to be with their husband and father and other members of the family.

Alexander was now entirely on his own.

Matti and Alexander were happy camping under the board pile, but winter was coming. Alexander suggested to Matti, Maybe we should ask if we could get into some handwork classes because it is October and it's getting cold. You could take carpentry lessons and I will ask Manner if I can take shoemaker lessons.

They left the sawmill and board pile. Alexander walked briskly down the street in Oulu to Manner's shoemaker shop. He was accepted as a student providing he got permission from his parents and two witnesses that Alexander was their son and that they would allow him to remain in school for three years. Alexander wrote to his parents in East Tawas, Michigan, and six months later a permit arrived along with a letter stating that the boy should be taught good manners, should learn to read and should be allowed to go to confirmation classes.

The shoemaking lessons started at 7 a.m. and lasted until 8 p.m. The first thing he had to learn was to make waxed thread and put a bristle on the end.

When he learned this he was allowed to repair old shoes. When the workday was over he proudly delivered the repaired shoes to the well-to-do families. Sometimes Alexander had to walk more than a kilometer and when he returned he was given a good but simple supper. In the morning he was given one cup of coffee. The apprentices were given two cups.

Alexander liked learning to be a shoemaker and was happy when there was work for him. He noticed that the apprentices were drinkers and he knew this was bad. He hoped he wouldn't start drinking when he became of age. Mother had warned him never to start drinking.

Confirmation

Alexander had been in shoemaker school for a year and a half when he went to confirmation classes. He was not accepted, as he couldn't read. The vicar asked him to leave. Crying, he returned to the shoe shop and on the way he decided not to try again and when he finished the shoemaker classes he would live the life of the apprentices—drink and fight.

Alexander's uncle got word of this and he came to talk to the shoemaker and the boy. The uncle was a lay preacher and he came regularly to teach the boy to read. Confirmation lessons started in the spring and while Alexander was afraid he would not be accepted the master shoemaker encouraged him and reminded him to behave and be courteous to the pastor and others.

Alexander was very happy when the vicar accepted him. The class lasted for several weeks and on St. John's Day (Juhannus) he and his classmates received Holy Communion. It was a festive and solemn occasion in the Oulu Church when they said their verses, made their vows and received a Bible as a gift. In the inside cover Pastor Holmström wrote memory verses and one was, Whoever comes to me I will not turn them away. Confirmation was a blessed time in Alexander's life and it was easy now to continue studying to become a shoemaker.

It was customary for those confirmed to give the pastor a gift. Alexander had only 2 marks and he gave them to the pastor, and the evening before confirmation he also brought the pastor new shoes that he had made.

When he entered the parsonage the pastor thanked him and said, "Alexander, I can't accept your money. These shoes are very precious, especially because you made them. So you keep the money and buy what you need. Thank you for the shoes. God bless you!"

Alexander was deeply moved and he vowed to attend church on Sundays when the Pastor Holmström was preaching. The pastor's warm sermons nurtured his faith and helped him remember his family across the ocean.

Alexander had a little over a year left to attend classes. One day he received a letter from America from his mother. It read as follows:

East Tawas, Mich. U.S.
Dear Son Alexander,

I am informing you of a great sorrow. Your father has passed away. He was very ill. We had a hard time when we couldn't get a Finnish pastor to conduct the service.

Be a good boy and go to the church office to inform them of his death. Emelia is fine and I am feeling fine. She has been attending school but we don't know how long we can go on with Father gone. I pray that God will take care of us.

We were happy that confirmation went so well for you. Be sure and bring this letter to the parsonage. Heartfelt Greetings from all of us. With love, Mother

When he was given permission from the master shoemaker Alexander went to the church office with the news. The rector said it couldn't be announced in church until there was an official notice from the pastor in America who conducted the funeral service. In tears Alexander returned to the shoemaker class. He realized he would never see his father again. He wrote a letter to his mother and told her what the rector had said. After a month he received an answer with a death certificate in German from the pastor who had conducted the funeral. The rector said he could announce the death in church but there would be a fee. The pastor heard this and asked how the boy could pay when he didn't earn any money and he offered to pay the fee. The rector accepted this and Alexander thanked him. When he returned to his class the master asked if a fee was required.

The boy answered, "Yes, but the pastor offered to pay it." An apprentice commented, "The pastor is a Christian and thank God that there is one in Oulu."

It is written, *All that you do for the least of them, you do for me.*

The Shoemaker's Apprentice

The Manner school was well known throughout Finland as it was there that many types of shoes were made from many types of leather. They made high tops, lower styles, hard soles, slippers and boots.

Alexander had been a student for nearly three years. He had become quite skilled and made first class shoes. The Master Shoemaker admired him because he was pleasant, playful, and animated and he did his work well and fast.

Finally the day arrived that Alexander attained the rank of shoemaker and could get his papers from the Oulu city hall. This was a big day for him. God had been good to him.

The Master Shoemaker asked him to remain at the school as a shoemaker. He promised to pay three marks a day plus room and board. This was good pay at that time so he decided to stay. He worked a ten-hour day and had 2 cups of coffee in the morning. He realized that education was worth it because not only did he get paid, he worked only ten instead of thirteen hours a day, and he got two cups of coffee in the morning.

Mother and Emelia wrote often and congratulated him for becoming a licensed shoemaker.

Alexander started saving money so he could join his mother. It took many months even working overtime. The shoemakers' workshop was filled with the rapa-tap-tap sound of the hammers.

Finally the time came to arrange his trip. His good aunt, Sanna, gave him socks, shirts, and lunch for the trip. His passport was ready and he bought his ticket in Oulu for 300 marks or 60 American dollars. He left at the end of June 1902. [This was right after his nineteenth birthday.] The day before he left he went to the parsonage and said goodbye to the pastor who had been so good to him. The pastor advised him to join a temperance society, as Finns had very few churches in America and much alcoholism. I am happy that you are going to help take care of your mother and your sister. Stay temperate. Remember your childhood faith in God. Remember that we are saved by grace and we receive forgiveness for our sins through the blood of Jesus. God bless your journey.

With tears in his eyes, Alexander left the parsonage. He still had to say farewell to his Uncle Jussi Anttila, who had taught him to read and had given him spiritual counsel. From there he went to say goodbye to other relatives.

The next day a group of young people were at the railroad station and they sang Farewell to Thee and Maumee Laulu, the Finnish national anthem. The train left for Hankoniemi. [Note from JRB: There is no such name on my modern map of Finland, but there is Hankö which is near Helsinki and is a seaport. *More than 12,000 Finns sailed from Hankö in 1901 because of political troubles with Russia—Encyclopaedia Britannica.*] The next day he boarded a ship named Polaris that brought the travelers to Hull, England. He went by train across England to Liverpool and waited nine days before boarding a ship. To pass the time they toured the city, museums and saw other interesting sights including beggars dressed in rags.

He finally boarded the elegant Cunard Line Saksonia (Saxon) for Boston, Mass., in the first part of July. America and Boston seemed very large and marvelous, but they didn't see much of Boston before they were on the train for East Tawas, Michigan. East Tawas reminded Alexander of Oulu.

At the small station, Maria, Alexander's oldest sister, who was married and had lived in America for several years didn't recognize the well-dressed young man who was her brother. She was expecting to find a young man in homespun clothes with boots on his feet.

They went to their mother's home and joined her and sister Emelia and Maria's husband for coffee. (Ten pounds of Arbuckle coffee cost a dollar.) There was a lot to talk about. The happiest person was Alexander who was reunited with his mother and favorite sister Emelia.

Mother asked about confirmation. She was pleased. It was common that when immigrants came to America from Finland the men got drunk. Alexander felt this was terrible and promised his mother he would never drink or fight. A person could find better things to do. In Oulu the young people sang:

> *Now to you Finland dear*
> *We make a vow*
> *That we are against drunkenness,*
> *We defend you forever,*
> *That powerful, poisonous river we will block entirely*
> —*K. Hammer*

The Iron Range

In East Tawas the only work was logging. The summer went and fall came and the men were taken into the woods to make railroad ties. Alexander was not like his father had been—logging was difficult for a shoemaker. The shoemaker's railroad ties were so twisted they would have made better windmill blades. Alexander decided to seek other work, and through his sister Wilhelmina (Minnie) God sent word that he should come to Mountain Iron, Minnesota, as there was lighter work and better wages.

Alexander left Michigan, telling his mother that he would send money to her and sister Emelia so they could come there, too. In Mountain Iron he found work on the railroad that paid $1.60 a day. With room and board at $10 a month he was soon able to send money so that Mother and Emelia could join him. They brought along a loom for weaving that Father had made.

The Merritt brothers had discovered iron ore about 1890 some 70 miles north of Duluth at a site they named Mountain Iron. The railroad that was built to bring that ore to Lake Superior was soon extended to other sites where ore was found and more towns sprang up: Hibbing, Chisholm, Buhl, Kinney, Virginia, Eveleth, Gilbert, Aurora, Biwabik, and others. Immigrants from many European countries including Finland arrived to work in the mines and on the railroads. Some immigrants built supposedly temporary homes thinking that when they got wealthy they could return to their native lands, but most remained in their new homeland.

Many Finnish people were among the immigrants and some were drawn to taverns, drinking and rough living. There was a great need for a church and a congregation to counteract this behavior.

Finally a pastor came and established a church and Alexander, Emelia, and Mother joined immediately. Pastor Salovaara rode horseback from one town to the next. There were many who had brought their faith in God and Christian principles from Finland and wanted to lead their fellow countrymen into a moral and devout life. They were inspired to establish a congregation and a place where God's word could be preached.

There were too few Finnish pastors to provide services every Sunday in each town. Since drunkenness was considered the biggest social problem among the Finnish immigrants, a Temperance Society was organized to provide good fellowship without alcohol. Alexander directed a drama club to present Christian-oriented temperance message plays, and they drank a lot of coffee. It was there that Alex met a young maiden, Hulda Hauta, who had just arrived from Finland in the summer of 1905 and was living in her sister's home.

Alexander bought a shoemaker business and lived with his mother and sister Emelia. In the fall Alex and Hulda became engaged and when Pastor Salovaara came at Christmas he performed their marriage ceremony on Christmas Eve, 1905. The wedding was held at the Temperance Hall where they had met.

Happiness and Sadness as Life Goes On

Alexander and Hulda moved into the home where he lived with his mother and sister. He built another small home for his mother and sister to move into, but he continued to provide for them. Hulda was his dear wife but his mother was also dear to him and he had promised that he would take care of his mother after his father died.

Alex and Hulda's marriage was made in Heaven. It was a peaceful home, which they established on a Christian foundation so that God could bless it as their isle of happiness here on earth.

The Temperance Society grew and was very active with weekly meetings. Alexander remembered his own difficult childhood and encouraged the Society to nurture its children. He was elected Sunday School Superintendent and made sure the children learned to read so they could attend confirmation classes without facing the disappointment he had. Young parents taught Sunday School at the Temperance Hall.

When Alexander and Hulda celebrated their first wedding anniversary they were happy to know that the next summer they would become parents. Their small home was furnished simply with furniture they received as wedding gifts and some cupboards made from boxes covered with lace. A much-used Singer sewing machine was also covered with a lace cloth. They couldn't afford artwork on the walls so they decorated with colorful pictures from business calendars.

Sister Emelia assisted Hulda often. Mother Wilhelmiina was living the closing days of her life devoutly, hoping and praying that God would let her see her grandchild before she died. She had been a midwife in her day but she was now weak and did little more than read God's word and pray. They had bought a large family Bible when they could afford it, knowing that it is the only foundation for life. This Bible remains in the family as a precious memory.

Winter went and spring came. Winter had been long, stormy, and cold. On June 10,1907, Alexander and Hulda's first daughter was born and was named Helmi Seliina. When Pastor Salovaara came to town, she was baptized. Grandma rejoiced with happy tears in her eyes. It was a hot July Sunday and it seemed as if the flowers of the field around the Keto home rejoiced in the heat of the sun while the Heavenly Son, Jesus Christ, entered the little one's heart. God's warm sunshine had been planted in this little one's heart to the joy of her parents, grandmother and Aunt Emelia. All were happy.

> *I am a seed planted in your garden*
> *And created for Heaven.*
> *And from birth desired in His care.*

In August, Mother Wilhelmiina's health failed further. One morning Emelia came running and asked Alex and Hulda to come, as Mother was ill and asking for them. She said her farewell and soon, happily trusting in God, moved into eternity. The pastor was asked to come and conduct the funeral services. In those days they had black carriages and horses for funerals. The pastor gave a good sermon and she was buried in the Virginia cemetery.

> *Now in my life I sing a new hymn*
> *And I leave everything when I die.*
> *The Lord Jesus is one I will never leave*
> *He won't abandon me But will bring me home.*

So this good and beloved woman moved into eternity but God had allowed her to see her precious grandchild, Helmi.

Children

In August Pastor Salovaara went back to Finland. The church members were sorry to see him leave, as there was a shortage of pastors and much work to be done in the Lord's vineyard.

The Temperance Society built a building with an upstairs hall and rented the ground floor to a hardware store. Young couples met regularly with their families in the large hall on the second floor, which was a center for social activities. Young couples often gathered there with their children. Alexander and Hulda added three more children to their family. After Helmi Seliina, had come Leah Aallotar, Maria Emelia, and Heimo (Herman) Andrew Aapeli.

At that time Pastor John Wargelin traveled from town to town to conduct church services. He baptized Leah Aallotar.

The Christmas program at the Temperance Hall was a memorable event for children. A huge tree was set up with candles. Gifts and candy from Santa Claus were under the tree to be distributed after the children's program. In the early years there was often no pastor available to speak so lay persons such as Lydia Kangas and Minnie Pesttula who were teachers at Suomi College spoke. Other speakers were Mrs. Edward Ala, Victor Frasa, and Alexander Keto.

When a church was finally built a pastor, M. E. Merijarvi, who lived in Eveleth, conducted services in Mountain Iron. Alexander was on the construction committee. At that time his sister Emelia was being courted by August Takala. She worked in the post office in Pat Hagen's general store. Aunt Emelia was special to the Keto girls, and often visited their home. When the next Keto child was born, Vaino (Wayne) Henry Alexander, she made Charlotte Russe, a special dessert to be served at the baptism. Wayne became a special favorite of hers.

Their home was always open for meetings of church groups as well as preachers of God's Word and children. The gentle and undemanding Hulda was a gracious hostess who never complained. Alexander loved her and held her in high esteem for teaching the children to be obedient and Christians.

The children were not allowed to miss any church events. They were given only two options after confirmation: to be a Sunday school teacher or attend a Bible study class. The boys chose the latter. The parents wanted the children to remain active in the church throughout their lives and worked hard to establish that habit pattern.

Life wasn't easy for the shoemaker. He had to provide for his family and remodel and enlarge the home as the family grew. In the evening after work they played music, sang and conversed together. He often had to leave for a meeting. He was a village council member for many years, a member of the library board for 8 years, Justice of the Peace for 12 years, president of the Minnesota Temperance Society for 20 years, a Knights of Kaleva member, Sunday School superintendent for 30 years, a church council member, chairman of the district church council, and a member of the board of Suomi College for 15 years. He also was the reporter and salesman for the Amerikan Suomitar and Paivalehti, two Finnish newspapers. As he was so busy and often away from home, most of the task of rearing the children fell to Hulda. She was quiet in temperament, but she enjoyed her children and the bonds of love between them were strong. The children had a lot of fun with her when Alex was on trips or at meetings.

Alexander insisted the children should be obedient. One night two of the older girls went to the library with orders to be home at 9 p.m. when the village whistle (curfew) sounded. The girls arrived home at 9:20 and the door was locked. When they knocked, Father came to the door, stared long, and asked, "Is it now 9:00? Let this be the last time you come in late." The girls said good night and quietly went upstairs to bed.

Emelia was a Sunday school teacher and attended church regularly. While working in the post office she remembered a little girl who had lost her front teeth so when she asked for the mail she said her box number as tuu tikti tuu instead of two sixty two. Emelia left her job in the post office after she married August Takala. She called the pastor for people, as many had no phone. She enjoyed doing this because Pastor Merijarvi was so friendly and courteous.

Emelia was very happily married and fixed up her home beautifully and artistically. One of her nieces, Marie, brought her mail on her way home from school. At Christmas she gave Marie a doll chest with an illustrated poem glued on the cover. Helmi received a bible and Leah a bible history.

One day Alex and his family received sad news. Emelia had died on July 4th. Her marriage had lasted only a short time. Others were celebrating Independence Day, but the Keto home was sad. The children climbed upstairs and cried. Father came to see if they wanted to go to the celebrations but when he saw them crying he again cried with them. Emelia was buried in the Virginia cemetery near her mother and after the funeral Emelia's husband came and they sang songs from the Sunday school songbook.

> *You have taken me away—No one can judge me,*
> *I am singing a joyous new song.*
> *The cage is broken—The bird is gone.*

[Note: She died in childbirth. Emelia was not much taller than four feet and probably not large enough to carry a baby to full term and delivery.

—Lillian Beck Fuller, Johan's daughter, and niece to Emelia.]

Life Calls

Hulda and Alexander had two more daughters, Tellervo Sylvia who was born shortly before Emelia died and Minerva Elizabeth who was born four years after Emelia's death. These two youngest sisters became very close.

The shoemaker wanted his seven children to be educated. After they finished high school they continued their education in whatever profession they chose for their life's work. The oldest daughter Helmi graduated from Duluth Teachers College with a B.A. degree. She taught or was a school principal in Virginia, Minnesota, for many years. She was also a Sunday school teacher and the secretary of the Minnesota Luther League board. She spent many summers at a Bible camp as a girls' chaperone. The Lord was an important part of her life and she not only volunteered her time for his causes, but also tithed to the church. She felt rewarded that God had blessed her life in every way, although there were many, many hard times, too.

While going to school, as all of the Keto children did, they earned money during summer vacations to help pay for their educations.

Alexander's Great Loss

When Hulda, Alex's wife, was the president of Hope Ladies Aid in the church she directed the study of a book Daavidin Huoneen Herra (The Lord of the House of David) over the winter. The following spring, three guest speakers came from Finland to participate in evangelistic services, which brought people from all over America to Mountain Iron. The event was a success: a refreshing and inspirational event for young and old. The women were kept very busy preparing meals for the people attending. These sessions were serious studies for faith strengthening, not emotionally rousing revival meetings.

Years passed and all of Alex and Hulda's children were on their own. All had married except two. Hulda's health was poor—her heart was weak and the children knew she could die at any time. The children and families spent their vacations with their parents. It was hard to leave, as they knew that they might not see Mother again. They loved her for her warm amiability, joyfulness and merriment as well as for her serious faith in God. She didn't travel much, but spent her time baking and cooking and accommodating the busy schedules of the members of her large family.

On the evening of October 10, 1944, their close friends Manda and Kusti Wainio had come to visit. They discussed church activities and world affairs. [This was during World War II.] Hulda fixed a lunch with coffee. She had a cup of coffee in her hand and said, "If people knew that this world isn't our permanent place…" and she dropped her head and the cup fell. Alex took her into his arms but death had come quietly and peacefully. Hulda had visited the cemetery earlier and told her neighbor that she would be there before long.

All of the children came to the funeral. Pastor Frank Pelkonen conducted the funeral service in the Messiah Lutheran Church, and his wife sang. Hulda was a noble, gentle wife, a Christian mother, and a good congregation member, and the church was filled with people and flowers.

The people sang the familiar:

> *Into thy hands, dear Lord, I give myself forever more.*
> *My soul, my body and my all*
> *Take them O Lord and accept them.*

They returned from the burial to the family home. Coffee an' was served. [A common Minnesota expression.] When other people were gone the children sat with their father and remembered their wife and mother. The youngest son, Wayne, remembered how he attended Bible class at Mother's insistence. He said he wouldn't be where he was if Mother hadn't made him go.

The youngest daughter Minerva couldn't speak a word nor could she cry. She had been with Mother after the other children had left home. She asked for her mother's robe as her mother looked like an angel in it. Others took pictures, jewelry, and flower vases, dishes, and furniture.

For a few days before they returned to their homes the children sat with father and sang familiar hymns. Finally, with tears in their eyes they kissed father goodbye and the shoemaker was left alone.

Loneliness

The shoemaker was lonesome in his quiet house. He thought he would weave a carpet out of the silk rags Hulda had been cutting. Then he moved Hulda's handwork out of sight into another room behind the sewing machine. He wondered how many rags Hulda had cut in her lifetime as well as how many socks she had darned and how many loaves she had baked when the children were home. Now she was gone and almost all of the children had moved away. Helmi, the oldest daughter, was in Germany with the Girl Scouts. The older son, Herman, still lived at home but he was courting Lempi, a schoolteacher of Finnish ancestry. That and his newspaper job which demanded his time at all hours kept him from seeing much of his father except for an occasional supper.

So Alex felt all alone. He walked around the room and looked out at the mountain ash trees he had planted years before. It was fall and loaded with berries. The gold-breasted warblers will soon show up to eat them. The long winter would soon arrive. He was annoyed by the tick-tock-tick-tock of the wall clock that broke the silence, and he almost hoped the clock would break down.

He went to the bookcase and took down a book of sermons and sat down to read. He was so engrossed that he no longer heard the clock ticking nor even its chiming. Finally he became tired, closed the book and said a long prayer. He thought about the next day. He would clean the stovepipes before winter comes. He was amused to remember how when Hulda was still alive he would lose patience and get angry trying to rejoin the pipes after they had been cleaned. Hulda would say, quietly, "Listen, Alexander, some things require a lot of patience," and soon the pipes would go back in place. Now he thought, Surely that Hulda was a wise wife not to lose patience with me.

Just as he was going to sleep the telephone rang. It was his youngest daughter Minerva calling from Washington, D.C. She was in the Army Nurse Corps and was getting a furlough and would fly into Duluth and come to visit her father. He went to sleep happily.

Helmi's involvement in Girl Scout work led to her being asked by the National council to go to Germany to work with girl scouts there after World War II. She traveled with a woman from Duluth. She wrote often to her widower father who lived with his oldest son. One day he received the following letter:

Thursday, Sept 18
Augsburg, Germany
Dear Father,

We are here now. There are five large groups that include Lithuanians, Latvians, Ukrainians and two Polish girls. They are being moved so we won't work with them. These are homeless girls. They are beautiful, happy, and well behaved. They sang songs and talked. Their leader invited us for coffee after the program. Their living quarters were in former German workers' apartments. Every family had one room.

At the Ukraine camp we were invited to attend their meetings. The children were so well behaved. No giggling or yelling.

There was a plan to move these 3700 people to another camp. They had lived here a year and arranged a school, church, and meeting place. But word came later that they wouldn't be moved. Their prayers were answered.

Today we were in Haunstetten Lager. There they were worried because many were going to be put out of the camp as they were anticommunist and Russia is a U.N member. These people had nowhere to go. Germany wouldn't feed them and the U.S. couldn't take them. War debts are so huge. Some criminals have gotten into these camps and they are being sorted out.

Father, I don't understand the world's politics.

UNRRA is trying to get these people back to their own countries. They didn't feed 800,000 people. The Polish are being repatriated back to Poland. It is sad when 69 pairs of shoes arrive and 700 people need them.

In one camp we were shown their workrooms. There were sewing rooms. Old clothes were made over from clothing sent from America.

In the city I saw the place where the Augsburg Proclamation was written in 1930. Sunday we are going to church at the 9th division chapel. The Red Cross will arrange a ride so we can see this old city on a tour.

It is late, have to get to bed. Tomorrow is another busy day. Hello to everyone. I am feeling fine. Don't worry. God is here too, Father.

Love, Helmi

On her return from Germany she made a side trip to Finland. She visited her mother's and father's relatives. She saw what had once been her father's home. She attended the Oulu church. She visited her uncle Nickolai in Oulu and met many cousins there. She attended her mother's church in Teuva and had an opportunity to see a cousin's baby baptized. From Teuva she went to Kaukajoki to visit her brother-in-law's relatives. One of them was a widow in a wheelchair who made cookies and cloudberry jam. Her late husband had been a school-teacher for over 40 years. She offered Helmi a book from her library and she chose the History of Finland.

On her way home she visited her sister Leah and family who were doing missionary work among the Finns working in gold mines in northern Ontario, Canada. She brought her sister's family souvenirs and greetings from Finland. She also took part in the dedication of a new church. When she came home her father and she had much to talk about.

Helmi also brought Leah's 12-year-old daughter with her from Canada. What a joy it was to Alexander to have his children and grandchildren visit, and especially to have a granddaughter who spoke really good Finnish instead of the Finnglish that most American-born younger Finns now spoke.

The youngest daughter Minerva who was married to a schoolteacher and lived in Los Angeles, California, also arrived for a visit.

When winter came and the shoemaker was alone again he decided to go to Michigan to visit daughter Leah who was a pastor's wife. Leah and her husband had finished their mission in Canada and returned to a rural parsonage in Michigan. One day he asked Leah what she would think if he remarried. The daughter said, No one can take Mother's place and what if the whole family falls apart as often happens?" The Shoemaker said he was lonely and that he didn't see anything wrong in widowers remarrying after a year. Leah then said it was her father's own business, "but you asked my opinion which I expressed without malice." This subject was dropped. The shoemaker left to go home but he had a woman on his mind whom he had met at Bible camp last summer. He went home to loneliness—only loneliness.

Alex finally told his daughter Helmi and son Herman, who lived with him in Mountain Iron, that he had decided to go out West to live or at least look around. The oldest son, Heimo (Herman), was about to be married and bought the home from his father. Helmi moved to an apartment near where she taught in Virginia, Minnesota. Helmi and Herman accepted without question their father's right to pursue his own life.

Seattle, Washington

Hilma Koski had been a widow for ten years and lived alone. Her son Eli, one of five children, was in the service in post-war Japan. Hilma had decided she would never remarry but in 1948 she went to a bible camp in Minnesota. There she met the shoemaker. They had many common interests and their friendship grew. She returned to Fort Lawton in Seattle to work at her well-paying job with the U. S. Army.

When the shoemaker arrived in Seattle he attended a Finnish church the first Sunday and then looked up Hilma to renew their acquaintance.

He made a trip to Los Angeles to visit Minerva and her family. He admired the flowers in bloom in the winter and the oranges ripening on the tree and thought about the snow-covered yard he had left in Minnesota. He was impressed with his son-in-law who was a high school teacher and appeared to be a good husband to Minerva.

He spent a week seeing the beautiful sights of southern California, which he concluded were indescribable. Minerva had no problems accepting the possibility of her father's remarrying, although she admitted it would seem strange.

Alexander went back to Seattle with its clean, healthy climate, the blue Pacific shoreline, and its snow-capped mountains—another place among the most beautiful of the Creator's handiwork. He and Hilma were married Dec 1, 1948 in the Suomi Synod parsonage of Pastor Otto Kaarto. They bought a home in Salmon Bay near Seattle with a beautiful view of the fishing boats and large ships traveling under the Ballard Bridge and at night the lights of the city.

Alex became a shoemaker again and set up a business near Fort Lawton where he served mostly servicemen. One day a general brought some shoes in to be repaired. He said he was going to Korea for the third time and he wanted a new pair of shoes made. The shoemaker wished him God's blessings; the general felt that God could use a shoemaker. The general asked Alex to pray for his safety, so they knelt to pray even though Alex could only pray in Finnish. The general returned later to thank the shoemaker for his safe return.

A Miracle

The shoemaker and Hilma took a bus one Saturday from Fort Lawton to Inter Bay. As they were crossing the street to board the Ballard 18 bus for home they were struck by a large truck. The shoemaker was unconscious, having been hit in the head. He was taken by ambulance to Maynard Hospital along with his wife who needed only first aid to her ankle. She was released the next day.

Doctors had little hope for the shoemaker's survival. Helmi flew to Seattle but her father was in poor condition, unable to recognize anyone, or speak or answer. She notified his other children, stayed a week and then returned to her teaching job in Virginia, Minnesota.

This was a difficult time for his wife and children. They and several church officials prayed for him. After 25 days he regained consciousness enough to be released to go home. His daughter Marie, a nurse, flew out from Detroit to care for him. He was lucid at times but sometimes unconscious. Marie suggested they sing hymns and the shoemaker joined in. She read him cards and letters that had come when he was hospitalized. Miraculously after four days his mind was clear as a bell—he had recovered. They sang:

> *Thanks be to God For all your grace,*
> *That during my life I have been able to feel.*
> *Thank you for the brightest spring like days,*

Thank you for the heavy sad days of fall,
Thank you that the prayers
Were heard by you in great numbers.

Faith and God's Will

When the shoemaker became well he gave thanks to the Lord. When he visited the doctor he told him he was a good doctor but there is a Greater Physician who had heard many prayers. The doctor agreed.

In the fall the shoemaker and Hilma decided to make a trip to California to visit Minerva and her family who were now living in Visalia where Minerva's husband was the school superintendent. They enjoyed their three grandchildren. It was warm and wonderful to sit in the swing and admire the surroundings. But the trip had to end and they returned to Seattle. They rested and sang a song about the home in heaven where there is no sorrow or worries.

A Wonderful Trip

The shoemaker and Hilma planned a trip after Christmas to visit all the children and grandchildren if God would allow it. They observed Christmas in their home with a small table tree.

In the spring they took a train to Duluth, Minnesota, where Helmi met them. She drove them to Virginia, Minnesota, where they joined sons Herman and Wayne and Wayne's three children. Herman had married Lempi and the family gathered at their new home in Virginia. [Herman was a newspaper reporter and columnist for the weekly *Range Facts* published in Virginia.] Younger son Wayne was tall and athletic and was a high school athletic coach and physical education teacher. One of Wayne's sons was named Alexander after the shoemaker. Wayne's little three-year-old daughter had long hair and Grandpa braided it. The shoemaker and Hilma stayed in Virginia with Helmi, making visits to nearby Mountain Iron to see Alexander's old friends.

They headed for Michigan where there were three more Keto daughters and their families. On the way they stopped in Ironwood, Michigan, to visit Hilma's daughter. The shoemaker was pleased to be welcomed warmly. In Pelkie, Michigan, they visited at Leah's home, the parsonage where many prayers had been said for him after his accident. A spring snowstorm gave them a chance to stay longer and rest from traveling. Evenings they drank coffee and talked. On Sunday they attended the Nisula church. After visiting for over a week they moved on to

Traverse City to Sylvia's home. Traverse City on Lake Michigan is known for cherry trees. They attended a non-Finnish Lutheran church.

Next in Detroit they visited Alex's daughter Marie, the nurse who had visited her father during his convalescence. They also visited a niece, Alex's older sister's daughter, who had suffered through many surgeries and were amazed that medical technology had been able to prolong her life. Marie's sons had matured and were impressively polite to the shoemaker and Hilma.

From Detroit they took a long train ride back to Seattle, which gave them time to reflect on their joyful trip. They arrived happily at their pleasant home on Salmon Bay with memories of having seen all the children loving the Lord.

Sitting in their recliners the shoemaker and Hilma sang

what a good and precious thing It is to thank our Lord
Who is our dear Father and gives us all our needs.
So now I wish with gladness
Bring Him thanks Admitting God's goodness
And all deep thoughts.
When here in God's garden
The seeds have been planted.
He at an older age
Will bring fruits aplenty.

THE END

EPILOGUE

Alexander Keto died at his home, 4211-21st Ave. West, Seattle, on January 27, 1955, at the age of 71 from an acute coronary occlusion. He was buried in Virginia, Minnesota.

He had been in Seattle for six years, and his memoirs were very likely written during that time.

His death certificate had no surprises: he was born in Finland on July 22, 1883, was a retired shoemaker, a citizen of the United States, and had a wife Hilma who survived him.

APPENDIX C

THE WORLD WAR JOURNAL
OF
J. LENNART BECK

FOREWORD
(By J. Robert Beck, 1990)

Sometime early in my life and probably shortly before I left home to join the Navy in World War II, my father, John Lennart Beck, showed me a small, red notebook he had stored in a steamer trunk in the garage of our home in Mountain Iron, Minnesota. He explained that this was a journal he kept during his service in the Navy in World War I and that I should remember to preserve it for future generations.

Just after he died, almost thirty years later, I remembered to locate and preserve that journal. The journal has now been in my possession for 21 years during which I made a few attempts to decipher the handwriting, but found the job more formidable than my time and patience permitted. Now, in 1990, inspired by the Mountain Iron Centennial and with more disposable time, I have finally deciphered and transcribed it. The thirty typed pages that follow are, I believe, a nearly perfect transcript. I have attempted to be faithful to the punctuation and spelling of the original, and have done no editing. I believe that I have deciphered all but perhaps two or three words exactly as they were written.

In most cases I cannot identify the people named. I expect that even if my father were living today he would not remember them all. There are a few, however, that I can identify:

Harry: This was Harry Slater. Lennart and Harry remained friends as long as they both lived. They rarely saw each other except at the reunions of the Fighting 7th Minnesota Naval Militia, but I think they corresponded fairly regularly.

<u>Helen:</u> Helen Slater, Harry's sister. I don't think she was ever a serious romantic interest for Lennart, but was a welcome correspondent, especially during the war.

Mabel: (Hanson) whom Lennart eventually married and who became my mother. Even though they had been high school classmates, it was interesting to note that she did not appear in this diary for the first several months, and at no time during these years was she or anyone else an obvious one and only.

<u>Leo:</u> Leo Beck was Lennart's next younger brother. They were very close, having been graduated from high school together and having entered college and later enlisted in the Navy together. They remained close friends until Lennart died in 1969.

<u>Uncle Chas.:</u> Charles Bygden, brother of Lennart's mother. He was born in 1892, and was thus only two years older than his oldest nephew, Lennart.

There were two historical references in the diary that I felt needed some research:

<u>Halifax</u>: This was a reference apparently to Halifax, Nova Scotia, Canada, where "About one tenth of the city area was devastated in 1917 by the explosion of a French steamer carrying 3000 tons of TNT on colliding with a Norwegian steamer on its way with a relief cargo to Belgium."—(*Encyclopaedia Britannica*).

"December 6, 1917—1,654 deaths." (*World Almanac*).

<u>Quentin Roosevelt</u>: Youngest son of Theodore Roosevelt who was killed in air combat over Germany.

THE JOURNAL OF J. LENNART BECK

John Lennart Beck, December 1917

Notes by myself during my life in the Navy, March 27, 1917 to
_____*[No entry, but it was Dec. 1918]*

Saint Paul	Killingholme, Eng.
Duluth	Liverpool
U. S. S. Gopher	Brest
Great Lakes, Ill.	New York
Cambridge, Mass.	Pelham Bay
Philadelphia, Pa.	

Having failed to chronicle the important and foolish events previous to this I feel that a few words of explanation will help anyone who is unfortunate enough to get a hold of the booklet.

During the exciting or rather turbulent week that we had at Macalester over the petitions sent out by our pacifist contemporaries, I, with several of my classmates, enlisted in the 7th Division of the Minnesota Naval Militia.

If I remember correctly my enlistment begins on March 27 1917, and unless the Kaiser dies of a broken heart and dynasty before the same date in 1920 I'll still be in the service of my Uncle.

After six weeks of drill and pleasure in the Saintly City we were sent to Duluth. We spent about three weeks in the Armory there. Duluthians entertained us royally. Invitations to dinner came so fast that we couldn't fill the bill. We received cakes, candy and cookies from benevolent old ladies and frivolous members of the younger set.

The Navy relief societies gave us comfort kits, ditty bags and sweaters as well as towels, soap and other necessary articles that the government had failed to provide. Bankers forwarded sums of money large enough to pay us off.

While in St. Paul, we had staged a vaudeville show under the direction of Mr. Lundberg, our steward. We decided to raid the range with it and did so, clearing about 1200 dollars on the deal. This money was used for underwear and shoes.

By that time through some mysterious source the naval authorities found out that we were in Duluth. They also learned through the same source that the Navy owned an old gunboat that was stationed in the Duluth harbor. We were taken aboard and until the first of August we cruised unless we were otherwise detailed.

On the fifth of July we overtook the Hundredth Grenadier Band of Winnipeg and I was one of ten sailors who were chosen to act as an escort for them while on their concert tour.

The reception while on the trip was wonderful. Banqueted at every town and entertained royally, especially on the range, the Canadians went back with the praise of the hospitality of the Yankees, I am sure.

Dewey, Weber, Larson and Fleeter, the Gopher quartet, were headliners. Lundberg made the crowds laugh and we brought the crowds to their feet with our peppy songs. A ball followed each concert and it's needless to say that I made good use of the fine floors and music. But then someone is always taking the joy out of life and we were jerked back to Duluth and landed here at the Naval Training Station (Great Lakes) on the first of August.

24 days we spent fenced in Camp Paul Jones. Discouraged and despondent upon our arrival we soon found that the change was doing us good. Moreover, we found that we were the luckiest devils on the grounds.

Many of our fellows had not received their uniforms. Camping out had done *some* damage to their civilian clothes. Using one's shirt for a towel doesn't make it look any better either. Those were the conditions the men had to undergo while taking their vaccinations and inoculations. As we had a complete outfit we were doubly fortunate. The texture of the goods used in uniforms had changed from broad cloth to serge and an increase in price made your clothes allowance look like pin money.

From this we were moved into the 2 regiment. Then the first. While here I played some baseball and acted as company clerk. The other fellows were less fortunate and were detailed to digging ditches, cleaning streets, piling lumber, etc. Some are still there.

I'm in the radio school and from now on will try to make this thing look like a diary.

J. L. Beck

Sept. 13 [1917]

This may be an unlucky day to begin this but Uncle Sammy paid us on this day. That throws the jinx way off. Some of the fellows visited the Gopher.

I accepted an invitation to dinner Sunday and a bid to a dance on Saturday in Chicago. I may have to buy a smaller pair of shoes, but it will be worth it.

Mailed a letter to the Mac Weekly

No mail.

Sept. 17

Back after a few days of liberty.

Sat. at noon I left with Bunkie Price for Chicago as guests of Chaplain Moore.

He turned us over to a kindly couple at the Fine Arts Institute. A rotten orchestra furnished music and 200 jackies (?) trod the light fantastic with some of the elite of Chicago. Solo dancing, a farce, singing, lunch, and dancing was the general program.

The various hallways filled with the likenesses of the warriors and athletes of old were enticing and many a sailor boy glommed a lady and strolled through these.

I had the pleasure of escorting one of the ladies to her home in Oak Park. Her name, Jeannette. She's coming out to see me Wed. and I'm to go to see her on Sat. or Sun.

Went to church yesterday and had dinner with a streetcar conductor and his family. We had a good feed. The people were real nice. She was an American. He a Greek. We stayed there until 3:15 p.m. Went to a couple of movies, had supper and returned to the station at 7:30 p.m.

Two letters.

Wrote six last night.

Four of us slept in one tent.

Sept. 18

Jack Nelson went to Dunwoodie as did several others of our original co.

Co. B-1 moved to Camp Ross. Expect to leave the station by Friday. Harry goes with them. He is trying to transfer to the aerial service. So is Steve.

I seem to be more interested in the math of the thing (radio) than I am in receiving and sending. The course here is interesting and a fellow can get a good deal out of it if he applies himself. I'll work like the devil until I am shipped to Harvard. After that, if necessary, I'll loaf a little. They tell us that quarters are excellent and that liberty is generously bestowed. I earned extra liberty this week because I was the first to hand in a problem this morning. Pretty soft, eh?

Sept. 25

I have neglected this terribly. But I have been busier than the Kaiser will be, making good.

Jae was out with her parents. Very kindly was I asked to dinner on Thursday evening. Most graciously did I accept for Leo, Price, and myself.

We, however, are and have been in straitened circumstances and have been hanging onto our coin. Today I received a card relieving us of all obligations. Our hostess thru family entanglement asks us to postpone the deal. Payday comes in the delay so we celebrated by buying one package of vanilla wafers and two of chocolate caramels.

As Leo was lying on his bunk resting this noon he yelled, "Beat it!" We did, and a moment later were glad that we had. The spark or primary broke down and its wires came swishing and coiling thru the air onto the instruction tents. No one was injured.

It gets dark early and as we have no means of illuminating our tents we are usually in bed at a decent hour. Usually we are up until as late as 7:30.

Slater and the rest of the gang are still in Camp Ross.

Dug a ditch yesterday.

Mail still continues to come in a microscopic stream.

Progressing noticeably in my receiving. My appetite is still enormous.

The physicians are enjoying themselves, too. Much to our sorrow. You can guess why.[1]

I mustn't forget Peewee our newly acquired Master-at-arms. Hard? Say, he's a regular guy! He's so hard that they don't let him scratch his head in an arsenal for fear that the sparks should ignite the ammunition. He a Northwestern product recently transferred from grant Park.

He's about as popular as cactus in pajamas.

My head aches a little so will wring off.

Sat. Sept. 29

Theodore Roosevelt was here Tuesday but we held classes as usual and I didn't get around to see or hear him.

Leo was one of a few who were fortunate enough to get away. Trust him!

Mail from everybody! Believe me, nothing is more welcome in a camp like this than a letter. It doesn't make much difference who it is from. The fact that it is from one who occasionally thinks enough of you to sit down and scribble a few cheering words make him your friend for life.

Uncle Chas. writes that he has a new car and plenty of room for the two of us any time we want to come and visit him.

He'd sent me two letters and in one I discovered that I am the owner of 8.54 of perfectly good dollars. School begins on Monday.

I took a test yesterday and I'm beginning to think or perhaps realize that I'm not as smart as I thought I was. Application, my dear boy, and concentration for you.

I'm going to get 12 words by next Friday or go bugs in the attempt.

The station foot ball plays Marquette University today. If I had had the necessary amount of cash I think that Milwaukee would have had the pleasure of my presence. The team is going to be a hummer or I'll miss my guess.

My M adorns my chest these days but under my jumper. It comes in mighty handy on these cold frosty mornings.

Lt. Bill wrote also. He's in the Dodge Training Camp, but expects to be in New Mexico soon.

Andy Johnson has been ordered to the U. S. then to France I spose.

Helen has been slow in answering so expect a letter any time.

---

1. Lennart told me that he and all others scheduled to go overseas were circumcised at Great Lakes if they had not been before, so I ssume that this is what he is referring to. JRB

Oct. 6

This was to have been payday but we poor N. N. V's didn't get a red penny. Uncle Sam thinks that if we won't save he'll do it for us, I guess. Anyway he wants to make sure of at least $35.90 worth of service to fine us on. That makes it necessary for us to continue my usual financial condition for another month. I am the possessor of $6.54 in real money in St. Paul and I sent a postal card after it yesterday.

I sold a pair of Price's sox for 35 cents and borrowed a dollar of Phelps. Had a pie-a-la-mode, cup of coffee. Purchased two boxes of Cracker Jack, a tablet, some envelopes, and 50 cents worth of stamps. Have been writing of my hard luck to everybody. See if it works!

Yesterday I got a package and a half. The whole package was from sweet Susan and contained rocks[2], sandwiches, candy and gum. I don't ever remember kissing her but I'll bet a pickle that I'm going to even if she's married when I get back.

The two Gilbertson girls sent Leo and I a package of dates jointly and if you think that our jaws didn't work for an hour or so without a let-up you're a long way off.

Fate decrees that I don't dine with the Flitcraft's again. I'd have car fare down but it's too blamed far to walk back. Besides I have an ingrown toenail.

Bonehead is on his way to Harvard. Good riddance! He means well enough but he's continually slapping some one just when he shouldn't or swearing or puffing a "fag"[3] or asking a ridiculously foolish question. Heaven knows I tried to convert the kid but what in hell was the use. If brains were money and cucumbers were a cent a bushel, he wouldn't have enough to buy a seed.

Of course I'm a smart guy myself. If I don't get a wiggle on Uncle Sam will have me down as a detriment instead of an aid.

Am going out for football.

Am mailing five letters.

Mary M. is again on my correspondent list. Beat that!

Sunday, Oct. 7, 1917

Retired at 7:10 last night. That is, I lit a candle, undressed, and crawled into my blanket and covered up with Phelp's. Then I read the Sat. Evening Post until he and she were married happily. Blew out the candle as soon as I had finished the Cracker Jack and slept peacefully until Price came in (12:30) and raved about the

---

2.   A kind of cookie.
3.   Cigarette

little actress that he had been out with. I slumbered again and didn't wake up again until the sentry threatened to pull me out.

Wrote to Amy and Lillian and Tommy. Nuf sed.

Oct. 13

I was Corporal of the Guard this week and didn't take the test. Leo is eligible for Harvard. L Rock wrote from Harvard and Jack from Dunwoodie. Both claim that each is in the best place in the world.

As Corporal I had the pleasure of accosting every girl that strolled the campus. I demanded to see the passes. Believe me, I was some Corporal. I spent 56 hours on the job and wallowed in the gooiest mud imaginable.

That near the surface was as oozy as cake batter. Underneath about three inches of the thick fluid was a more glutinous substance that insisted on sticking to your boot and to itself so strenuously that unless one trod carefully he'd place a clean sock into the ooze.

Tomorrow I expect to play foot ball against Pee Wee's company. If I don't break my neck I'm going to make the Harvard draft. No Bull either.

At last Co. B-1 leaves for the coast, Dolly, Schmitty, and O'Neill excepted.

Thursday we were told that unless we purchased coupon books ($5) from the Navy Relief we'd get no liberty. Saturday, due to some unknown reason the order was cancelled until payday. Here's hoping I'm no longer here.

Birthday coming. Expect eats from various sources. Watch this book for results.

Lee had an offer to teach geometry at the Y. He refused.

Steve is teaching algebra and arithmetic.

Oct. 22

I've a new pen now and ought to do better with this than I have been doing.

We were paid last Thursday and unexpectedly Uncle Sam gave me 50 bux.

Thurs. also took an exam or rather another fellow did for me and I became eligible for Harvard. Leo did, too, but this morning I was on the draft and Leo wasn't. My throat was cultured this morning and I'm all set for a trip across the continent to Cambridge.

We moved into barracks Sat. and slept in hammocks. It was the first time for many and a fellow next to me nearly broke his neck. After two attempts he gave it up for a bad job and slept on the floor.

As we had no lights we all turned in before seven. The next hour and a half was spent in the art of balancing and in rapid-fire exchange of remarks.

I tried to scour the grease out of one of the large iron kettles in the new mess hall but didn't have enough time Sunday morning. We went on liberty to Chicago at about 4.

Leo and I bummed around until midnite and retired at the Y Hotel. Rode in on a train this morning.

Some time hence I said I expected eats for my birthday. I got some but from a source totally unexpected. Mabe sent dates and fudge. Helen sent me a trench mirror and a scarf.

We go down to the main mess hall (about 2 miles) for our meals. They tell us that those jaunts are over and that we chow tonite in the new ones. My feet aren't kicking atall.

There goes assembly so must wring off.

Tues., Oct. 23

Yesterday we passed in review before Sec. Daniels. I read his speech in the papers last nite while on liberty in Waukegon

Oct. 24

Looks like another day of rest. All the fellows are sprawled along the walls reading or writing.

Yesterday thru the Parents' League in St. Paul I rec'd a letter from a Minnette Warren. She tells me she is a pianist (solo) with the Chicago Symphony. Her home is in St. Paul. Will have to look into this.

Last night about midnight we were all awakened by a loud noise that resembled a bursting bomb. While discussing what it might have been we heard another. Silence. We slept and this morning we found that our weight had pulled our hammock braces and the boards they were in from the wall.

I fully expected to be in Harvard by this time but here I am. If we don't get word to move today I'll give up hope of ever reaching the old place.

Should get a couple of letters today from ladies loyal.

Oct. 25

Letters from Bill and Mabel.

I've given up hope of ever getting to Harvard. I've been standing by ever since Monday and here I am still. The monotony of this is getting unbearable. Classes began this morning but I went on a work detail. A company or two went on a long hike.

Eats are fine here and things would be fine if we'd have something to do that would give us exercise. Another thing we ought to have is stools. These floors make hard seats.

I've been getting all kinds of mail so guess I'll stick. I finished the jam today. Guess I'll mosey over to the canteen and get some pie.

I'll bet I wrote 2 doz. Letters already this week.

Oct. 26

Sherman was right! Here I am still waiting to go east. This was just a repetition of the days that preceded. Here's the schedule: Reveille at five a.m. Dressed in the dark and washed. By the time everybody had his own clothes, enough light had trickled thru the east to permit sight of the deck. It was swabbed. Hammocks were lashed in time for chow at 6:45. Sausages & oat meal, coffee, bread & butter.

Muster at 7:45. Hung around till 9:30. From then on I spent my time until 11:00 in the code room. 11:45 muster and chow. 1 to 2:15 we laid around. Then assembly and we were marched down to the drill hall. Why? Nobody knows yet, although Pee Wee did make a speech. Just before chow Ensign Nichols addressed us and told us he was leaving tomorrow for France. Lucky Stiff!

We chowed at five and I am spending my evening writing letters & this. Now for the Merry Wives of Windsor.

Oct. 28

Oh, Boy! I'm going to Cambridge Tuesday. We signed up yesterday and all we'll have to do is pack up and go.

Yesterday I had been in the service seven months. I haven't got a commission yet, either. Just wait awhile, zats all. The Kaiser pulled one on me yesterday, too, indirectly. I was detailed to assist in the galley. I wasn't mad but I wept all the time I was there. You would too if you peeled and sliced onions. That wasn't the joke, however. I went to Chi on Liberty. Every time I met a wop up goes my nasal organ in disgust. Naturally anyone passing at precisely the same time would imagine that poor Antonio or Izzy was the one who smelled like a popular vegetable. It threw off suspicion but made me feel so uncomfortable that I bought a wristwatch. What my motive was I do not know but I sure purchased a peach.

I enjoy a good joke but when Kaiser Bill makes me smell so much like a wop that I walk into an Italian restaurant because I don't want to spoil the reputation of a strictly decent grub joint I won't stand for it. True, I'm not one of the 500 but some German is going to catch the devil for this.

Watch me.

My Prima Donna sent me a box of fudge and a splendid letter. Too bad she'll be in the city when I'm not here. Just my luck anyway.

Cousin Lil tells me she'll kiss me at Detroit. Gee, that makes me sore!

Nov. 1

She did! So did the rest of the family. We had a fairly good trip deducting, of course, the blizzard, rain and bus connections. The hills of N. Y. and Mass. were about all the scenery that I enjoyed. Got interested in a game of cards and a few stories.

We hit the place about 11 o'clock last night and it sure was a dead place. No sleeping arrangements had been made so we were turned loose on our own hooks and purses. Some of the fellows slept in the basement of this place but I, Plute, took a sub to the Hub. Slept at the Commonwealth and swiped all the loose stationery and one perfectly good towel.

The increased rate in postage goes into effect today and that's going to leave me flatter than a pancake financially.

Of course, to put on the old dog I had to address everything, I expect, Harvard U., etc. We are quartered in the attic of one of the old buildings. Still, you know, I might be in a trend! The grub is about as good as we had at Great Lakes. It was this noon. The fellows who have been here for some time say the feed is fine. Well, let's hope so. I can't say that I am crazy about the place yet because I haven't seen it all.

Nov. 2, 1917

I came, I saw and am conquered. Yesterday afternoon I just strolled around and studied the boastful church signs and leaning tombstones. All the churches evidently were built in the 18th century and are relics. Also everybody who ever died here for a while either did so at Bunker Hill or else was wounded so that he died as late as fifty years afterward from the effect.

Harvard itself I'll not attempt to describe as I couldn't do so. We are stationed in the Hemingway gymnasium. In the attic. It's a little cool and I think that studying here will be impossible. I possess all of ten cents and postage is 3 and 2 cents. Payday comes????

I was looking over a map and concluded that I have placed quite a distance between myself and home.

I slipped one over on our dear Uncle yesterday—mailed 15 pieces of mail.

Last evening Morgan, Edwards and I strolled. We started down the street to Harvard Square, the down toward the river. It was a beautiful night and the weather was zippy enough to make hiking good. Our friend was an architect and knew or recognized most of the beautiful buildings that we passed. Whenever in doubt we would go to the entrance and peruse the plate. Dropped into a movie and sat in front of a bevy of tickled women. Anyway they tittered nearly all the time.

Heard an interesting appeal to save food. Walked back and went to bed tired but well satisfied.

Eats are served to us with music, and by negroes. We had beans but if they are Bostonian, deliver me! Great Lakes for beans! The rest of the chow has been all that one could expect.

I'll have to buy a camera! If I try to tell anyone anything I can prove it. The West may be ok, but it hasn't the class! See?

I am not certain but I think that this is the first letter I ever wrote to Leo.

Nov. 5

A despondent letter from Leo and a different one from home. Leo is not on the draft yet and I'm afraid he's scheduled to spend a month or so more at Great Lakes. The poor kid feels rotten over it, too.

This town is teeming with women, mostly wild. I was out and spooned a bit last night and may have found a home. But—my financial condition is, well—rather strained, and I may lose out.

I began my course here today. Magnetism and Code. It will be the same all week. The proof we got is inexperienced and none too well versed with the scientific point of his subject. He knows that it's there but the why of it is as vague as it is with me. He graphed one thing today but could not give the formula. But he's so funny that he is interesting. Being from Minnesota, too, helps a lot even if he is from Duluth.

Barker, one of our number is inclined to be curious. Yesterday he came back about twenty minutes after dark. He was pale around the gills. It seems that he saw a large fire in an enclosure and went to a window for a peep. As he did so he saw the men slide a couple of caskets into the crematory. He's feeling none too well today, either.

Fortune smiled on me. I borrowed a dollar from Rock and missed all the guard duty and working parties.

Things are going to be busy with me from now on. If I fail to make entries in here from time to time you'll know why.

Nov. 9

I've been feeling rotten the last few days. Am on the binnacle list now. La Grippe.

Today is the ending of our first school week. The subject has been magnetism and we take finals this morning. I'll take it if the doctor permits me to. They are calling for understudies for deck ensigns. Am going to look that up.

Got a bunch of mail yesterday.

Nov. 10

Fortunately somebody in the record department failed to get me into a company. As I didn't have to muster I beat it to the Y and wrote three letters. My neck is a little stiff but I feel pretty good otherwise. May stroll over to Bunker Hill. I've a date tonite but as I am a little low on kale may plead off. That remains to be seen, however.

Decided not to go into the deck end of the deal. Will take a chance in this line.

Nov. 17

I've been been writing letters all week it seems and yet I couldn't catch up.

Mabel is writing letters that seem to be inspired by a rather strong liking for me.

Stayed in every night but one this week. Then I was in before eleven. Model young man.

Pulled down a 3.4 in Statics. Brings my average up to 3.2.

We, the Radio, are giving a big dance Friday. I must get out and find a nice girl some place. I just want to step the old dance off the worst way. When I get back home I know I'll be a regular *cut up*. The navy hasn't hardened me any but it surely has made me appreciate that little old neck of the woods that I call home.

Harry writes, may get into aviation. However, I've been a 'gob' too long to really expect it.

Leo writes: "Am on a special draft. May go to Frisco or I may go to the Receiving Ship at Boston or may join you at Harvard." That's all very well, Leo, but it is so indefinite!

Mother writes: "I sometimes wish I were a man and young enough to enlist."

Helen Slater says: "I hope Harry gets his chance and sends his German to his fair or smoky future and I hope he whacks over a couple for me."

My! The warlike women!

Nov. 21

Yesterday was payday and I'm almost broke again today. This evening I step out with a real nice young lady. Friday I may take her to a dance.

Leo has had a run of hard luck and is now in isolation at Great Lakes. He says it's like a brig. He says he's taking 15 words so he isn't faring badly at all. That's more than I can take.

Nov. 26

It's been a big week!

First of all my theory was absorbed so wonderfully that I pulled down a 3.8. This makes my average 3.4. My operating is rotten!

Saturday I rung in on a party and today I'm glad I went.

We began at a movie house and the place was loaded with kids. Doug Fairbanks was starring in a Western Comedy and the kids whooped and cheered. Talk about noise! It beat any ball game I've ever been to.

After the show we were turned over to our host and hostess, Mr. and Mrs. Paine of Winchester. They took us to their home in a big car and after dinner gave us our choice of going out or staying in for the evening.

Roy Hettinger (Wis.) and I felt that we would enjoy nothing better than just staying home.

Mrs. Paine worried over our colds and doctored us as though she were our mother.

Sunday a.m. after cutting myself with Mr. Paine's Gillette we broke our fast, went to church and just as we reached the house on our return the car balked.

Had a fine dinner and spent the afternoon very quietly while Mr. Paine and three machinists tinkered with the car.

Supper and then the car being ready we went for a ride which ended at Hemenway Gym. Doesn't sound wild but I must say I enjoyed it far more than I can express.

Nov. 29—Thanksgiving

Pulled down a 3.6.

Ate Thanksgiving Dinner at the Boston Ath. Ass'n.

Am standing a fire watch so I can get off for another big feed tomorrow.

I'm trying to catch up with my correspondence. Mail last week brought me:

1 pr. sox (Mpls. Assn.)

1 scarf (Anti-Suffrage)

2 Mac Weeklies

2 Boxes Candy—Ida Y and Helen

The other night we were all called out of bed and put on report for chewing the fat after taps.

No doubt many a fluttering heart and vibrating knee will endeavor to face the music about Wednesday or Thursday next.

I am Co. Reporter so I spose it's up to me to waste a few drops of ink in advertising the ninth company.

Dec. 1

I have been loafing all morning. The weather is ideal for it, too. The snow has melted and old J. Pluvius and his sprinkler butt in on dad Winter's nice big flaky snow. The condition of the streets can easily be imagined.

Yesterday Andy (Arn) and I were the guests of a Swedish Episcopal minister and family. Two grown up daughters entertained and were entertained by us. We indulged in eats (of course), singing, dancing, cards and checkers. The family name is Sundelof, Roxbury, Mass.

Edwards and I are attending a little party for four this evening. I don't feel at all lonesome but I certainly will feel that way about Xmas if Leo isn't here. It will be my first Xmas away from home. As they are in quarantine I don't even get letters from them. Leo writes often, though. I've missed the mail now for two days and just feel that I have some dandy letters.

Indications are that we are in the war for some time. To many fellows that doesn't mean much. To me it means that I may have to give up all hopes of ever attaining a degree and taking a course in journalism. If possible I am going to try to help dad out. He is getting old[4] and still has an ideal (Roosevelt's) family to bring up. If I should happen to be killed my insurance will be an aid as I intend to take out $5,000 with the gov't.

The U. S. isn't half bad. Here I am, getting an education, being paid, clothed and fed. I get nearly as much time to myself as I did in civil life and have less to worry about. If I wished to worry I spose I could. You know I may never touch the good old American soil after I once leave it, or I might lose a leg or an eye, who knows? Besides, who cares?

Yip Owens plays foot ball here today and I ought to look him up. But they have forced us to watch games so that it's going to be a fine day before I watch a foot ball game again this winter.

---

4.   At that time, John Beck, Lennart's father was 44 years old.

Northcliffe says that the U. S. will win the war. How well we know it! Now for a beauty sleep and then the party! Au revoir!

Dec. 9

A 3.6 this week.

Rock, Hazleton and I called on Miss Tiffany last night and we had a very good time gossiping and swapping news.

Lot of society last week and all kinds of variety.

A box of candy from Mabel.

Mrs. Wargstrom, the little Merry Widow is dead. The news came in a letter from Estelle and left me dazed for a moment. It doesn't seem long since she chased me around the house in Costin and I stepped on the nail. Her description of me: You crossy kit.

She wasn't young nor winsome but she was a lively old lady who could see the humor of almost any situation.

Monday Morning, Dec. 10

Began the week right. Caught sleeping in. For two weeks I'll be a regular stay at home.

Didn't get what I expected so have been free to move around as usual.

No mail for three days.

Heard Countess Mazzucchi on the Red Cross in Italy Saturday afternoon.

Assigned $15 per month to the folks. Am getting philanthropic, am I not?

Dined with Mr. and Mrs. Jackson Sunday. While there we met a man who had been to Halifax. His description of the awful disaster was most vivid.

Fire watch Sunday so I guess it's up to me to stay right in Cambridge during our vacation.

May be able to pick up a dollar or two standing watches for some of the fellows who want to go home.

Saw my proofs and I guess they'll do. I ordered 13 and now I'll have to figure up a mailing list. They won't be ready until Monday. That means that they won't get home until New Years. Probably won't get lost, anyway.

Dec. 26

Cash on hand	.05
In debt	10.00
Liabilities	9.95

That's another thing Kaiser Bill will have to answer for. Here I am $9.95 in the hole and 1900 miles from home and Xmas has just slipped by.

But—It was some Xmas at that. Feast, wine, women, mistletoe, music, dance and song! Lots of mail and even a few gifts. And all I sent out was a few cartoons pasted on cardboard!

Xmas was spent with the Rev. Sundelof and family of Roxbury and we did it in the good old Swedish style.

I played the part of Santa in the usual uncomfortable way.

I have been writing letters all day. Here's Andy! Guess we'll go out.

Dec. 30

Leo's of age tomorrow.

He expects to be out of isolation before long. Here's luck to you.

Poor Steve is in too.

Nothing really interesting has happened the last few days. We get Tuesday, Jan. 1 off.

The gym is colder than Minnesota these nights but we are hard and guess we'll live thru it ok.

In my Xmas articles (?) I forgot to mention Karin. Nice li'l girl.

Letter from mother yesterday and one from Mrs. Brookes today.

A rumor afloat that 600 will be sent to sea next week. I don't take 12 yet so guess I'm safe in saying that I won't go.

Feb. 27

The past two months or so have been busy ones.

But don't imagine for a moment that it's been all work. Far from it! In fact I don't believe in letting my education interfere too much with my good times even with the fate of the nation at stake. Some say that even Marc Antony was the same kind of a guy.

But I've finished my course and am going out of here as an Electrician (Radio) 3rd class. My assignment to duty will reach me today and as I've applied for and have been examined for aviation I have no doubt half a chance of become one of the many bird men of the nation. Time alone will tell and I'll know in a very few hours.

March 12, 1918

The few hours turned out to be a week and I failed to get in to the aerial service but was assigned to the armed guard out of Philadelphia.

I was transferred and reached there on the 3rd of March.

Hung around there for a week and a day. Chief called for two volunteers for aviation. Cation and I stepped out and here we are steerage passengers on the SS New York all set for France. Bon Voyage.

March 13

I began my trip by being a trifle sea-sick. Fortunately I didn't suffer very much and am feeling pretty good today.

In fact, I feel like eating a little but the grub has been fairly rotten.

Probably my condition is the cause of the above statement but I should worry. Only ten or more days of this rolling around the best part of the sphere and then?

A gob was nearly washed overboard. Was watching the waves roll in on the lower deck and an extra large one slopped in over the railing. Gobby had the presence of mind to fall on his stomach. That saved him but he sure got a dunking.

A couple of crap games furnished excitement for the rest of the morning.

Mar. 19

This has been about the longest week I ever spent in my life. I've had the pleasure? of being sea sick and sure will be glad when we get settled in France on good solid ground.

I've sized up sea sickness as the sister of Pessimism and am sure that a real pessimist will never be happy until he gets sea sick on this very craft.

You have to wear a gas mask to get by the galley into the dining room. And the grub sure has been rotten.

I've slept more and eaten less in the last few days that I ever expect to do again in the same length of time.

We are in the war zone and are being convoyed by American destroyers.

I need a bath, shave, hair cut and a square meal. I own 40 cents. They tell me money goes a long way over here, but I'm afraid my wants will never depreciate or my money stretch enough to satisfy me.

I sure have an awful bunch of letters to write. Lord knows when I'll get any mail myself.

March 23, 1918

Well here I am in the British Navy as it were detailed as a dry land sailor.

We are quartered in concrete bungalows. Twenty or so to each one. Our bunks are 3 soft pine boards mounted on two horses each a foot high. I sure wish I were fat now. My hip bones get sore sleeping on the blamed things. My N.N.V. blankets, too, are proving their inefficiency and I'm mighty glad that spring is here.

I was turned over to a chief radio electrician this morning. We have to learn the British Mag forms.

Grub is good but is handed out in rations. Got plenty this noon but my appetite is a little too large for some of the meals. Here's hoping that the U.S.A. soon takes over this place and gives us real beans. Get up from the table hungry and you'll live longer. That may be so but as our chances of being Zepped are good I'd like to go West on a full stomach.

The place is being sought by Germans and a week ago Tuesday nite a Zep flew over. The place is camouflaged and the hangars look as though they'd been wallpapered by a wop hanger and designed by a coon.

Lots of liberty is granted and I guess our money will go a long way toward having a decent time whenever we get any.

I just happened to think that every time I write in here I am broke. Can't go ashore and must do something so I read and then scribble in this or my diary.

There is a rugby game on this afternoon. May go.

Saw a Lima (Britisher) shooting craps with some gobs. Some of the fellows don't like 'em but I've yet to see a disagreeable one.

We are out in the country on a river bank. Sun's shining. Birds are singing and I don't feel right. My eyes are bothering me a little. Will report to sick bay tomorrow morning.

We were inspected (Tummy) this afternoon.

Guess I'll write to Mabel.

April 4

When I said I've yet to see a disagreeable Lima I must have been in a trance. One, a W.L. man, is continually casting slurring insulting remarks at the U.S. and if I weren't a peace loving chap and he was a little bit larger I'd show him a little bit of the bloomin' Yank doncherknow.

The eats situation here is rotten just now and we all hope for a good old American ship to come storming into the Humber with beans, coffee and other American delicacies.

Several machines have crashed but no one has been injured severely.

We are all looking forward to a pay day. Tomorrow is a scheduled one but time alone will tell whether tomorrow evening finds me ashore and flush or in the barracks and broke.

As we get about four times as much as the average lima we spend a deuce of a lot more. They resent this especially in the canteen and I wouldn't be at all surprised to see a small sized riot take place there.

The English seem to resent the fact that we, the Americans, are so free and easy going. They waste more time getting ready to do anything than we do in the execution. It's no wonder the war has lasted as long as it has. What these people need is a little touch of American push and aggressiveness. I hope for England's sake that this isn't a fair sample of England's fighting force.

I'm in a barracks with general electricians and others connected with the power plant. We all stand watches. The rest of our time is our own. We spend it reading, playing cards, and chewing the fat.

So far I have neglected to state that this station is at Killingholme, near Grimsby on the Humber River, England.

April 15, 1918

Feed is a whole lot better and the paymaster called on us last week.

The Germans, too, paid us a short visit and carelessly dropped a bomb here and there as they flew over.

They didn't do much damage but dropped a few within a mile of us.

Considering all things they have our location and no doubt on a clearer night would have blown us west or to Blighty.

Spent Friday evening and about a pound in Hull.

Yesterday went to Grimsby and Immingham. Fed up! Steak, bacon, eggs, cake, etc. No limit.

We take over the shack today. I'm on 4 to 8. Some ham.

Bill Thompson arrived Friday. Reports a package for me at Phila. Hope it gets here.

No mail for me yet

Probably I've been forgotten by them all.

April 28, 1918

I suppose that the first I ought to comment upon is the mail. So far I've received 10 letters and a card. They trickled in thru a period of three days.

I've spent all my money for eats and when one stops to consider that most of it went for eats he begins to think that something is radically wrong with our commissary.

It hasn't been candy, either. Rice pudding, coffee and sweetless cakes is about all you can buy. And you're blamed lucky if the old lady who bosses the canteen doesn't stint you.

Hospitality was never bred in England. Rather than appreciate the fact that we are here because we, the U.S., are doing our utmost to help them, some of them even try to run us down. In the states we, or rather the civilians, try to make things as nice as possible for the British Tar when he is ashore.

Here you can have a swell time if you pay for it.

We, the Yanks, take over the shack tomorrow and yours truly stands the initial watch. The U. S. Naval Forces also take over all the Shorts.

Only wish we were nearer the German coast so that our machines could get into some real action. A little American aggressiveness may make things hum, however.

More orders regarding restrictions in letter writing came out so that now we can write about the weather and our health.

I intended to hike out to a nearby Abbey today but the early liberty parties were stopped because of the flights and to turn to and haul in a few machines.

Friday we unloaded stores and I lost my knife and broke my watch crystal. The latter was really by own fault. Too chivalrous or generous. Last Sunday I donated my guard to a munition worker in Hull.

I also managed to get a little sugar.

Payday we Radio guys are going to purchase a coffee pot and skillet. Night watches will be great when we get good hot Jamoch.

Maybe mother will have to keep the old waffle iron hot when I get back. And when I get back I'm going to stick right in the good old U. S. until I'm pretty sure that the world has plenty of eats.

This stinting your stomach may be healthy and all that, but—

May 2

Cold and damp today.

Went out to play ball but was too late to get into the game.

Some mechanic turned out a bat and somebody taped a base ball. There is noticeable shortage of baseball gear but the genuine American doesn't need all of it to have a game.

Eats are a whole lot better and the fellows are all talking of saving their money. Naturally I'm one of those and I guess I'll do it.

If I get enough of it I won't have any way to spend it. Am almost tempted to begin smoking, but what's the use? It's too blamed expensive here. Shortage of money has brought many of our fellows down so far that they are actually "shooting snipes."[5]

The papers are more optimistic over the war just now and even claim an allied victory.

Guess I'll roll in for a nap as I have the 8 to 12 tonight. Expect to be paid tomorrow! Will need it for my life insurance.

Am getting a little more confidence in myself as an operator and no doubt I can make good enough to go up a notch before summer is over. If I don't get too lazy I may try two before Xmas.

Killingholme July 14, 1918

Seemingly I've been here for nearly a century but my diary never lies and that booklet tells me I've been here just one week less than four months.

On June 12, I was rated second class. That rates higher than a corporal in the army but doesn't quite equal a sergeant.

Am expecting to qualify for flying very soon. Unfortunately, about forty camouflagers have been especially trained for work that I think I can do if given the opportunity. What's more I'm going to make that opportunity or die in the attempt.

We have over fifty seaplanes (made in U.S.A. Liberty motors and everything) here now and altho our pilots are scrapping a few machines per week I expect to see this station a hummer before long.

Whiting, our commanding officer, is here and even more in evidence is his executive officer Leighton. He's a man whose middle name must be Regulation.

---

5.   I believe this means picking up cast off cigarette butts and salvaging the tobacco.

At any rate all non-duty men roll out at 5:30 and take a little Swedish before Breakfast. Fortunately I rate it only two out of five mornings.

Eight o'clock muster gets me as often.

Liberty is granted just often enough to make us want to go crazy to leave the place for a few hours and jazz 'em up. I've met a little girl who I like quite a lot for her straight forwardness. She doesn't beat about the bush and hem and haw, but if she has something to say she says it. She's a brick and a promise from her is always kept. He name's Dora and she's fairly good looking.

Mail from home comes regularly and if it were not for the monotony of our menu, the rottenness of the weather and a few other aggravating discomforts we could imagine that we were in some country place in the states.

Camouflaged buildings, long days, ancient architecture, the lack of automobiles, real coffee, ice-cream and good American girls are the details which make it Un-American.

We celebrated the fourth here and a letter to each of us from King George featured. Can you imagine his ancestor turning in his resting place in the Abbey?

Our baseball team is one of these naval political affairs. I'm not kicking but feel that I rate a berth on it.

The YMCA takes over athletics so I'll see whether I do or not. It may be that I'm getting old.

Colors just went so will get ready to turn in.

July 17, 1918

Quentin Roosevelt's death was announced in the mess hall this evening. He was probably one of many who died yesterday yet because his father is T.R. he gets his name shoved before public. I'm sure that his mother doesn't feel any worse over the loss of her boy than mine or anybody else's would. But the newspapers must publish it in big black print on the front page.

It is true the young man made the greatest sacrifice in his power. But so have thousands and thousands of others. Here's a fact. I've only heard of three men being wounded or killed during the last week. They have all been Roosevelts. Surely it can't be that advertising publicity is the cause. I would hate to believe it, but why can't Mr. Nobody's deeds be broadcasted also?

I wrote a letter to Bill Scott today and another to Ida Y. I mailed the former but decided not to mail the one to Ida Y. It's the first time I ever did anything like that and am wondering if I've changed any. I've eaten several sheep since I came here. That may be the cause of any change for the worse.

Dusty Matthews gave me a photo today.

Bill Thompson left today for a hospital in Scotland. Expects to get back to the States before long.

July 22, 1918

Fairly decent day.

I worked two machines this morning.

The Yanks have taken this station over completely and the Limies are leaving in droves today.

Saturday the English flag came down at noon and now Old Glory in all her splendor waves fearlessly alone.

Friday an American crew on an H-12 got a submarine. They had an explosion and were obliged to take to the water. After being afloat 3 1/2 hours they were picked up by a trawler. Trawler also rammed the disabled sub and took nine German prisoners. The H-12 was lost. Nobody injured. Same crew is on aerial patrol this morning. Stuff to gill' them, eh?

Meanwhile our khaki brothers are raising Holy Hell in France.

Roosevelt wasn't killed after all![6]

Have decided to become ambitious. Watch my smoke. Just watch!

I often wonder if I'll ever amount to a deuce of a lot. Folks will expect me to marry some time but the independence of bachelorhood will appeal to me more than the blissful? life of a benedict.

I'm afraid that my ability to wield a pen will never pay my board but am more than willing to try it.

If I want to roam I've my wireless experience. Harry and I expected to knock around some after peace is declared but I guess little old Afton will look blamed good to him by that time.

Altho' I'll be twenty-four I feel that I'm not a success. I don't feel like a winner, either. My best days are coming but I'm not worrying.

Until the war is over I'm a gob. After that? I don't know but I've confidence enough in myself to know that I'll get along.

July 26, 1918

Poetically inclined.

Weepy weather the cause, I guess.

We're winning! Germans being driven back.

---

6.   Quentin Roosevelt had, in fact, been killed on July 14, 1918, as announced. This is an example of the false rumors that are common among troops during wartime.

Duty

This? Oh a Song of Seaplane
Creaking Shrieking Seaplane
Throbbing bobbing seaplane
With its moaning groaning wire
The Engine—missing again!
One cylinder never fires!

Give me Earth again!
This is the song of a gob
A trying flying gob
A one thrilled now chilled gob.
The pilot. The man at the wheel
Turns 'round with a sickly grin.
Making Jack hair bristly feel
High? Well I'm thinkin'!

This is one thought of J. L.
For a tuppence I'd sell
Some good chances to Hell
And he swallows his heart in haste
As downward groundward they float
A Bump! Kersplash! Lights out! All waste!
Getting gobby's goat.

This Oh! A song of a gob
A dazed crazed gob
A relieved peeved gob
As he swims and stroke upon stroke
He'll swim as long as he can
Sea Planing? Not all joke.
It's Life! For a Man!

Aug. 7, 1918

Night before last our enemy paid us a visit. He didn't do any damage. Our losses were great in sleep, though.

Anti-air craft guns in action are almost as annoying as a rookie bugler trying to blow reveille.

Last night we were rolled out again. Black Bess our pet fighting plane went up in smoke. Origin of fire unknown. Possibly Hun-known. The sentries had a swell time trying their guns out. The wings of the other planes were burned.

They are standing out on the concrete now like a couple of moths who ventured a bit too near the flame.

Lovelace is the meteorological officer here.

Leo's on the U.S.S. Henderson. Started across but caught fire two days out. He got back to Phila on a destroyer.

Gunner says we are ok. Sounds good!

Dec. 28, 1918, Pelham Bay, N.Y,

Since the armistice was signed Nov. 11 things have happened pretty suddenly.

On Nov. 30 about 300 of us left Killingholme and went aboard the U.S.S. Leviathan at Liverpool. After a couple of days we steamed to Brest, France, where we cooled ship, took on water and a few troops.

The trip across was rough and my poor sensitive stomach just pretty near died of generosity. It just gave up everything it had as freely as the Red Cross dealt out cigarettes.

I was alright as long as I lay in my bunk and Benny smuggled me enough eats to keep me alive.

We were stuck on a sand bar for twenty-four hours before entering Hoboken so I had a chance to recuperate enough to enjoy the reception we got. Whistles tooted, bands played, etc.

We came direct to Pelham and are standing by to be released.

Radio men have a mighty slim chance of getting out but I am still hopeful.

Guess I'll go and get some coffee and cake.

Spent Xmas in New York. Fairly good time!

Dec. 30

Still here and things don't look a lot better than they did a month ago. This station was never an efficient one and the officers are living up to the pre-peace standard.

I've received two letters from Karin since landing but no news from home.
I go on guard duty again tomorrow morning.

THE END

NOTES TO WORLD WAR I JOURNAL OF J. LENNART BECK (by J. Robert Beck)

I wrote the following letter to Gerald Beck, Leland Beck, Lillian Beck Fuller, and Roland Beck on December 5, 1990:

Enclosed is a copy of my father's World War I diary, which I hope you will be interested in having. While the diary needs no further explanation beyond the foreword I have included, I cannot resist presenting some of my own observations.

I am also enclosing a brief biographical summary. Even though this is unnecessary information for you, I am including it for anyone who may come across this in future years and be curious about who this person was and what happened during the rest of his life.

I was impressed that this whole diary was written with almost no corrections of any kind. Lennart was obviously able to create sentences with correct spelling and grammar and to convert them into writing without errors. This was a really unusual talent, I assume no less rare in his generation than today, and is an indication that he really did have the basic tools to become a wordsmith. This diary barely hints at the excuses he was to use in later years to justify his reluctance to exploit this talent.

You will certainly note the use of some slang words of the time which are now archaic. You will also note the overgenerous use of quotation marks, which I believe was an annoying but standard practice of the time. Some words such as foot ball have been changed with time. Most notable of all, I thought, was his very careful avoidance of what would have been considered strong slang words in those days (hell, damn, e.g.) and the total absence of the use of those bathroom and bedroom words that so commonly dilute the effectiveness of today's writing and conversation.

On the other hand, his totally unapologetic use of such terms as wop and coon was a bit of a surprise because nowadays the use of derogatory ethnic epithets, real or perceived, is usually carefully avoided. I should have expected to find this in Lennart's writing, however, since his mind set for all of his life was to classify everyone he met by his or her ethnic heritage. I remember that even on his last visit to us he shocked our dinner guests and me by saying: Mountain Iron is a wonderful place to live. We don't have any problems and that's because we don't have any Jews or niggers living there.

It was surprising that except for a passing reference to a letter to Tommy there was no mention in the diary of any of his siblings except Leo. There was also no mention of the birth and death in June 1918, of a younger brother named Donald Stanley. We can probably assume that his family elected not to inform him of that event until he returned home.

I was at first surprised and disappointed to find little or no indication of intellectual curiosity or speculation about the important historical events occurring during the time span of the diary. Then I remembered my own years in the service during a war. The big picture and the historical long term implications were totally lost in the day-to-day attitude that our only goal was short-term survival for as long as possible—with luck, to the end of the war. This even applied to those like me who never came within thousands of miles of the shooting war. We must remember, too, that during both of these wars the international political news was heavily censored, or often misrepresented.

It was most disappointing that there was no coverage of his activities during the last three months of the war.

I was struck by one difference between Lennart's expressed attitude toward World War I and mine in WW II, attitudes I believe are representative of the two eras. This diary shows a gung-ho, rah-rah, flag-waving patriotism for a contest against what were perceived to be the German clones of a demoniacal Kaiser. It indicates a desire to participate directly in what seemed to be naively looked upon as just a big athletic contest between the good guys and the bad guys, sort of like a high school football game.

My peers in World War II were much more resigned to having to do a dirty job requiring a very great personal risk, which they were willing to face, but without much idealistic hope that this would save the world forever. There was not a great deal of patriotic fervor and, surprisingly Hitler seemed to be less the perceived villain of the war than the Kaiser had been, even though Hitler was probably far more deserving of being seen as an evil villain.

This diary brought into focus for me how brief the U. S. participation in WW I really was. Lennart and Leo enlisted immediately when the U. S. declared war. They both spent the Christmas of 1917 still in training in the U. S. By the following Christmas, 1918, the war was over and Lennart was back in the U. S., having been overseas only about 7 1/2 months before the Armistice. It is not revealed in this diary what Leo had done between Dec. 30, 1917 and Aug. 18,

1918, but we did learn that in August, 1918, only three months before the end of the war, Leo was in New York awaiting a ship.

Transcribing this diary, I believe, brought me closer to my father than I ever was during the 45 years that our lives on earth overlapped. I was for the first time able to sample even fleetingly his inner thoughts, aspirations, doubts, hopes and his daily life during formative years.

He was 30 when I was born, and probably 35 going on 65 by the time I began to observe him as a person. By that time he had subscribed to a number of cast-in-concrete principles including, but not limited to:

I will never move again in my life.
I will always vote Republican.
I will forever and without question be a Presbyterian.
WASPs are the superior people of the world.
Finno-Scandinavians are almost as good as WASPs.

I tended to be inquisitive, studious, and skeptical, and liked to explore multiple facets of answers to questions about things like politics, religion, philosophy, and maybe even sex. I soon learned that my questions about these sorts of things made him uncomfortable, and that his standard answer was "You'll find out when you are older," without attempting to give a rational answer for his own unwavering beliefs.

It was interesting to learn that he had perhaps not always been so rigid (or was it defensive?), and it would be even more interesting to have a diary covering the next ten years to find out how he became the man I knew—or perhaps never did know.

I hope you enjoy the fruits of his and my efforts, and find it an interesting addition to your library.

BIOGRAPHICAL DATA: John Lennart Beck

John Lennart Anderson was born Oct. 17, 1894, in East Tawas or Tawas City, Michigan. The family name was changed from Anderson to Beck sometime before his brother Leo was born in 1896.

By 1896 the family had moved from East Tawas, Michigan, to Oscoda, Michigan, and moved again to Cloquet, Minnesota, before they finally settled in Mountain Iron, Minnesota sometime before 1905. Lennart and his siblings were educated in the Mountain Iron schools, and he was a member of the first high school graduating class in 1915 when he was 20 years old. His brother Leo and Lennart's wife-to-be were also among the nine members of the class.

He entered Macalester College in St. Paul, Minnesota, in the fall of 1915 and continued there until he enlisted in the Navy in April 1917.

He was married on February 28, 1922, to Mabel Leila Hanson in Mountain Iron. They had two children, John Robert born July 16, 1924, and Roderick Gerald born November 26, 1930. Mabel died on April 9, l952, and John Lennart on October 11, 1969.

John Lennart was known mainly as Lennart. After he returned from his service in World War I he lived the remainder of his life in Mountain Iron, Minnesota. From 1922 to 1936 he was the postmaster there, and in conjunction with the post office had a small business selling tobacco, candy, ice cream, magazines and non-prescription drugs. In 1937-38 he was the village clerk.

For the remainder of his working life he worked in the iron mining industry, first for the Wheeling Steel Corporation at its Wacootah Mine in Mountain Iron, and later for U. S. Steel as a warehouseman in its shops in Virginia, Minnesota.

He was very active in the local American Legion Post between World War I and until the end of World War II. He was active and increasingly so in his later years in the Mountain Iron Presbyterian Church. He joined the Masons in his middle years but was never especially active in that organization.

His father was John (Keto/Anderson) Beck, born in Inankyla, Finland, on May 16, 1873, to Antti (Andrew) Keto and his wife Wilhelmiina. Lennart's mother was Hulda Bygden Beck, born August 28, 1879, in Finland near Karleby to Swedish parents Johan Petter Bygden and Maria Eriksson Bygden. John and Hulda Beck had a total of 10 children, seven of whom survived to adulthood: John Lennart was the oldest followed by Leo Emil (baptized Emil Lionel, 1896); Lillian Augusta (1902); Clarence Royal (1905); Laurence Randolf (1908); Charles Joel (1910); and Roland Arthur (1913).

Appendix D

DESCENDANTS

I am sorry that I do not have time to expand this volume or write a second volume to cover the generations beyond mine in the same detail as I have tried to cover my and previous generations. There were 20 in my generation all of whom I have known at some stage of their lives. There are 49 in the next generation most of whom I have rarely if ever seen. To write about them fairly I would want to meet and interview each one, so I feel it is a job I must leave to someone younger, interesting though I am sure it would be.

My generation has certainly included many very successful cousins. They are mostly good, solid, middle or upper middle class citizens with traditional professions: lawyers, doctors, professors, teachers, engineers, managers, and military officers. The next generation has some of these, too, but I also hear about such jobs as vice-president of Time-Warner, guiding satellites, geneticist, Doctor of Music specializing in the valveless (French) horn, and dealer for Las Vegas Poker Tournaments. I would love to have the time and energy to interview and write about all 49. I am sure there is a great and interesting story there. But since I don't feel it would be fair to do less than the whole job, I am not going to attempt it.

All I will say is that the more I hear from and about the next generations, the more impressed I am with the fruitfulness of the family tree. And we must not forget that the tree is increasingly cross-fertilized with other family trees as the generations proliferate.

Even of the twenty in my generation, only Gerry and I share both the Beck and Hanson grandparents, so I expect the rest of you will be more interested in one side of my story than in the other.

I do, however, feel that I should at least list all of those who can trace their ancestry back to either the Hansons or the Becks or both for the future reference of those who may be interested. That is the purpose of this appendix.

Bans and Bertha Hanson and John and Hulda Beck pushed hard to have their children get the education they had not. I don't think any of the four finished more than six or seven grades, and it appears that John never went to school. That may be why John, especially during the depression, sometimes wavered and felt that high school and a job in the iron mines was enough for his children to aspire to. Hulda would have none of that and insisted that all of her children at least try college. Bans and Bertha were together in encouraging their children to go to college and were successful with all but Orville, who, as Bertha once commented to me, was not only the most brilliant of her children but had a mind of his own.

Here's how successfully the message was transmitted to subsequent generations:

GENERATION	NO COLLEGE		SOME COLLEGE		BA/BS DEGREE		ADVANCED DEGREE	
	#	%	#	%	#	%	#	%
I	4	100%	0	0	0	0	0	0
II	1	8%	11	92%	8	67%	3	25%
III	1	5%	19	95%	18	90%	8	40%
IV	2	4%	47	96%	41	84%	17	35%

Generation I are John, Hulda, Bans, and Bertha.

Generation IV still has young enough members so that the numbers attending college and attaining bachelor and advanced degrees will almost certainly go higher. Generations V and VI are too young to be included in a college survey.

This does not mean that I believe that college is for everyone. People who are not good at academics can be very successful and some who are good at academics can be unsuccessful in life. Some who are not super intelligent, intellectually curious, or highly creative can achieve academic success. And intelligent, curious and creative people may have trouble achieving academic success. But it appears that members of these families have most often achieved success in their lives through higher education.

I have numbered the Becks and Hansons as a means of determining who belongs to whom on the table that follows listing all of the 130 descendants. Refer to the family number code. After each listing there is a number showing who is the parent of the listed person. If you want to know who 063 Kristie L. Beck's parent and grandparent are, for example, you can look up 25 (Douglas

Charles Beck, parent) and that will lead you to 8 (Charles Joel Beck, grandparent).

FOLLOWING IS A LIST OF THE DESCENDANTS OF JOHN AND HULDA BECK AND BANS AND BERTHA HANSON AS OF INFORMATION I HAVE RECEIVED IN MAY, 2005 (EXCEPT THOSE WHO DIED BEFORE ATTAINING MATURITY).

001 John Anderson Keto Beck
001 Hulda Maria Bygden Beck
002 Ben (Bans, Bernt) Hanson
002 Bertha (Bergit) Johnson Hanson
003 John Lennart Beck-1
003 Mabel Leila Hanson Beck-2
004 Leo Emil Beck-1
05 Lillian Augusta Beck Fuller-1
06 Clarence Royal Beck-1
07 Laurence Randolf Beck-1
08 Charles Joel Beck-1
09 Roland Arthur Beck-1
10 Harry Albert Hanson, Sr.-2
11 Orville Hanson-2
12 Ethel Ragnild Hanson Forder-2
13 Benjamin Raymond Hanson-2
14 John Robert Beck-3
15 Roderick Gerald Beck-3
16 Leland Whitcomb Beck-4
17 Faith Fuller Wick-5
18 Bruce Beck Fuller-5
19 Mary Ellen Beck Ganzer-6
20 Joyce Elizabeth Beck-6
21 Beverly Joan Beck Hatherly-7
22 Gary Laurence Beck-7
23 Joellen Margaret Beck Hawkins-8
24 Bruce Lennart Beck-8
25 Douglas Charles Beck-8
26 David Wallace Beck-8
27 Bradley Thomas Beck-9
28 Brian Arthur Beck-9

29 Gwen Harriet Hanson Reichert-10
30 Harry Albert Hanson, Jr.-10
31 William Robert Forder-12
32 Karen Louise Hanson Wilson-13
33 Theodore Hanson-13
34 Bryan Lennart Beck-14
35 Stephen Charles Beck-14
36 David Robert Beck-14
37 Barbara Jean Beck (Anderson)-14
38 Thomas Jeffrey Beck-14
39 John Charles Beck-15
40 Karen Lynn Beck-15
41 William Lennart Beck-15
42 Charles Leland Beck-16
43 Thomas Eric Beck-16
44 Anne Whitcomb Beck Cottingham-16
45 Timothy Bruce Wick-17
46 Kimberly Anne Wick Anderson-17
47 Jonathan Joel Wick-17
48 Heidi Faith Wick (Christianson)-17
49 Gretchen Faith Fuller-18
50 Christine Rae Ganzer Lannan-19
51 Karen Rae Ganzer Jennings-19
52 Mark William Hatherly-21
53 Kirk Laurence Hatherly-21
54 Todd Christopher Hatherly-21
55 Steven Laurence Beck-22
56 Karen Sue Beck Painter-22
57 John Charles Watson-23
58 Andrew Bruce Watson-23
59 Emily Lynn Beck-24

60 Brian Richards Beck-24
61 Lauren Elizabeth Beck-24
62 Katherine Ann Beck-25
63 Kristie Lynn Beck-25
64 Ashley Catherine Beck-26
65 Grant David Beck-26
66 Madelaine Wallace Beck-26
67 Eric Roland Beck-27
68 Jason David Beck-28
69 Jeffrey Michael Beck-28
70 Diane Elaine Beck (Vincent)-28
71 Susan Reichert (Thomas)-29
72 Ann Reichert Croll-29
73 Douglas Reichert-29
74 Harry Albert Hanson III-30
75 Bradley Hanson-30
76 Belinda Hanson Thomas-30
77 Nancee Forder Bray-31
78 Robert Forder-31
79 Katherine Louise Inman Johnson-32
80 Deanne Marie Inman-32
81 Eric Hanson-33
82 Shari Hanson-33
83 Allison Lee Baxterbeck-35
84 Ariel Nicole Baxterbeck-35
85 Forrest Leland Beck-42
86 Carson Price Beck-42
92 Karin Michele Anderson-46
93 Molly Alyssa Wick-47
94 Nathan Andrew Wick-47
95 Forrest Walker Christenson-48
96 Zoe Aurora Dancer Christenson-48
97 Zachery Patrick Lannan-50
98 Amy Lynn Day-50
99 Steven E. Jennings-51
100 Andrew Scott Jennings-51

87 Sonja Anne Beck-43
88 Oliver Beck-43
89 Samantha Bethany Wick Kemp-45
90 Seth Stephen Wick-45
91 Kristin Anne Anderson-46
101 Rebekah Darleen Hatherly-53
102 Seth Laurence Hathery-53
103 Leah Hope Hatherly-53
104 Tyler John Hatherly-54
105 Katelyn Anne Hatherly-54
106 Trevor Lee Hatherly-54
107 Whitney Catherine Beck-55
108 Lauren Ashley Beck-55
109 Taylor M. Beck-55
110 Daniel David Painter-56
111 Taylor Thomas Beck-67
112 Ethan Arthur Beck-68
113 Galen Andrew Reichert Thomas-71
114 Jared Scott Reichert Thomas-71
115 Grace Lauren Reichert Thomas-71
116 Sara Croll-72
117 Robert Croll-72
118 Christopher Reichert-73
119 Natalia Reichert-73
120 Samuel Hollingsworth Hanson-74
121 Thomas Jeanes Hanson-74
122 Louisa Grace Hanson-74
123 Leigh Hanson Thomas-76
124 Katherine Terry Thomas-76
125 Ashley Bray-77
126 Amber Bray-77
127 Taylor Bray-77
128 Duane Raymond Johnson III-79
129 Kade Stryder Kemp-89
130 Logan Dane Kemp-89

There are 115 living descendants of John and Hulda Beck and Ben and Bertha Hanson.

There are 13 more who lived to maturity and have died.

There are 10 more who died in infancy or childhood.

Total descendants: 138 (that I know of.)

Those who lived to adulthood or are children still living:

I. Grandparents generation: 4 (0 living)

II. Parents generation: 12 (0 living)

III. My generation: 20 (19 living)

IV. Next generation: 49 (all living)

V. Next generation: 45 (may increase)

VI. Next generation: 2 (will increase)

Appendix E

FAMILY TREES

These will map the way to get from long gone ancestors to you—or at least to my parents, and I hope that by now you can get from there to you.

If you can't, give me a call. If it's too late for that, try one of my children.

Bob

THE SKJUSTAD/HANSONS

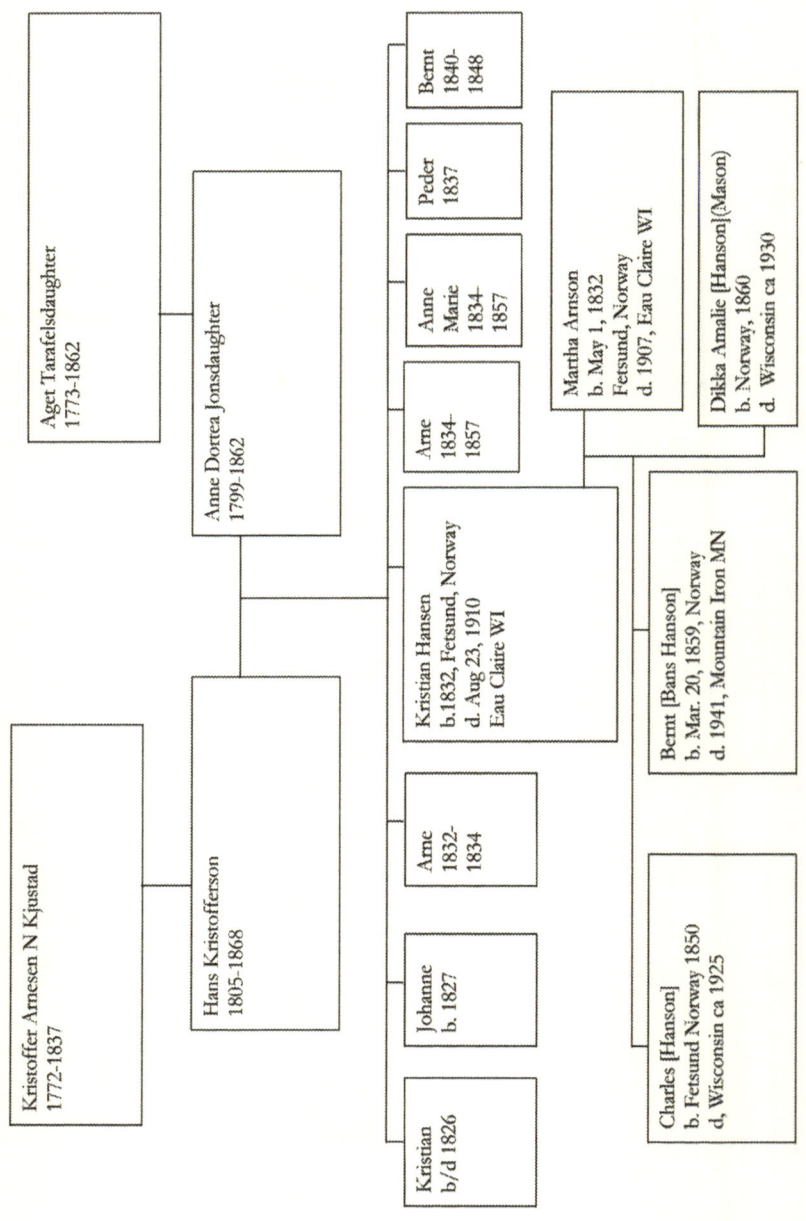

THE BYGDEN/ERIKSSONS

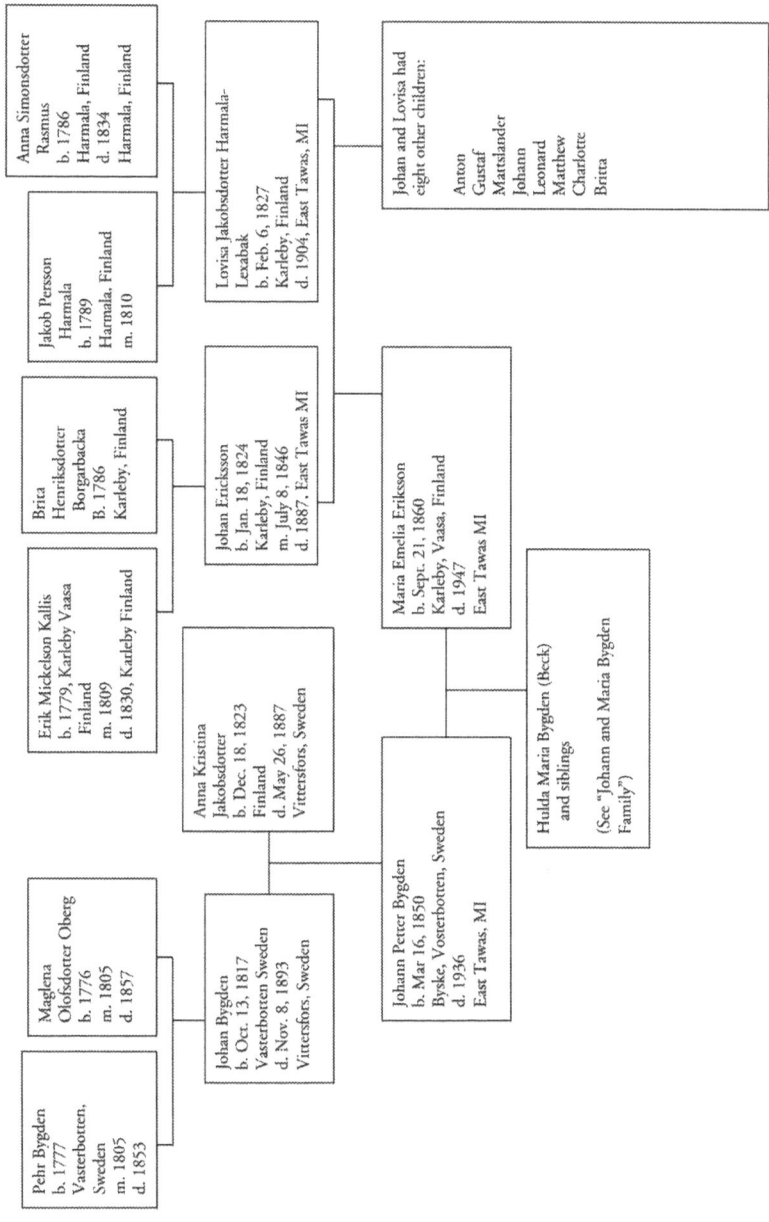

Anna Simonsdotter
Rasmus
b. 1786
Harmala, Finland
d. 1834
Harmala, Finland

Jakob Persson
Harmala
b. 1789
Harmala, Finland
m. 1810

Lovisa Jakobsdotter Harmala-Lexabak
b. Feb. 6, 1827
Karleby, Finland
d. 1904, East Tawas, MI

Johan and Lovisa had eight other children:

Anton
Gustaf
Mattslander
Johann
Leonard
Matthew
Charlotte
Britta

Brita
Henriksdotter
Borgarbacka
B. 1786
Karleby, Finland

Erik Mickelson Kallis
b. 1779, Karleby Vaasa
Finland
m. 1809
d. 1830, Karleby Finland

Johan Ericksson
b. Jan. 18, 1824
Karleby, Finland
m. July 8, 1846
d. 1887, East Tawas MI

Maria Emelia Eriksson
b. Sept. 21, 1860
Karleby, Vaasa, Finland
d. 1947
East Tawas MI

Anna Kristina
Jakobsdotter
b. Dec. 18, 1823
Finland
d. May 26, 1887
Vittersfors, Sweden

Hulda Maria Bygden (Beck)
and siblings

(See "Johann and Maria Bygden
Family")

Maglena
Olofsdotter Oberg
b. 1776
m. 1805
d. 1857

Johan Bygden
b. Oct. 13, 1817
Vasterbotten Sweden
d. Nov. 8, 1893
Vittersfors, Sweden

Johann Petter Bygden
b. Mar 16, 1850
Byske, Vosterbotten, Sweden
d. 1936
East Tawas, MI

Pehr Bygden
b. 1777
Vasterbotten,
Sweden
m. 1805
d. 1853

THE FAMILY OF ANTTI AND WILHELMIINA KETO

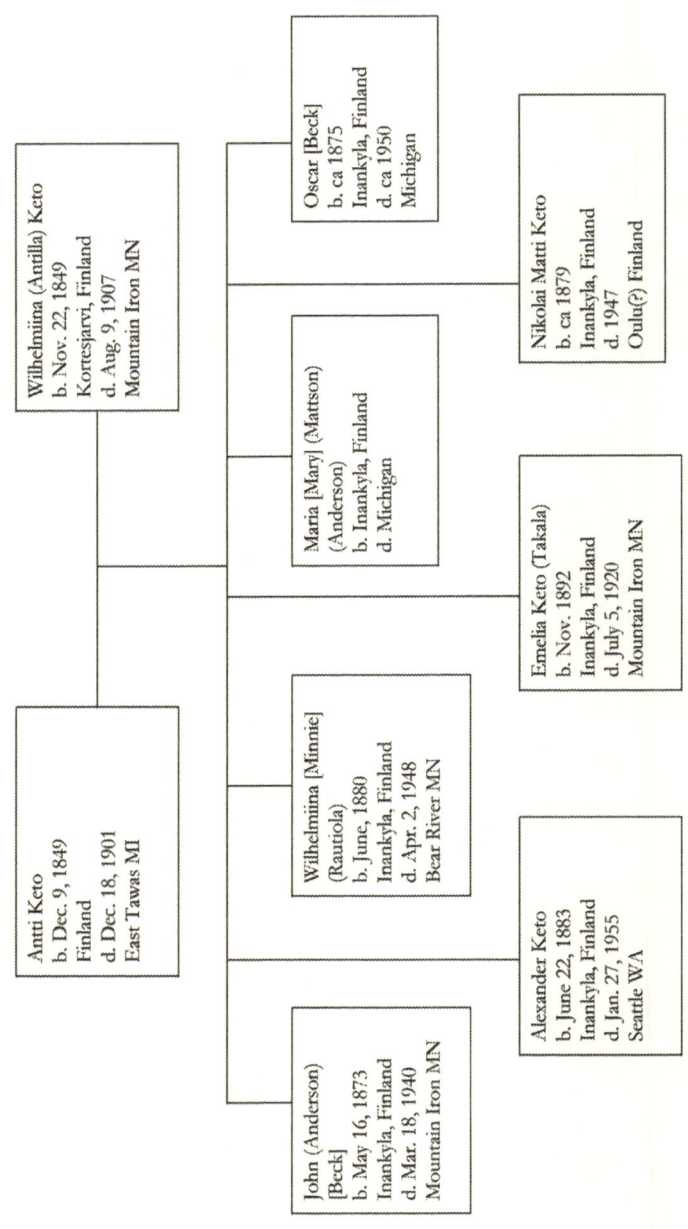

THE BYGDENS

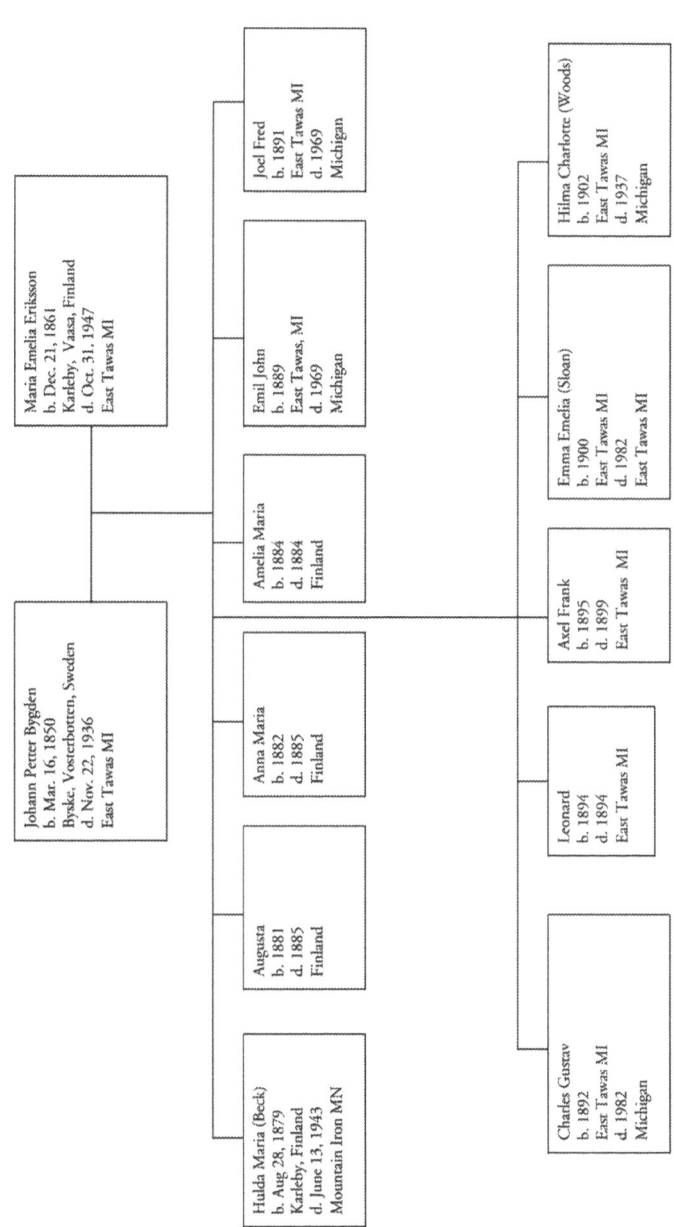

Johann Petter Bygden
b. Mar. 16, 1850
Byske, Vosterbotten, Sweden
d. Nov. 22, 1936
East Tawas MI

Maria Emelia Eriksson
b. Dec. 21, 1861
Karleby, Vaasa, Finland
d. Oct. 31, 1947
East Tawas MI

Hulda Maria (Beck)
b. Aug 28, 1879
Karleby, Finland
d. June 13, 1943
Mountain Iron MN

Augusta
b. 1881
d. 1885
Finland

Anna Maria
b. 1882
d. 1885
Finland

Amelia Maria
b. 1884
d. 1884
Finland

Emil John
b. 1889
East Tawas, MI
d. 1969
Michigan

Joel Fred
b. 1891
East Tawas MI
d. 1969
Michigan

Charles Gustav
b. 1892
East Tawas MI
d. 1982
Michigan

Leonard
b. 1894
d. 1894
East Tawas MI

Axel Frank
b. 1895
d. 1899
East Tawas MI

Emma Emelia (Sloan)
b. 1900
East Tawas MI
d. 1982
East Tawas MI

Hilma Charlotte (Woods)
b. 1902
East Tawas MI
d. 1937
Michigan

THE ODEGAARD/JOHNSON FAMILY

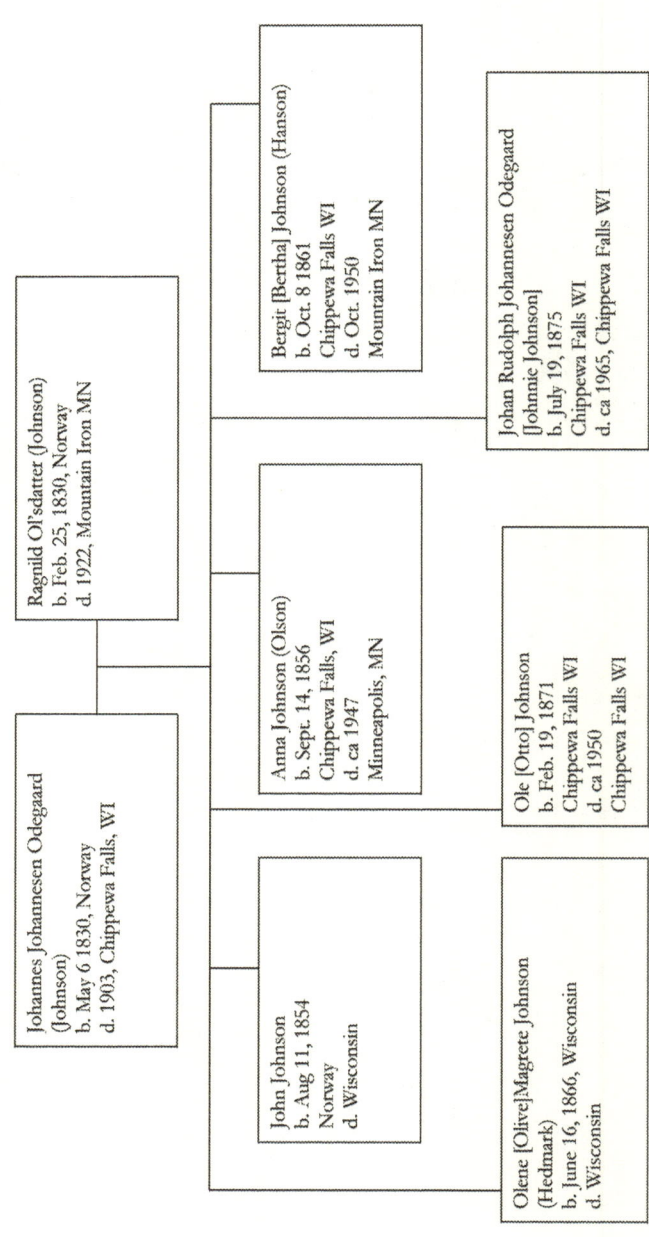

Johannes Johannesen Odegaard (Johnson)
b. May 6 1830, Norway
d. 1903, Chippewa Falls, WI

Ragnild Ol'sdatter (Johnson)
b. Feb. 25, 1830, Norway
d. 1922, Mountain Iron MN

Bergit [Bertha] Johnson (Hanson)
b. Oct. 8 1861
Chippewa Falls WI
d. Oct. 1950
Mountain Iron MN

Johan Rudolph Johannesen Odegaard [Johnnie Johnson]
b. July 19, 1875
Chippewa Falls WI
d. ca 1965, Chippewa Falls WI

Anna Johnson (Olson)
b. Sept. 14, 1856
Chippewa Falls, WI
d. ca 1947
Minneapolis, MN

Ole [Otto] Johnson
b. Feb. 19, 1871
Chippewa Falls WI
d. ca 1950
Chippewa Falls WI

John Johnson
b. Aug 11, 1854
Norway
d. Wisconsin

Olene [Olive]Magrete Johnson (Hedmark)
b. June 16, 1866, Wisconsin
d. Wisconsin

THE FAMILY OF BANS AND BERTHA HANSON

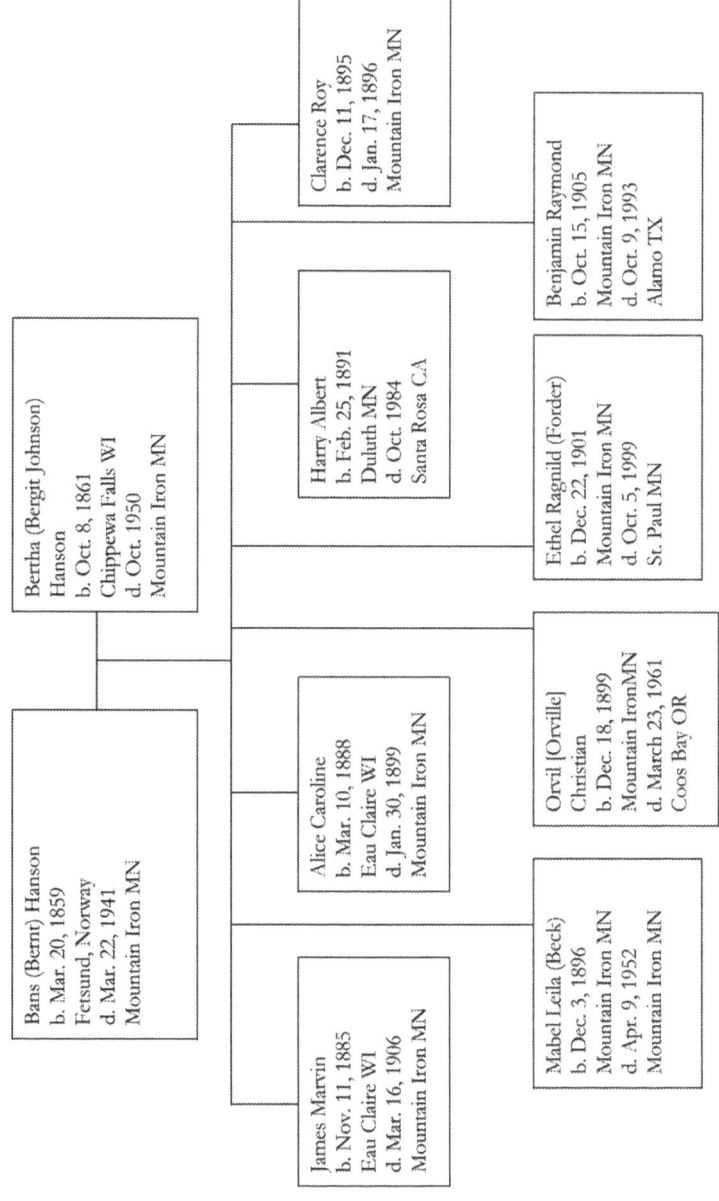

THE FAMILY OF JOHN AND HULDA BECK

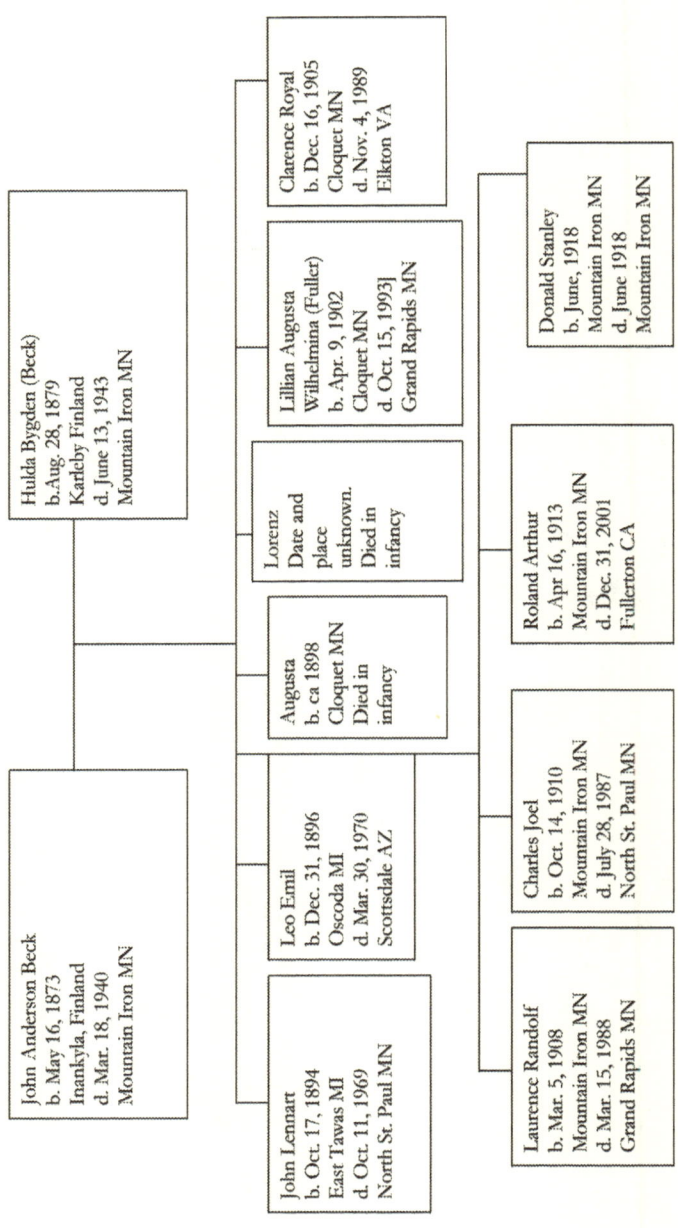

978-0-595-35772-7
0-595-35772-5